Richard S. Fisher

The Spanish West Indies

Richard S. Fisher

The Spanish West Indies

ISBN/EAN: 9783337318673

Printed in Europe, USA, Canada, Australia, Japan

Cover: Foto ©Andreas Hilbeck / pixelio.de

More available books at **www.hansebooks.com**

THE SPANISH WEST INDIES.

CUBA AND PORTO RICO:

GEOGRAPHICAL, POLITICAL, AND INDUSTRIAL.

CUBA:
FROM THE SPANISH OF DON J. M. DE LA TORRE.

PORTO RICO:
BY J. T. O'NEIL, ESQ.

EDITED BY RICHARD S. FISHER, M.D.,
AUTHOR OF "PROGRESS OF THE UNITED STATES;" STATISTICAL EDITOR OF "COLTON'S ATLAS OF THE WORLD," ETC., ETC.

Illustrated by a New and Accurate Map.

NEW YORK:
J. H. COLTON,
No. 172 WILLIAM STREET.
LONDON: TRÜBNER AND CO., 12 PATERNOSTER ROW.
1861.

ADVERTISEMENT.

This volume contains two separate memoirs on the Spanish West Indies : each is also distinct as regards authorship.

The " Memoir on Cuba," composing the first part of the volume, is a translation from the Spanish* of *Don José Maria de la Torre*, of Havana. It embraces a complete review of the physical geography and the political, social, and industrial condition of one of the fairest islands of the world, and one to which public attention has of late years been significantly directed.

The " Memoir on Porto Rico" has been compiled by *Don J. T. O'Neil*, a native of San Juan, and at present a resident of New York city. Though not so extensive in design as that on Cuba, it will be found to be sufficiently comprehensive for all practical purposes.

The editor has made no alterations in the original text, further than required in the adjustment of idiomatic peculiarities. Where necessary, his remarks are made in the foot notes ; and he has added largely to the statistical tables.

In issuing this work, the sole object of the publishers has been to disseminate information.

---

* *Compendio de Geografia, fisica, politica, estadistica y comparada de la Isla de Cuba, por Don José Maria de la Torre. Habana:* 1854.

CONTENTS.

PART I.
CUBA: PHYSICAL, POLITICAL, AND INDUSTRIAL.

PHYSICAL GEOGRAPHY.—Position, Figure, Boundaries, Neighboring Lands, Advantages and Disadvantages, Extent, Surface or Area, Coasts, Gulfs, Peninsulas, Capes, Islands, etc., Straits and Channels, Mountains, Volcanoes, Valleys, Caverns, *Sabanas* or Plains, Rivers, Waterfalls, Lakes and Lagoons, *Cienagas* or Swamps, Salt-fields, Harbors, etc., Climate, Diseases, Animals, Vegetation, Minerals, etc., etc. .... Page 7–44

POLITICAL AND INDUSTRIAL GEOGRAPHY.—Population, Religion, Territorial Divisions, Government, Laws, Ethnography, Idiom, Character and Customs, Public Instruction, Manufactures and Arts, Agriculture, Navigation, Commerce, Revenue, Expenditure, Intercommunication, Coat of Arms, Measures, Weights, Currency, Forces, etc. 44–70

ADJACENT ISLANDS.—Isla de Pinos, etc. 71–73

DESCRIPTION OF THE JURISDICTIONS.—Capital Towns, Villages, Petty Districts, Communities, Productions, Peculiarities, etc., of each 74–103

ANCIENT GEOGRAPHY. 104–109

HISTORY OF THE ISLAND.—Discovery, Conquest and Colonization, Organization, Civilization, Era of Prosperity, etc. 110–117

STATISTICS OF CUBA.—Population of the Island in 1853, Progress of Population, Towns of 1,500 Inhabitants and upward, in 1841, 1846, and 1853; Rural Establishments, Distribution of Land, Chief Agricultural Products in 1852, Staple Exports, Navigation and Commerce, Sugar Exported from 1791 to 1850, Other Exports from 1826 to 1850, Copper Exported from 1841 to 1850, Value of Commerce with Foreign Nations, Commercial Movement, Revenue of the Island from 1826 to 1850... 118–127

APPENDIX. 128–131

PART II.
MEMOIR OF THE ISLAND OF PORTO RICO.

PHYSICAL GEOGRAPHY.—Position, Form, Boundaries, Extent and Area, Coasts, Capes and Points, Adjacent Islands and Keys, Reefs and Shoals, Channels, Mountains and Valleys, Lagoons, Salt-ponds, Harbors, etc., Currents, Climate, Diseases, Animals, Vegetation, Minerals... 133-145

POLITICAL GEOGRAPHY.—Population, Religion, Administrative Divisions, Exchequer, Church, Army, Navy, Laws, Education, Character and Customs, etc. 146-154

INDUSTRIAL GEOGRAPHY.—Manufactures and Arts, Agriculture, Navigation and Commerce, Communication, Weights and Measures, Currency, etc........... 155-163

DEPENDENCIES.—Vieques or Crab Island, Culebras, etc...................... 164, 165

EARLY HISTORY 166, 167

THE CAPITAL AND THE DEPARTMENTS.—San Juan Bautista, Bayamon, Arecibo, Aguadilla, Mayagües, Ponce, Humacao, Guayama, etc...................... 168-185

STATISTICAL APPENDIX. 186-190

CUBA:

PHYSICAL, POLITICAL, AND INDUSTRIAL.

PHYSICAL GEOGRAPHY.

Absolute or Astronomical Position.—The Island of Cuba is situated in the torrid zone, between longitudes 67° 51′ 8″ and 78° 40′ 22″ west of the meridian of Cadiz,* and latitudes 19° 48′ 30″ and 23° 12′ 45″ north. It therefore falls short about 16 minutes of the tropic of Cancer, where the temperate zone begins.

Relative Position.—Relatively to the surface of the globe the island is advantageously situated in the Atlantic Ocean at the entrance of the Gulf of Mexico, and between the two Americas; for which reason it is called the " Key of the New World," " Queen and bulwark of the Antilles," and, also, because the largest and most westerly of the islands, " Mother of the Antilles."

Extremities.—The points which constitute the extreme ends of the island are—Cabo San Antonio on the west, and Cabo Maisí on the east; although are also remarkable—Punta Francés (on the northern extremity of Cabo Hicacos), as being the most northerly point of the Cuban continent; Cabo Lucrecia; Punta del Inglés (near Cabo de Cruz), which is the southern extremity of the island; Punta Gorda or de Mangle, on Cabo Matahambre; and Punta de Aguirre, the southern extremity of Cabo Corrientes.

Figure.—The form of the island is long and narrow, appearing as an irregular disc, with its convexity facing the north. The territory comprised between Cabo San Antonio and the meridian of the Mariel runs

---

* The Morro light at Havana is in 76° 4′ 40″ west longitude of Cadiz, and in 23° 9′ 26″ north latitude. The meridian of Cadiz, used throughout this work corresponds to 6° 17′ 14″ east from Greenwich; hence by adding such sum to the sum of the given meridian, that commonly used by English and American astronomers is obtained.

from south-west to north-east; that comprised between the meridians of the Mariel and of Cárdenas, from east to west; and that comprised between Cárdenas and Cabo Maisí, from north-west to south-east.*

Boundaries.—On the west and north-west is the Gulf of Mexico. On the north, the Florida channel, which separates it from the peninsula of the same name, the southern mouth of the new channel of the Bahamas, the Canal de los Roques, the old Bahama channel, and the Atlantic Ocean. On the west, the Maisí passage, which separates it from the island of Hayti or St. Domingo. On the south, the sea called Columbian, Caribbean, or of the Antilles. On the south-west, the passage or strait of Yucatan.

Neighboring Land.—At the north, the peninsula of Florida, whose Cabo Tancha, Arena, or Ají lies 32 maritime leagues from Cabo Hicacos;† Cayos de los Roques, of which the one called Sal is 15 maritime leagues off;‡ and Cayos Guincho, Lobos, Punta de Diamante, Múcaras, and Santo Domingo, on the southern edge of the Grand Bank of Bahama, at a mean distance of about 12 leagues from the coast of this island. At the east, the British island of Great Inagua, 15 leagues from Cabo Maisí. At the south-east, the island of Hayti, whose Cabo Mole or San Nicolas is at a distance of 14 leagues, and Cabo Doña Maria on the south, 37 leagues from Cabo Maisí. At the south, the British islands of Jamaica (25 leagues from Cabo Cruz), Great Caiman, and Little Caiman, at a distance of about 50 leagues from Cienfuegos.|| At the south-west, the peninsula of Yucatan, whose Cabo Catoche is only 38 leagues from Cabo San Antonio; and at the west and north-west, the coasts of the Mexican Gulf, from Tampico to Florida.

Advantages and Disadvantages of the Form and Position of the Island.—Its length and narrowness, and the great number of its magnificent harbors, doubtless constitute its greatest advantages, affording, as they do, great facilities for a sea-trade, which is so much more economical than communication by land; but, at the same time, they offer the

---

* In this manner the periphery of the island may be easily traced, drawing first two parallel lines in the directions indicated, and bearing in mind that the parallels of the first course given are in extent as 2, those of the second as 1⅓, and those of the third as 7⅓ of the 11 parts into which the length of the island is to be considered divided.

† The reefs or chains of keys projecting into the sea west of Cabo Tancha (the chief of which is *Cayo Hueso* or Key West) are only about 30 maritime leagues distant from the nearest coast of Cuba, with which they form the Florida channel.

‡ Until very recently the island was almost supplied with salt from this islet, but at present the English owners of that bank prohibit Spaniards from extracting the article as an object of trade.

|| More to the south, the American continent comprised between Honduras and Santa Marta.

disadvantage of requiring a large maritime force to guard the coast, as well against smugglers as against the invasion of enemies. Situated as the island is, at the entrance of the Gulf of Mexico, it becomes almost necessarily the stopping-place (especially its flourishing capital) of all vessels bound for Vera Cruz, and other places within said Gulf.* And how vastly will not the advantages of the superior position of Havana be increased when the projected union of the Atlantic and Pacific oceans through the isthmus of Tehuantepec shall be realized? Or the gigantic undertaking of a railroad from New Orleans to the Pacific? Neither is the position of the island less favorable from lying between the enterprising and commercial Anglo-American nation on the one hand, and the growing Spanish-American republics on the other, since, being the stopping-place for vessels, and likewise the depôt of European merchandise, it derives benefit from the trade of all those countries.

Extent.—The greatest extent of the island is from east to west, or from Cabo Maisí to Cabo San Antonio. If we draw a line through the centre of the irregular disc formed by the island, we shall find a length of 220 maritime or 376 itinerary leagues. Its greatest breadth, from Cabo Lucrecia to Cabo de Cruz, is 45 maritime leagues; from the mouth of the port of Nuevitas to the mouth of the port of Mota, 37; from the mouth of the Mariel to the Bay of Majana, 7½; and from the mouth of the harbor of Havana to Batabanó, 9½ maritime leagues. The average breadth is about 16 leagues.

Surface or Area.—The area of the Cuban continent is 3,804 square leagues (20 to the equatorial degree); and adding 68 for the island of Pinos, and 101 for the other adjacent islands and keys, we have a total of 3,973 square leagues.†

---

* Nature, so lavish in benefiting the Mexican territory, denied it any ports worthy of the name, for which reason Havana was not entirely forgotten during the dependence of Mexico on the Spanish monarchy, as, failing of good harbors in that republic, government found it necessary to build and maintain almost always its squadrons at Havana.

† Equal to 85,757 square geographical miles, or 47,278 square English miles. Thus the territory of the island is equal to a little more than the fourth part of that possessed by the monarchy on the Iberian peninsula (15,260 square leagues); to the half of the Philippine Islands (8,000 square leagues), and to more than nine times the island of Porto Rico. The area of the island is greater than that of Portugal, Holland, Switzerland, Denmark, and Greece: than each of the Italian states, and those of the Germanic confederation (except Austria and Prussia); than the principalities of Moldavia, Wallachia, and Servia, and the whole of the Ionian Islands. It is equal to Belgium, England proper (without Wales), the States of New York, Pennsylvania, Mississippi, North Carolina, and Louisiana, and greater than all the other Antilles together, which are only 3,814 square leagues. Although the general surface of the Cuban territory is pretty well ascertained, the same is not the case with the interior divisions, such as the jurisdic-

1*

Circumference.—Following the straightest line along the coast, the island presents a frontage to the sea of 573 maritime leagues, of which 272 correspond to the north coast, and 301 to the south coast.

Coasts.—Considering that the island has a sea-board of 573 leagues (272 on the north, and 301 on the south), it will be seen that it comprises a greater extent than that of the peninsula of Spain, which is only 487 leagues. The coasts of the island are bold and unobstructed in the spaces comprised between Bahia-Honda and Cabo Hicacos, between the peninsula of Sabinal and Cabo Maisí, between the latter and Cabo Cruz, between Trinidad and the Bay of Cochinos, and between Punta Francés and Cabo San Antonio; but the rest are surrounded by islands, islets, keys, and shoals, which encroach within a few leagues, presenting obstacles to navigators unacquainted with the channels or guts affording a passage between them to the harbors and anchorages. The greater part of the outline of the coast consists of a zone of very low land, in some places nearly level with the water, and very subject to inundation, giving rise to permanent, and, in some instances, very extensive swamps. This is especially the case on the southern coast. These marshes are almost invariably lined with mangroves. The coasts are indented by a large number of harbors, bays, creeks, and *embarcaderos* or embarking places; and among the harbors are many that surpass or rival the best on the face of the globe.

Gulfs.—Six great and remarkable influxes of the sea may be so styled, viz., that of Guanahacabibes, an open gulf at the west of the island, between Cabo San Antonio and Santa Isabel Bay (ensenada); that of Barajagua, also open, between Cabo Lucrecia and Sagua de Tánamo River; that of Gacanayabo, also open, between Cabo Cruz and the Najaza River, with the bays of Birama and Buey; the open Gulf of Ornofay, between Punta Macurijes and the Jatibonico River; the closed one of Matamanó, between Cabo Matahambre and Punta Carraguao; and the open one of Guaniguaníco (known as Ensenada de Cortés), between Punta de la Fisga and the so-called Cabo Francés. In the island of Pinos we may also consider as a gulf what is called Ensenada de Siguanea.

Peninsulas.—Guanahacabibes, at the west end of the island, between the inlets or albuferas (miscalled ensenadas) of Guadiana and Cortés; La Rosa, in the lagoon of Ariguanabo; Zapata, between the bays of Broa and Cochinos; Hicacos, which is five leagues long, and closes on the north-

---

tions, districts, etc., and the differences observed between the statistical returns of 1827 and 1846, and the great general chart of the island, arise from the fact that other data have been used in the case of some territories. Thus the area of Pinos Island appears in said documents as 810 square miles, and we have assigned only 614, as calculated by Sr. Lanier by order of the government.

west the vast Bay of Cárdenas; Sabinal, between the bay of the same name and the port of Nuevitas; and Entre-Casco, between the ports of Mayarí and Cabonico.*

Capes and Principal Points.—On the north coast are—Cabo San Antonio (the western extremity of the island), with a light-house called Roncali; Punta de Abalo or de los Organos, north of the inlet of Guadiana; Punta de la Gobernadora, west of the port of Bahia-Honda; Punta Brava on the west, and Punta Bacuranao on the east of Havana, which are remarkable only for their proximity to the capital of the island; Punta Tarará, west of the mouth of the river of the same name; Puntas Guanos, Ubero-Alto, Sabanilla, and Maya, at the entrance of the port of Matanzas; Cabo Hicacos, running from south-west to north-east, and at its northern extremity Punta Francés (the most northerly of the Cuban continent), and at its eastern extremity Punta Mola; Punta Curiana, adjoining the Bay of Jigüey, and remarkable only as a point of demarkation to the maritime division; Punta Brava, at the western extremity of the port of Guanaja; Punta del Sabinal and Punta Maternillos, at the mouth of the port of Nuevitas, with a light-house called Colon; Cabo Lucrecia, at the north of the port of Nipe; Cabo Guarico, near Moa; Cabo Maisí, the eastern extremity of the island, low and sandy. On the south coast are—Punta Verraco, a cape near the port of Cuba; Cabo Cruz, one of the most remarkable in the island; Punta de Macurijes; Punta Casilda, at the entrance of the port of the same name; Punta San Juan, between Trinidad and Jagua; Punta Don Cristóbal, remarkable only as the boundary between the maritime provinces of Trinidad and Havana; Cabo Matahambre, western extremity of the Zapata swamp; Punta Mayabeque, at the mouth of the river of the same name; Punta Salinas; Punta Comegatos; Punta Carraguao or Mediacasa, at the east of the estuary of Dayaniguas; Punta del Gato; Punta de la Fisga; Punta Francés; Cabo Corrientes, with Punta Aguirre at its southern extremity; and Punta del Holandés, near Cabo San Antonio. In the island of Pinos the chief are—Punta del Este; Cabo Francés, and Punta Buenavista, at the entrance of the Bay of Siguanea.

Adjacent Islands, Keys, and Shoals.—Bordering upon the Island of Cuba are four distinct and well-defined archipelagos : two on the northern coast, and two on the southern. In that of Guaniguanico,† on the

---

* We do not mention the peninsula of La Herradura, in the port of Cabañas, because there are similar ones in almost all the principal ports of the island, the most notable among which being that of Cayo Juan Tomas, in the same port, and the one lying between the ports of Banes (eastern) and Nipe.

† This name and that of the following group have been bestowed by the author with reference to the aboriginal provinces to which they are most contiguous.

most westerly part of the north coast, are to be distinguished the following keys and shoals: Sancho Pardo, an isolated shoal, lying six leagues north-west of Cabo San Antonio, of little extent, but much feared by navigators; Santa Isabel and the Colorados, long and dangerous shoals, extending from near Punta de Abalo into Bahia-Honda; the Cayos de Buenavista, Rapado, Diego, and Jutias; the two Cayos de Inés de Soto, with watering-place; that of Lebisa; the small group of Alacranes, and Cayo Blanco. The other northerly archipelago extends from Cabo Hicacos to the peninsula of Sabinal. For the better classification of the islands, keys, and shoals that compose it, we shall divide it into two groups: one we shall term Sabaneque, from its proximity to the old province so called, and the other Jardines (gardens) del Rey, which name was bestowed upon it by the discoverer of the island (doubtless because of the luxuriant appearance it derives from the mangrove, coco-plum, and other shrubs, which clothe or line most of them); the remarkable break descried at the north of Turiguanó island will serve to divide the two groups. That of Sabaneque comprises Cayo Monito, Cayo Piedras (with a light), and Cayo Mono, which are the most westerly of the group; Cayo Diana (with a light), near Punta de Mola, on Cabo Hicacos; Cayos de Cupeyes, near the Bay of Cárdenas: all these present a picturesque and pleasing appearance to passengers by sea between Matanzas and Cárdenas; Cayo Cruz del Padre, where a light is about to be erected; Cayo Blanco; Cayo de Cinco Leguas, very singular and remarkable; Cayo Bahia de Cádiz, with good anchorage; Cayo Verde; Cayo Sotavento; Cayos Cristo, Fragoso, and Francés, which are considerable, the last containing a spacious bay termed de Caldera, wherein a squadron may anchor; Cayo Cobos, and Cayos de Santa Maria. In the group of Jardines del Rey are to be distinguished Cayo Media-Luna; Turiguanó island; Cayo Guillermo; the island called Cayo Coco; the island called Cayo Romano, which is the largest of the archipelago;* Cayo Paredon del Medio, to be furnished with a light; Cayo Paredon-Grande; Cayos del Barril; Cayo Cruz; Cayo Confites, which is small, and shows a light, and, together with the four last, lies on the edge of the old Bahama channel; and, finally, Guajaba island. The portion of coast comprised between the mouth of the port of Nuevitas and Cabo Maisí is in general rocky and clear, there being only the small Cayos Moa and Burro, the latter at the boundary of the districts of Cuba and Baracoa. Of the two archipelagos on the southern coast, one faces the space comprised between Cabo de Cruz and Trinidad, and the other the coast extending between Cochinos Bay and the inlet (termed lagoon) of Cortés; the first retains the name of Jardines

---

* This island, as well as those of Turiguanó, Coco, Guajaba, and Pinos, will be especially mentioned in the sequel.

de la Reina, bestowed by the discoverer (although also known as Laberínto, or Cayos de las doce Leguas, which name is peculiar to the keys at the south of this archipelago); the second we shall call Canarreos, as it was termed by the natives. Among the Jardines de la Reina we shall notice the Cayos de Manzanillo, Bajo de Buena-Esperanza; the Laberinto, or Cayos de las doce Leguas, which is a chain running from southeast to north-west, composed of the largest and most northerly keys of this archipelago; those at the east end being called Jamaicanas, and the most westerly, Cayo Breton; Cayo Piedras being distinguished by having been visited by Columbus on his second voyage, and who named it Santa Maria; Cayos de Ana Maria; Cayo Saza, south of the landing-place of the same name; and Cayo Guayo, at the entrance of port Casilda. Between the archipelagos De la Reina and Canarreos lie the isolated shallows of La Paz and Jagua. In the archipelago of the Canarreos are observed— the bank of Los Jardines and Jardinillos, south of the Zapata swamp, containing Cayos Rabihorcado and de Pasaje, and the islet of Cayo-Largo, with watering-place; Cayos Blanco, Diego, Perez, Flamenco, and Bonito, adjoining the Bay of Cazones (coast of the aforesaid Zapata swamp); Cayos Juan Luis and Guanimar; Bajos Patatillos; Cayos de los Indios, and·de San Felipe (within view of vessels from La Vuelta-Abajo); and, above all, the important island of Pinos, which merits the especial description given in the sequel.

Straits and Channels.—Such as are near to the island we shall style *common*, or belonging to all nations, and *adjacent* such as are annexed to the government of the island. Under the caption of common are—the Florida channel, formed by the keys or reefs of Florida, and the north coast of this island from the port of Havana to the Canal de Hicacos; the new Bahama channel, between the open peninsula of Florida and the Grand Bank of Bahama (as its currents tend toward the north, it serves, in the transit to Europe, for vessels going out of the Mexican Gulf or from the coasts of this island); the Canal de Santaren, between the shallow of Los Roques and the Grand Bank of Bahama; the old Bahama channel, between the Grand Bank and the northern coast of the island, from San Juan de los Remedios to Cabo Lucrecia (as its currents flow toward the north-west, it serves for vessels coming from Europe to the north coast of the island or to the Mexican Gulf); the Freo de Maisí (or *de los pajaros*), between Cabo Maisí and Cabo San Nicolas in Hayti; Freo de Colon, between this island and Jamaica; and, finally, the Estrecho de Yucatan between Cabos San Antonio and Catoche on the open peninsula of Yucatan. The adjacent ones are as follows: in the Sabaneque group, the passage or Boca de la Manui (east of Cárdenas), separating the famous Cayo de Cinco Leguas; the Canal del Pargo, front-opening through which runs the river of the same name; the Jiquíma, north-west of Madruga and 100 *varas* high; Sierra de Madruga, Cayajábos, etc., east of the town of Madruga; Sierras de Caobas, Limon, Santa Ana, and Gonzales; and the Lomas de Cabaljan and Jacan, containing copper ores, south of Limonal, and commanding a distant view of the sea; Loma de Cantel, on which is the town of the same name; Tetas de Camarioca, a notable ridge six leagues from Matanzas, presenting two conical peaks 400 *varas* high, which serve as landmarks to mariners; Loma de Triana, north of Lagunillas, and Lomas de las Quimbámbaras, south-west of the town of Roque. In the *Sabaneque* group may be comprised the comparatively low Sierra de Limones and Sierra Morena; the Jumaguas, isolated hills west of Sagua la Grande; Sierra Matahambre, 600 *varas* in height; Sierras Bamburanao and Centeno; Lomas de Meneses, Canoa, and Babuya, and Sierra de Jatibonico, whence arise two rivers of the same name. The group *Cubanacan* comprises the remarkable and craggy Sierra de Escambray, source of the copious rivers Sagua la Grande, Sagua la Chica, and Agabama, contains mines of copper, and, according to history, of gold and silver. In the group *Guamuhaya* the principal are, Sierra de Jagua, between Cienfuegos and Trinidad; Pico Blanco and Cabeza del Muerto (which mariners call Cabeza de San Juan), 1,000 *varas* high; Cabagan; Pico Potrerillo, north of Trinidad, 1,094 *varas* high, and visible on fine days at a distance of 21 leagues; Sierras de San Juan de Letran; de Guaniquicál; Trancas de Galvez; Sierras de Yaguasal; Lomas de la Rosa, and de Banao (1,000 *varas* high); Pan de Azucar; Pico Tuerto, and Sierra de la Gloria, boundary between Trinidad and Santo Espíritu. Of the *Camagueyano* group the chief are, Sierra de Cubitas, whose summit is the lofty Loma de Tuabaquei, which, with that of Limones, forms a land-port, called Boca de Cubitas: this ridge contains the largest and most remarkable caverns in the island; Loma Camajan; Sierra de Judas; Cerros Cascarro and Bayatabo, where a rich copper mine is being worked; and, south of Puerto Principe, the Sierras Guaicanamar and Chorillo. Among the group *Maniabon* we distinguish the Mesa de Manatí, west of the mouth of the port of that name; Sierra Dumañuecos; Lomas Rompe and Carcamisas; the Mesa de Jibára, which is a landmark to navigators, and the Lomas de Almiquí, south-west of Holguin, where gold has been found. Group *Macaca* extends from Cape Cruz to the Baconao River, and is known as the Sierra Maestra; it consists of the highest mountains of the Antillian system, the most remarkable being the Ojo de Toro, a striking peak near Cape Cruz, 1,200 *varas* in height. Pico Turquino, the nucleus of the Antillian system[*] towering

---

[*] In 1845, while in Cuba with the commission of forming the statistics of the eastern

to the height of 2,800 *varas*, and presenting a majestic appearance; Sierra del Cobre; Sierra Armonía de Limones, part of the Sierra Maestra, north-east of Cuba, replete with coffee-plantations, producing the best in the island; the Gran-Piedra, a remarkable mountain, 2,600 *varas* high, in the form of a truncated cone, on the top of which rests a vast rock, as if fallen from heaven;* Loma del Gato, 1,179 *varas* high; and Loma de la Guinea, 1,213 *varas* high. In the group *Sagua-Baracoa* are the Sierra de Nipe, the Sierra de Cristál, and Cuchillas de Santa Catalina; Sierra de la Vela, which forms the boundary of Saltadero, Cuba, and Baracoa; Sierra de Moa; Cuchillas de Toa; Sierra del Yunque, east of Baracoa, and the most striking of the group; it is a truncated cone, which, added to its height (1,000 *varas*), makes it a guiding-point to navigators; and Cuchillas de Baracoa, south of the city of that name.

Volcanoes.—There are no active ones in the island, but the pumice-stone, and other substances found in the Cabaljana and other mountains, prove them to be extinct volcanoes, as also the pyramidal forms of the imposing Turquino, the Ojo de Toro, Tetas de Camarioca, and others; and the lake crowning the conical and isolated Yunque indicates an old crater.

Valleys.—That of Ceja Ana de Luna, south-east of the Chorrera, or Consolacion del Norte; that of Güines, one of the most extensive in the island, and presenting such a magnificent appearance when viewed from the Loma de Candela, that Humboldt declares it unequaled; the remarkable and picturesque valley of Yumurí, east of Matanzas, formed by the hills which, extending along the Cumbre and the coast to Punta de Guanos, close in toward the Pan, Palenque, etc.; the valleys of Siguanea and Jibacoa, north-west of Trinidad; the picturesque valley of Los Injenios de Trinidad, and many others in the mountainous jurisdiction of Cuba.

Caverns.—Many of the innumerable caverns piercing each of the mountainous groups are exceedingly curious, but we shall mention only

department, the author intended, in company with the intelligent engineer M. Sagebien, who was provided with an excellent barometer, to measure the principal heights of the Sierra Maestra, but was prevented from doing so. The measures of many of them have been furnished by M. Sagebien, but, unfortunately, not those of the loftiest points of said ridge.

* La Grosse-Roche, as it is termed by the Frenchmen who first cultivated those mountains, is a parallelopiped whose upper face is 52 feet long and 19 wide. For some time the southern bed of it has been crumbling away, and the earthquakes have formed a hollow round its base. It is reasonable to suppose that the rains have subsequently undermined it, and it may fall in the course of the present century. When this shall happen the concussion will be perceived at a very great distance, and it is likely that the mass will not stop short of Juragua, at a distance of at least two leagues from its present site.

a few of the best known. One in the Sierra del Rosario, on the road to San Cristóbal, where several of Narciso Lopez's party sought refuge; those of Jaiguan, with a stream of excellent water running through them, and affording a convenient bathing-place; the remarkable one of Cotilla, six leagues from Havana;* those of San Juan de los Remedios; those of Cubitas, the most notable in the island, as well for their extent as for their singular features; and, finally, the vast number that are found in the broken ground on the east of the island, and which, besides being remarkable in themselves, contain in many instances osseous remains, idols, and utensils of the primitive inhabitants.

Sabanas or Plains—There are many at the east of the district comprised between Cape San Antonio and the jurisdiction of Matanzas; in the jurisdictions of Cárdenas, Sagua la Grande, Villa Clara, Cienfuegos, and even San Juan de los Remedios; but the most extensive (in some cases limited only by the horizon) are those of Santo Espiritu, Puerto Principe, Holguin, and Bayamo.

Rivers.—On the northern coast are the following: Pan de Azucar, small, but with a strong current, and serving as the boundary between the jurisdictions of Pinar del Rio and Bahia-Honda; Ortigosa, or Santiago, bounding between Bahia-Honda and Mariel; Banes (formerly Bani), small, but with good anchorage, a tower, and salt-water baths near its mouth; Baracoa, boundary between Mariel and Santiago; Marianao, boundary between Santiago and Havana, is a small river running near the town of that name, and whose waters are exquisite, and even medicinal; Chorrera (formerly Casiguaguas) rises in the Loma del Gallo, near Tapaste, under the name of Jicotea, extends into Lake Curbelo, then takes successively the names of Jiaraco, Chorrera, Catalina, Calabazar (on passing by the town of that name), Almendarez (where an excellent spring is received, and from which it is purposed to supply Havana), running along the Husillo, at a distance of two leagues from Havana (whence water is at present furnished to the capital), Puentes-Grandes, on passing by the bathing-town of that name, and finally resuming the name of Chorrera at its mouth; Luyanó (vulgarly Villanó), which is remarkable only for disemboguing at the south of the harbor of Havana, and as the dividing line between Havana and Guanabacoa, from its mouth to Rio Hondo, and having formerly served to supply the city of Havana; Jaruco, part of which, together with the Guanabo, more to the west, is the boundary between Guanabacoa and Jaruco; Yumurí, a narrow river, five leagues in its course, watering the picturesque valley of that name, and passing through a remarkable

---

* A description of this and other caves has been published by Sr. Carles in the *Diario de la Habana* for August, 1847.

opening, disembogues at the north of the city of Matanzas, separating the fine district of Versalles, and serving as a channel for large lighters for a distance of half a league from its mouth; San Juan receives the San Agustin and other rivulets which dilate it, and under various names disembogues at the south of Matanzas, separating therefrom the ward of Pueblo-Nuevo, and spanned by two bridges communicating between that ward and said city: like the Yumurí it is navigable for lighters for a space of one league; Canimar, a magnificent river with a course of six leagues, and, like the two preceding, emptying into the Bay of Matanzas, being navigable nearly two leagues by schooners, and for a greater distance if its windings are followed; Camarioca, with anchorage east of the Bay of Matanzas; San Anton de la Ancgada, east of the Júcaro station; Júcaro,* which rises in Sabanilla de la Palma, and disembogues (like the Canal of San Mateo) in the Bay of Santa Clara; La Palma, a considerable river, emptying opposite the Canal del Pargo, and serving, like the latter, as a boundary in the maritime division: it is navigable as far as its embarking-place, one league distant; Las Cruces, opposite the Canal de Nicolas Sanchez, and spreading its waters into the swamp of the coast; Sierra Morena, limited in its course, has served as a boundary between the western and central departments, and is such at present between the division of the districts of the Audiencias and for the Intendancies of Havana and Puerto Principe; Sagua la Grande, the largest river of the northern coast, rises in the Sierra del Escambray, runs a course of 35 leagues, and passes by the towns of Santo Domingo and Sagua la Grande, whence it is navigable for schooners as far as its mouth, a distance of seven leagues, and very tortuous;† Caonao, one and a half leagues in length, from its mouth to the estuary of Granadillo, and serving as a boundary between Sagua la Grande and Villa Clara; Sagua la Chica also rises in the Sierra del Escambray, is 25 leagues long, having the Embarcadero del Santo a league from its mouth, and serving as a boundary between Villa Clara and San Juan de los Remedios; Jatiboníco del Norte rises at the south of the Sierra de Jatiboníco (where Jatiboníco del Sur also has its origin), disappearing at a short distance and reappearing a league off in boisterous cascades; it disembogues east of Punta Judas, after a course of 15 miles, and serves as a boundary between Remedios and Santo Espiritu; Los Perros (called *Chambas* at its head) rises in Sierra Matahambre and passes by Hato Camagueyano; La Yana (called *Arroyo Pablos* at its origin) empties itself on the east of Laguna Moron, and serves as a boundary of the chief military and ecclesiastical divisions; Caonao arises at the north of Puerto

---
* The station, and even the railroad of Júcaro, have therefore been improperly named.
† In a straight line the distance is but about four leagues.

Principe, and passes near the parish of Mulato; Jigüey rises at the south of the Sierra de Cubitas, and disembogues east of Punta Curiana; Mácsimo, a short river that empties into the Bay of Sabinál, and remarkable because it is supposed that Columbus made his first landing in the island at its mouth, calling it the San Salvador, the 28th of October, 1492; Saramaguacan, 20 leagues long, rises near Puerto Principe, and empties into the bay of Mayanabo, port of Nuevitas; Las Cabreras, that used to be the dividing line between the eastern and central departments, empties itself before reaching the coast; Yariguá disembogues in the port of Manatí, and has its borders covered with brilliant pebbles; Tacajó, that empties into the Bay of Nipe; Mayarí, that rises in the Lomas de Tiguabos, passes by the town of its name, and disembogues three leagues thence in the port of Nipe, after a course of 35 leagues; Sagua de Tánamo, 22 leagues long, copious and navigable as far as the town of that name, four leagues from its mouth; Cabreras, distinguished only as the boundary between Baracoa and Cuba; Moa, a short river, which disappears at its origin, and forms on its reappearance a cascade of 100 *varas*; the Toa, a considerable river, rising in the heights of the same name, and emptying itself north-east of Baracoa; Macaganigua and Miel, small rivers disemboguing near Baracoa, with bars at their mouths, rendering them dangerous, as was experienced by Hernan Cortés.

On the southern coast the rivers are as follows: Sabana-la-mar, boundary between the Saltadero and Baracoa; Yateras, 24 leagues in length; Guantánamo, about 25 leagues long, receiving at its right bank the Tiguabos, and emptying itself by the western coast of the Bay of Guantánamo; Aguadores, a short river; Yarayó, short, and disemboguing at the north of the port of Cuba; Turquino, a short river at the foot of the lofty peak of the same name, and serving as a boundary between Manzanillo and Cuba; Bicana; Yara, bordered by fine tobacco-lands or *vegas*; Jicotea, the boundary between Bayamo and Manzanillo; Buey, of little extent, but overflowing in its course, forms the swamp of the same name; Cauto, the longest and most copious river of the island, having a course of 60 leagues: it rises near Villa del Cobre, at a place called Macuto, receiving on its left margin the rivers Contramaestre and Cautillo (which form the eastern and western boundaries of Jiguaní), and the Bayamo, which passes by the city of the same name; and on its right margin, the rivulet Cayo del Rey, and the deep and broad Salado, 25 leagues long, into which flows the Playuelas rivulet, boundary of Holguin; the Cauto is navigable for schooners a distance of 22 leagues (as far as the town of Cauto del Embarcadero); the Jobabo, which used to serve as the boundary between the central and eastern departments; Sevilla, boundary between

Bayamo and Puerto Principe; San Juan, Najaza, or Santa Cruz, with a course of 23 leagues, empties itself a short distance east of the port of Santa Cruz, after irrigating the broad savannas at the south of Puerto Principe; San Pedro or Santa Clara, 33 leagues long, receiving at its origin the rivers Tínima and Jatibonico, which cross the city of Puerto Principe; Altamira or Durán, which disembogues into the bay of Santa Clara; Sabana-la-mar, a rivulet serving as a boundary between the dioceses and the military divisions; Jatibonico del Sur, having a course of 25 leagues, rises in the Sierra de Jatibonico (which also produces the river Jatibonico del Norte), and passes by the town of San Antonio Abad del Jíbaro, whence it is navigable for schooners as far as its mouth, a space of three leagues; Sasa, 35 leagues long, rises in the Sierra Jatibonico, passes three leagues east of Santo Espiritu, and afterward by the Embarcadero del Algodonal, whence it is navigable as far as its mouth, in the anchorage of Benitez, and serves for the shipping-trade of Santo Espiritu which is authorized for the purpose under the denomination of *puerto seco* or "dry port;" the Iguanojo, boundary between Trinidad and Santo Espiritu; the Agabáma, 26 leagues in course, rises in the Escambray Mountains, in the chain called *Peña del Agabama:* it receives the river Ay (called *De los Negros* at its head), which is lost in the splendid valley of Jibacoa, but reappears by the Sierra Yaguasal; the Guanabo or Táyaba, a short river, but navigable by lighters for the space of a league, or half the distance to Trinidad; San Juan, a short river, and the boundary between Trinidad and Cienfuegos; Arimao, with a course of 14 leagues, rises in the Sierra Escambray, waters the beautiful *vegas* of Manicaragua and Mandinga, and passing by the hamlets of Cumanayagua and Arimao, disembogues near the mouth of the port of Jagua, with which it unites by an arm crossing the lagoon of Guanaroca, which arm is known as *Derramadero de las Auras:* the *encomiendas*[*] of the celebrated Father Las Casas and his friend the good Pedro de Renteria were situated at this place.; the river Hanabanilla, which is one of the affluents of the Arimao, produces in the Hacienda de Siguanea a cascade of 120 *varas* fall; Caonao, navigable four leagues, rises in the Sierra Escambray, passes near the hamlets of Camarones and Caonao, and empties into the port of Jagua, south of Cienfuegos; the Salado, navigable six leagues, also disembogues in the port of Jagua; Damují, 18 leagues long (six of which are navigable and very deep), empties at the north of said port of Jagua, and serves as the boundary between the Intendancies of Havana and Puerto Principe: it contains formidable alligators; Hanábana, with a course of 10 leagues, receives the rivulet

---

[*] A grant of land and Indian servants.

Mayabon, serves as the boundary between the jurisdictions of Cienfuegos and Cárdenas, and disembogues in the Laguna del Tesoro, north of Cochinos Bay; Hatiguaníco or Atibonico, formed by the Gonzalo rivers, divides the jurisdiction of Cienfuegos from those of Cárdenas, Matanzas, and Güines; Madruga rises in the Loma de Madruga, and disembogues in one of the Guanamon lagoons; Guara, receiving the Rio-Blanco, which serves as the boundary between Bejucál and Güines; Mayabeque (formerly Onicajinal), known at its commencement as the *Catalina*, from arising in the source of the same name, and successively as the Bija, Yamaraguas, and also as Güines: it courses nine leagues through land of the richest description, suitable for all the productions of the climate, and is the only river whose waters have been availed of for irrigation; Govea, flows at its origin between Santiago and Bejucál, and, after fertilizing a multitude of farms, empties into the lagoon of Ariguanabo, serving as the boundary between San Antonio, Bejucál, and Santiago; San Antonio takes its rise at the junction of the Govea and the Ariguanabo lagoon, passes by the fine town of San Antonio, at the south of which it disappears at the foot of a leafy *Seiba* tree (whose roots form a singular arch), and appears again in several caves, among which is that of Jaiguan; Cajío, a short river, supposed to be an outlet of the San Antonio; Capellanías, which, like the San Antonio, hides itself at the south of the town of its name, reappears and empties itself before reaching the coast; Macurijes disappears at its origin in a mountain of the Guaniguanico group; San Diego (formerly *Caiguanabo*), has a course of 11 leagues, three of which are navigable, and is remarkable for disappearing in the Portales (a species of natural arches), and especially for the baths of its name; La Coloma, river and port, rising in the Sabánas de las Ovas; Guamá, rising in the Organos and passing by Pinar del Rio; San Juan y Martinez, rises in the Organos and receives the Palmillas, Negros, and Papaya, disemboguing near Punta de Cartas; Galafre has its rise in the Contador, receives the Alvarado and Yaguas, and empties into the bay of its name; Cuyaguateje, the greatest river of the Vuelta-Abajo, being 23 leagues long: it rises in the Organos Mountains, runs through a natural vault, known as the *Resolladero*, and disembogues north of the inlet of Cortés.

Water-Falls.—Although there are several in the declivities of the mountains, we shall mention only the following : the falls of the Manantial River (affluent of the Bayate), 80 *varas* high; the remarkable ones of the Siguanea, or Salto de la Hanabanilla (affluent of the Arimao), from a height of 120 *varas*, on the Hacienda Siguanea, which is the boundary point between Cienfuegos, Trinidad, and Villa Clara; the falls of the river Ay (affluent of the Agabama), about 60 *varas* high; those of Moa, 100 *varas* high. There are many others in the eastern part of the island, among them the falls del Indio, 120 *varas* high, being a greater height than those of Niagara.

Lakes or Lagoons.—In the peninsula of Guanajacabibes there are, among others, the following: the Laguna de Melones, near the Bay of Corrientes; that of Algodonal and of Lopez, near the inlet of Guadiana; the Laguna de la Siguanea; Laguna de Ahoga-Caballos, in the district of Consolacion del Norte (Puercos River); Lagunas del Gato and Masio, near the estuary del Gato, at the mouth of Rio-Hondo; Laguna de Macurijes, south of the Palacios; Laguna de Piedra, in Hato Guanacaje, west of Bay Majana; Laguna de Fuente-Paloma, west of the port of Cabañas; Laguna de Ariguanabo, which is a union of three, viz.—the Biragua, Loreto, and Guandambú, merging into one during the rainy season, containing four keys, and forming quite a peninsula, called La Rosa; it is then a veritable lake, covering a surface of two leagues, and in some places three fathoms deep; it is abundantly supplied with fish; it receives the Govea River, and gives rise to that of San Antonio; on the north it communicates with two or three notable lagoons; Laguna de Zaldivar, south-west of Ubajay; Laguna Ahoga-Mulas, between Santiago and Ubajay;[*] Lagunas Berroa, Larga, and del Cobre, near Bacuranao; Laguna de Curbelo, at the origin of the Almendares River; Lagunas Fabelo, Bainoa, Manajay, or Tibo-Tibo and del Reló or Guayabo, between Jaruco and El Aguacate; Ojo de Agua, in the Catalina River, a spring remarkable for its extent and picturesque aspect, and for giving rise to the river Güines or Mayabeque; Lagunas de Guanamon, abounding in fish, south of La Nueva Paz, one of them receiving the Madruga River; Laguna de Maya, of considerable extent, east of the bay of Matanzas; Lagunas de Macurijes and del Masio, east of Corral-Falso; Laguna del Tesoro, which receives the Hanabana River, north of Cochinos Bay, and is unfathomable; Laguna de Caobillas, south-west of the town of that name; Laguna de Guanajayabo, near the Recreo station, on the Júcaro railroad; Laguna-Nueva, south-east of Guamutas; Laguna Asiento-Viejo, origin of the Hanabana River; Laguna Guanaroca, communicating with the Arimao River and the Bay of Jagua; Moron or Laguna-Grande, miscalled lagoon, since it is a passage between the continent of this island and Turiguanó island: however, it is said to contain fresh-water; Laguna de la Sigua (in Cuba), remarkable both for its extent and the excellent fish abounding in its waters.

Cienagas or Swamps.—As said before, the stretches of coast fronting the four adjacent archipelagos are almost all swampy; we notice the following: Cienaga del Gato, near the estuary of that name, Cienaga de

---

[*] The coast comprised between Banes and Marianao River is bordered by a great number of lagoons.

Dayaniguas and Carraguao, south of Los Palacios; Cienaga de Majagüiyal, divided by the Canal of San Mateo, east of the Júcaro; Cienaga de Zapata, the most notable in the island, since it extends from the Gulf of Matabanó to the Bay of Cochinos; Cienaga de Yaguaraguas; Cienaga de Buey, between the rivers Buey and Cauto; Lagunas de Salsipuedes and Laguna-Blanca, in the district of Cauto-Abajo; the first, three leagues in circumference, and the latter two.

Salt Fields.—In those places where the tides, especially the lunar and equinoctial tides, flow into the coasts, are formed extensive salt lagoons, which in years of drought, produce considerable quantities of salt, sufficient for the consumption of the interior. These lagoons are generally more common on the northern than on the southern coast. We shall notice only the following: those of the Bay of Majana; those of Cape Hicacos and Chocó, which yield over 4,000 *arrobas* per annum; those of the Cienaga de Zapata, toward Punta del Padre; those of the Bay of Cochinos; those on the south coast of Santo Espiritu; those of the ports of Malagueta, Padre, and Nipe,* and those at the mouth of the River Sagua de Tánamo; that north of the Bay of Birama; and those of Guantánamo, which are very productive.

Harbors, Bays, Inlets, Anchorages, etc.—NORTH COAST—In *Pinar del Rio:* the Guadiana, an inlet (albufera) miscalled bay; San Francisco and Mantua, embarcaderos or embarking-places; Los Arroyos, embarcadero, three leagues from Mantua, and stopping-place of the screw-steamer "Veguero;" Santa Ysabel, embarcadero; Garnacha and Bája, bays. In *Bahia-Honda:* El Rosario, a large bay with two embarking-places; Rio-Puercos, a port, but no town; La Mulata, a port of the third class, with town; Playitas, embarking-place; El Morillo, embarking-place north of the town of Las Pozas; Manimaní or Maniman, a fine bay in the mouth of the River San Miguel or Manimaní; Bahia-Honda, a port of the first class, 22 maritime leagues from Havana, with anchorage in some places for the largest ships: its spacious entrance is defended by a fort; La Ortigosa, a port in the mouth of the River Santiago. In *Mariel:* Cabañas, a port of the second class, two leagues long and one wide, 16 maritime leagues west of Havana, with anchorage for frigates: it is divided into two parts by a peninsula called Cayo de Juan Tomás, on whose northern extremity is a fort defending the entrance; Dominica, a port in the mouth of the river of that name; Mariel (formerly Marien), an authorized port† of the second class, 12 maritime leagues from Havana,

---
* That of Yarayal, near Mayari, has not crystallized since 1844.
† Authorized ports, or ports of entry:
    1st class, authorized for all foreign trade, inward and outward.
    2d class, where foreign vessels are limited to the coasting trade as regards imports, but can export produce.
    3d class, limited to the coasting-trade in vessels of the island.

with anchorage for frigates: its entrance is somewhat obstructed by a shoal; it is defended by a tower, and nearly at its bottom lies the town of the same name; Mosquitos, an estuary in the mouth of the river of that name, and has a tower; Guaijabon, a port, with tower; Banes (formerly Bani), a port, eight leagues from Havana, with a tower and a small hamlet at the bottom; Baracoa, in the mouth of the river of that name. In *Santiago:* Santa Ana, embarking-place, in the mouth of the River Bauta or Santa Ana, with a small town; Jaimaníta, a port with a hamlet. In *Habana:* Marianao, a port, in the mouth of the river of that name, with a tower and hamlet; La Chorrera, a port of the fourth class, in the mouth of the river of that name, with a tower and hamlet; La Habana (formerly Carenas), a port of the first order, with a narrow entrance, well sheltered and defended: it comprises the bays of Marimelena, Guasabacoa, and Atarés, and has a bonded warehouse. In *Guanabacoa:* Cojímar, a port, in the mouth of the river of that name, with a tower, and town of the same name; Bacuranao, a port, with tower and hamlet, in the mouth of the river of that name; La Boca, embarking-place, with hamlet, in the mouth of the River Guanabo; Rincon de Sibarimar, embarking-place, with hamlet; Jaruco, with tower, and a hamlet called La Boca, in the mouth of the Jaruco River. In *Jaruco:* Santa Cruz, an anchorage, with hamlet, in the mouth of the river so called: it is dangerous from the reefs that surround it; Rota, a bay, for vessels drawing 10 feet; Jibacoa-Rutinel, embarking-place, with hamlet, east of the River Jibacoa. In *Matanzas:* Canasí, an anchorage, with hamlet, in the mouth of the river of that name, and having warehouses toward the interior; Puerto-Escondido, an anchorage, with warehouses, in the mouth of the river of that name; Bacunayagua, an anchorage in the mouth of the river so called; Matanzas (formerly Yucayo), a great bay, deep enough for the largest ships: it is an authorized port of the first class, defended by a castle and three batteries, and is also the terminus of the Matanzas Railroad; Canímar, embarking-place, inland three leagues from the mouth of the river of that name, and whither is transported the merchandise of its great trade; Camarioca, an anchorage of the fourth class, with a hamlet, in the mouth of the river of that name. In *Cárdenas:* Siguapa or Las Guásimas, embarking-place in the most western part of the Bay of Cárdenas; Cárdenas, a bay, and port of the second class, with the flourishing town of that name: it is also a railroad terminus; Siguagua, embarking-place; Júcaro, an anchorage, with a straggling hamlet and very long piers, supporting the branches of the Júcaro railroad; Canal de San Mateo, with embarking-place in the Bay of Santa Clara, where considerable business is done: it is two leagues long; La Palma, an inland embarking-place, three leagues from the mouth of the river of that name, with a large trade; La Teja, embarking-place, where the Sagua la Grande steamboat stops; Santa Clara, embarking-place; Ganuza, embarking-place. In *Sagua la Grande:* Sierra-Morena, embarking-place half a league east of the mouth of the river of that name; Pozas, embarking-place and stopping-place of the steamer *Jejen;* El Mallorquin, between Pozas and Sabanilla, whence it is intended to build a railroad to connect with that of Júcaro at Pijuan; Sagua la Grande, an authorized inland port of the second class, distant (by its windings) seven leagues from the mouth of the river of that name: it has a town which is the head of a district, and will soon be a railroad terminus; Carabatas, embarking-place west of the river so called, and a league from its hamlet. In *Villa Clara:* Granadillo, an inland embarking-place, three leagues from the mouth of the Caonao River. In *San Juan de los Remedios:* Tesíco, a port in the great bay which also comprises Caibarien; Caibarien, a bay serving for the shipping trade of the authorized "dry port" of the first class, San Juan de los Remedios, distant three leagues south-west; Mayajigua, a "dry port" whose shipping-place is the Estero Real. In *Santo Espiritu:* Los Perros, Mamon, or Chambas, a port at the mouth of the river so called; Moron or Laguna-Grande, an estuary, with a depth of eight or nine feet, formed by the island of Turiguanó and the Cuban continent. In *Puerto Principe:* Santa Gertrudis and Santa Marcelina, embarking-places; Sabana-la-mar, an embarking-place west of Caonao River; Guanaja, a bay and authorized port of the second class, where the shipping trade of Puerto Principe is done: of this, however, it has lost a good deal since the completion of the Nuevitas railroad; Jigüey, a bay of little depth in the mouth of the river of that name. In *Nuevitas:* Sabinal, an extensive bay, through the mouth of which, called Boca de los Carabelas, it is surmised that Columbus entered on the discovery of the island, October 28, 1492; Nuevitas (formerly Puerto Principe), is an authorized port of the second class, with an area of 57 square miles: the entrance is long and narrow, furnished with a light, and defended by fort San Hilario; in the interior are several keys and the bays of Mayanabo, Pueblo-Viejo (the original site of Santa Maria de Puerto Principe), Guincho (where the railroad to Puerto Principe begins), Granadillas, Santa Rosa, and Santa Lucia, and in the south side is the town of Bagá; Nuevas-Grandes, a long and narrow estuary, with several keys within it. In *Tunas:* Manatí and Malagueta, excellent ports. In *Holguin:* Puerto del Padre, very deep; Jibára, an authorized port of the first class, with a fort and the town of Punta del Yarey; Jururú; Bariay; Vita; Naranjo, a small, but deep and excellent port; Samá, and Banes, good ports. In *Cuba:* Nipe, the largest port in the island, having an area of 65 square miles; its entrance is narrow and free; it is deserted, and its great extent, reaching almost to the horizon, prevents it from affording vessels a good shelter from the winds; Mayarí, an embarking-place within the port of Nipe, and three and a half leagues from the town of Mayarí, which also is an embarking-place, with eight feet depth at high water; Lebisa or Libisa and Cabonico, ports with only one entrance; Cebollas, Cananova, and Yaguaneque, small ports; Sagua de Tánamo, an inland port four leagues* from the mouth of the river of that name: it does an extensive trade in timber, tobacco, and cattle. In *Baracoa:* Moa, a port with a good depth and well sheltered, and having in front the key of that name; Baracoa, an authorized port of the first class, with the city of the same name; Mata, the most easterly port of the island.

SOUTH COAST—In *Baracoa:* Jauco, an anchorage. In *Saltadero:* Baitiquerí, a port; Puerto-Escondido; Guantánamo, a large bay (called Cumberland Bay by the English) 20 leagues east of Cuba, and three leagues south of the town of Guantánamo: its entrance is 8,000 *varas* wide, and has a fort at the narrowest part of the interior: its area is 27 square miles, and contains a number of ports, among which are those of Joa and La Majagua; its trade, consisting in live-stock, cotton, and timber, is trifling. In *Cuba:* Baconao and Altáres, bays; Juragua and Aguadores, anchorages east of Cuba, the latter defended by a battery; Cuba, an authorized port of the first class, of great extent, and affording good shelter: the entrance is narrow and defended by three castles, the Morro, Santa Catalina, and La Estrella, and a battery near the city, which is situated on the eastern margin, almost at the bottom of the port: it contains the keys Raton and Smith,† the port and hamlet of Socapa on the western shore, and the Punta de Sal, fronting Cuba, is the terminus of the Cobre railroad: it is an excellent port, well sheltered, of smooth waters, and has a light. Cabañas, an anchorage with a battery: Nimaníma, Quibiján, and Rincon de Sevilla, anchorages. In *Manzanillo:* Turquino; Mota, a port south of peak Ojo de Toro; Portillo; Mora; Limones; Manzanillo, a bay, authorized as a port, with the town of the same name, and defended by a fort. In *Bayamo:* Cauto del Embarcadero, an inland embarking-place, 25 leagues from the mouth of the Cauto River, and six from the city of Bayamo: it might be the New Orleans of the island, and the banks of the Cauto bear many cities,

---

* Along the river, for in a straight line the distance is only three leagues. At the mouth there is five or six feet draft, and continues the same depth as far as the place called Los Cocos, two leagues from the town, and whence only lighters can navigate, and then only at tide. The north banks are covered with *vegas* of tobacco.

† The latter is large and of good soil; it is the property of Dr. Robert, and is inhabited by a few fishermen.

if its mouth were not obstructed ;* Birama, a spacious bay, with swampy coasts, and salt fields in the vicinity. In *Puerto Principe:* Junco, an estuary, noticed only as a boundary in the maritime division; Santa Cruz, a bay and authorized port, with the town of the same name, 22 leagues south of Puerto Principe; Santa Maria, an inlet where the English pirate Morgan landed in 1666; Vertientes, an anchorage, which used to be authorized for shipping; Sabana-la-mar, embarking-place near the southern boundary of the episcopal division. In *Santo Espiritu:* Sasa, an inland embarking-place on the River Sasa, authorized as a port, and having a town: it is seven leagues south of Santo Espiritu; Algodonal, also an inland embarking-place on the same river, and a short distance from that of Sasa, but more generally used, as it admits vessels of greater draught; Goleto or Caney, an estuary fronting the Key of Sasa. In *Trinidad:* Manati, an anchorage at the mouth of the Agabama River; La Seiba, embarking-place; Brujas, a bay; Jobabo and Caballones, bays with swampy coasts; El Masío, a port two and a half leagues east of the port of Casilda; Casilda, a port authorized for shipping, and serving for the trade of the " dry port" of Trinidad, a league north of it; Guaurabo, an anchorage, with a battery, at the mouth of the river of that name, navigable by skiffs for the space of a league, or within one mile of Trinidad. In *Cienfuegos:* Jagua, the most magnificent port in the island, and perhaps in the world, with an area of 56 square miles: its entrance is narrow and protected by the fort of Los Angeles: within it are the bays of Jucaral, Majagua, and Guaicanamar, the Caleton de Don Bruno, and Cayos Carenas, Ocampo, Alcatraz, and Loco: it is an authorized port, and has the flourishing town of Cienfuegos on the northern extremity of its eastern coast, where the Villa Clara railroad commences; even were it not " the best, nor is there, perhaps, its like in the whole world" (as expressed by Father Las Casas, who resided in its neighborhood), it is destined to be the chief port of the " Key of the New World," and is at the present day styled by foreigners *The great port of the Americas:* in the mouth of this port, and piercing the centre of its waters, is a spring of fresh water;† Cochinos, a large bay with embarking-place at the bottom; Cazones, a bay at the south of the Zapata swamp; Matahambre, near the cape of that name; La Broa, a vast bay, deep enough

---

* Until 1616 this embarking-place was one of the chief commercial places in the island, as is proved by the remains of the ancient custom-house (the first in the island); but in consequence of a flood of the river in that year a great bar was formed at the mouth, shutting in over 80 vessels, and ruining its trade, for at present only vessels within 200 tons can enter, and that at high tide.

† These phenomena occur at several places in the island, among others east of Los Jardines and Jardinillos, and in the Bay of Cochinos.

for brigs. In *Güines:* El Caimito, an estuary with a battery and hamlet; El Rosario, embarking-place, with a hamlet at the mouth of the river of that name. In *Bejucál:* Batabanó, an anchorage and port at the mouth of a small draining channel; it is situated a league from the town of the same name (although there is besides a small hamlet on the beach), and has an extensive pier, which is the terminus of the branch railroad of San Felipe; it was visited by Columbus on his second voyage. In *San Antonio:* Guanímar, embarking-place at the mouth of the river of that name. In *San Cristobal:* Majana, a bay where the river of that name disembogues; Sabana-la-mar, an estuary; Dayaniguas, a bay between the rivers San Diego and Los Palacios: it is the stopping-place of the steamers from Vuelta-Abajo, south coast; it is provided with warehouses and an establishment for sea-bathing. In *Pinar del Rio:* Cortés, an inland embarking-place, two leagues from the mouth of the San Diego; El Gato, an estuary, with an inlet connected with a lagoon called the Masío, at the mouth of the Rio-Hondo; La Coloma, embarking-place, with considerable trade, a river, port, and baths, six and a quarter leagues from Pinar del Rio; Punta de Cartas, a roadstead with warehouses and baths; Colon, an inland embarking-place one league from the mouth of the Coloma River, and five and a quarter leagues from Pinar del Rio: the entrance is picturesquely bordered by mangroves: there are warehouses and baths; Noda, within the Bay of Galafre, a port, with a town in project; Garay, an anchorage and hamlet in the mouth of Arroyo-Puercos;* Cortés, an inlet known as the Laguna de Cortés; Juan Claro, a bay between Cabo Corrientes and Cabo San Antonio.

Bridges.—The principal ones are as follows: that of Diego Velazquez, built in 1850 over the rivulet of Mordazo; it is entirely of hewn stone, and one of its arches is the greatest ever built in the island; that of Puentes-Grandes, over the Almendares, old, but solid and built of wood with buttresses of mason-work; that of Arango or Marinao, consisting of a single and small Gothic arch, but with broad terraces and high walls of mixed construction; that of Las Casas (called so in memory of the worthy governor Las Casas), in the town of Arroyo Arenas, entirely of stone, with three equal elliptical arches, finished in 1849; that of Santa Cruz, a league from the preceding, built of mason-work and wood; the old bridge of Calabazar, with one medium-sized arch and four smaller ones in its spacious wall, which serves rather as a dyke when the river overflows; that of Arroyo-Jíbaro, of a single stone arch, with wooden abutments; that of Alcoy, on the Luyanó River, on the road between

---

* The name of Bailen, bestowed on it by the company owning the steamers running to the Philippine Islands, is applied especially to their warehouse, which is situated there.

Havana and Guanabacoa, composed of three arches: it is finished with stone, and remarkable for its elegant and bold proportions; that of Bailen, in Matanzas, on the San Juan River, formed of two arches: also a fine stone work; that of San Luis, on the same river, built of wood; that of Canimar, at the point where it is crossed by the railroad: built of wood, and with a single arch, but in bold style; that of Yayabo, in Santo Espiritu, of stone, with five arches, and well constructed.*

Climate.—ASTRONOMICAL CLIMATE.—According to the stated astronomical position, the island of Cuba is comprised in the third *climate of hours*, the longest day (21st of June) being 13 hours 24 minutes, and the shortest (21st December) 10 hours 42 minutes. The longest summer day in Havana is from 5.13 A. M. to 6.47 P. M., and the shortest from 6.39 A. M. to 5.21 P. M., from sunrise to sunset, exclusive of twilight.

PHYSICAL CLIMATE.—We shall indicate the atmospherical phenomena according to meteorological classification.

Aerial Phenomena.—As in almost all the countries situated within the torrid zone, the air is less dense than in cold climates. The mean pressure at Havana is 759.84 millimetres: the maximum, in January, 770 millimetres, and the minimum, in October, 747.† With regard to temperature, as the island of Cuba lies between 20° and 23° north latitude, it will be conceived that in the half comprised between 20° and 21° 30′ it is lower than in the more northerly section. However, its proximity to the continent of America occasions frequent changes of temperature, and when the north-north-west wind is high, cold is experienced even at Santiago de Cuba, situated in the most southern part, although much more sensibly on the northern coast, and especially on the highlands of the interior, where the nights and mornings are cool enough to require extra clothing, and even to render a fire agreeable. The average annual temperature of Havana is 25° centigrade :‡ the highest, 32° (observed June,

---

* There are many others smaller, but well built; and at present it is intended to build simple, solid, and economical bridges on the central road, and on that of Vuelta-Abajo, from San Luis de la Seiba to Pinar del Rio.

† The barometer in the tropics attains the maximum between 9 and 9½ A. M., falls slowly until 12 M., and a little faster until 11 P. M., when it is somewhat lower than at 9 A. M.: it falls slowly through the night till 4 A. M., and reascends until 9 A. M. Of the two maxima, there is one greater than the other, which occurs at 9 A. M., and likewise of the two minima, one is least, and takes place at 4 A. M. This minimum of 4 A. M. has been found by Don Andrés Poey, as neither Humboldt nor other authors make any mention of it. During the great hurricane of 1846 the barometer fell as much as 730 millimetres.

‡ 0° Cent. = 32° Fahr.   21° Cent. = 69.8° Fahr.   31° Cent. = 87.8° Fahr.
 10°   "   = 50° "   25°   "   = 77°   "   32°   "   = 89.6° "
 14°   "   = 57.2° "   27°   "   = 82.6° "

1826), and the lowest, 10° (December, 1826) ;* or, deducting extremes, 31° and 14°. The average temperature of the warmest month was 27°, and of the coldest 21°. The average humidity of the atmosphere, as shown by the hair hygrometer, is 85° ; the maximum, in November and December, being 100°, and the minimum, in April, 66°, or 97° and 75°, without the extremes.

Winds.—North-easters, called *brisas* in the island, prevail at almost all seasons from 9 to 10 A. M. till sunset. They begin in the east-south-east and go as far as east-north-east, at which point they are termed *brisa alta.*† The most prevalent winds, when electrical discharges occur, are the south and south-south-west. Their duration is very variable, but they rarely last longer than a day, and occur 30 to 40 times during the year. The west and north-west winds are unfrequent, and always accompanied by rain. The northers, occurring from September to March, usually last two days, subsiding on the third, and blow six or eight times a year. They are regularly preceded by the south wind, which, veering to the west, causes some showers before the norther sets in. Windspouts or whirlwinds are of frequent occurrence during the dry season; sometimes, although seldom, doing injury to the plantations. Waterspouts also are sometimes seen.

Aqueous Phenomena.—The dew falls very copiously, especially during the dry season, but chiefly in December and January. Fogs also occur principally in the season of drought. The rain has so fixed and definite a period as to determine the seasons, which are divided into two, viz., the *rainy season* and the *dry season*, or season of northers. The first commences between May and June, and ends in November, being most active in September and October ; the average number of rainy days at Havana is 102, and the extremes for several years 135 and 75 days; 22 days is the maximum for a month, and 2 days the minimum. The average fall of rain at Havana is 1,029 millimetres ; the most, recorded for a year, is 50 inches 6 lines, and the least 32 inches 7 lines. The most for a month (August) 11 inches, and the least (November and December) 2 lines. The average of the most rainy months shows 6 inches 4 lines, and of the least 1 inch 4 lines. In the interior of the island 133 inches of rain have

---

* Don Antonio Robledo observed in 1801 a minimum temperature of zero (Reaumur, or 32° Fahr.) in the interior of the country. Don Francisco Lavallée declares that in Trinidad, among the mountains, the mercury falls to freezing point on cold nights, among which he instances the 13th of February, 1841. In Madrid, during the summer of 1853, it is stated that Reaumur's thermometer indicated as high as 35°, equal to 110⅔° Fahrenheit.

† At Santiago de Cuba the south wind is termed *brisa* (which means north-east wind), because, coming from the sea instead of the land, as is the case at other points of the north coast, it is cool and agreeable.

fallen in one year, of which 57 inches fell during the most rainy month. There is no notice of snow having fallen, but it hails almost every year in several parts of the island, particularly the eastern department, between February and July.

Electrical Phenomena.—The average annual number of thunderstorms at Havana has been 18. The greatest number during one year 32, and the least 7. The most during one month 13, while in others not one has occurred. They are most frequent in June, July, August, and September, and in the two first-named months thunderbolts sometimes literally rain down in the country. At Havana silent lightnings are common, appearing almost every night from June to October, and especially in July and August. Oftentimes they are seen in every quarter, but most frequently in the south-east and south-west. These lightnings correspond to the *second class,* which, according to M. Arago, are such as, instead of forming sinuous gyrations, almost without apparent extent, embrace on the contrary a vast expanse of the horizon. They are neither as white nor as swift as those of the *first* or zig-zag class, and generally appear of a bright red, blue, or purple color, which are the most common; they dart from the centre of the clouds, encircling them with a vivid light. On the night of 4th August, M. Poey counted during 10 minutes 110 of these lightnings in a south-westerly direction, and 11 zigzag flashes.*

Meteors.—The appearance of these phenomena is subject to a certain periodicity. At such times they are abundant, and are occasionally seen as a luminous shower, like that of the night of November 12 to 13, 1833, when a literal shower of fire was visible from Jamaica to Boston.† Prof. Olmstead is of opinion that the point whence these meteors issued was at a height of 800 leagues, and consequently beyond our atmosphere. Humboldt has assigned the following periods: April 22–25, July 17–26, August 10, November 12–14 and 28, 29, and December 6–12.‡ We would here call the attention of meteorologists to the following fact, stated by our friend Don Andrés Poey:|| this gentleman having observed the meteors during the nights of August 9–12, and November 11–15, 1849 and 1850, could not count more than 5 or 6 per hour, while on the same night of August 9, 10, 1850, there were counted at Yale College (United States) as many as 451 in the space of two hours and a quarter. Although we have no notice of the fall of any aerolite in the island, no doubt can be entertained of it in view of the frequent appearance of fire

---

* See "Anales de la Real Junta de Fomento, y Sociedad Económica," Vol. iii., No. 1.
† See Professor Olmstead's fine article in Silliman's Journal, XXV.
‡ Cosmos, Vol. i., page 472.
|| "Anales," etc., cited in 1st note, Vol. iii., No. 1.

balls and other similar phenomena, among which is the above-mentioned meteoric shower of November, 1833.

Phosphorescence of the Sea.—The only data we possess on this point as regards the Island of Cuba are the result of observations made by Don Andrés Poey, in 1850, 1851, and 1853, on the water within and without the harbor of Havana; and the following are the conclusions of that gentleman:* 1st. The phosphorescence of the sea observed in the harbor of Havana seems to increase from the new moon to the first quarter, attaining its maximum intensity at the full, and diminishing in the second quarter, when it is less than in the first quarter; consequently the first maximum is at the full moon, and the second at the new moon; and the first minimum at the first quarter, and the second at the wane. 2d. The phosphorescence increases with the greatest high and low tides of January. 3d. It increases also during low water more that at high water. Respecting the temperature, M. Poey has observed not only a certain connection between it and the phosphoric intensity of the water, but also with the phases of the moon, when the sky is clear and that orb shines brightly.†

Haloes, Mock Suns, etc.—Haloes and mock suns are of rare occurrence, although both phenomena were observed in 1852.‡ Solar rainbows are very common: the contrary of lunar rainbows, of which a remarkable one was observed at Havana in 1849. Of the zodiacal light and aurora-borealis there is record of only two instances of the latter seen at Havana, the 14th November, 1789, and 17th November, 1848. The longest twilight lasts one hour, and the shortest three quarters of an hour. During one year the average of clear or alternately clouded days may be set down at 285, and only 80 overcast. The maximum of cloudy days during any year has been 107, and the minimum 87. Cases wherein the 24 hours have elapsed with an entirely clouded sky are exceedingly rare.||

---

* Inedited memoir on the increase of phosphorescence of the salt-water of the harbor of Havana, in connection with the phases of the moon, the tides, and the temperature of the water; and on the dynamic power of the waters considered as a producing cause of the temperature of seas and rivers.

† 1st. Under a clear sky the temperature of the water was greater at the full of the moon than at her other phases, and the phosphorescence likewise was greater. 2d. Both increased at high water and at low water. 3d. They likewise increased more at low water than at high water.

‡ See the notice of a mock sun given by the author of "Apuntes del Terremoto de Cuba de Agosto, 1852."

|| The want of a meteorological observatory in an agricultural country of the importance of Cuba is daily more sensibly felt. Its establishment was recommended to the Junta de Fomento by the author in 1848. In 1850 our industrious and intelligent young

Earthquakes occur seldom in the western part of the island, but are frequent in the eastern part, although not so much so as in the other Antilles. They are most common in the district of Santiago de Cuba, where the shocks are successive.*

Diseases.—From what has been said under the head of *Physical Climate*, it may be inferred that the temperature of the island is mild, although humid and warm; and if the diseases arising from these last circumstances are common, such as originate in great thermometric variations are, on the contrary, of unusual occurrence, especially those induced by intense cold, as violent pulmonary affections, acute athritis, obstinate neuralgia, etc. The better to classify the diseases incident to the climate we shall divide the year into three periods, viz.: 1st, from December to May, the season of drought and of the finest weather; 2d, from May to September, a period of excessive heat, rain, and of most atmospheric electricity; 3d, from September to December, the season of

---

friend, Don Andrés Poey, established one, but a temporary absence of that gentleman from the island occurring a year after, it was relinquished. At the author's instance Messrs. Charlais and Fernandez, booksellers, No. 114 Obispo Street, have imported a complete set of compared meteorological instruments of the first class.

* The most remarkable earthquakes have been as follows: 11th February, 1675; one in 1682, which destroyed the cathedral; June, 1766; July, 1826; May, 1842; and, above all, those of the 20th August and 26th November, 1852, which seem to have traversed the globe, since, on the 19th of August, a shock was felt at Cervera (Spain); on the 20th there was a splendid eruption of Mount Etna; in Austria a shock that rang the bells; the 18th it was felt at St. Domingo; the 25th in Georgia (United States); and the 16th of September the inhabitants of Manilla experienced the most violent earthquake on their records. At Havana only two very slight shocks have been observed—on the 7th of July, 1777, and 7th July, 1852. The effect of the earthquake of 20th August, 1852, in the copper mines of San José, near the Villa del Cobre, is thus described by an eye-witness. "I was in the gallery No. 132 (264 *varas* below the surface) of the San Juan shaft, directing the work of a gang of 24 men, when we heard a strange and fearful noise, as if the whole mine were collapsing. We then felt the earth rising and sinking, and were thrown from one side of the gallery to the other. We seated ourselves on the ground to escape instant death, for we considered death inevitable in the end. The lights that were fixed to the walls were thrown down and extinguished, adding total darkness to the horrors that involved us. The timbers of the vaults cracked with a noise like that of a huge bonfire fed with green wood, and the filtration of water greatly increased. The mine seemed like a thickly-leaved tree laden with dew, and shaken by the storm or by the hand of God. We observed a sulphurous smell, and the great noise of stones and earth falling from the upper to the lower cavities. Although so many of us together, we dared not speak, and I believe that we all imagined ourselves sepultured forever. The noise lasted over four minutes, although the shocks had already ceased. It was some time ere we mustered resolution to attempt our exit, and as we ascended the ladders we had another shock, which would have thrown us off if we had not been prepared for it. After great sufferings we finally emerged from the mine, experiencing a degree of pleasurable relief not easily described. Our oppressed bosoms expanded like that of a criminal reprieved at the foot of the gallows."

deluging rains and of the greatest atmospheric changes. During the first period the following complaints prevail: catarrhs and catarrhal fevers (due to the cold air and drizzling rain, usually occurring until February); ephemeral and intermittent fevers; sore throat, croup, rheumatism; and, in some years, pleurisy, inflammation of the lungs, and eruptive fevers. During the second period the most predominant are—diarrhœa and other disorders of the digestive apparatus; yellow-fever, small-pox, liver complaint, and, since 1850, Asiatic cholera and eruptive fevers; at the same time instances offer of violent congestion, pulmonary inflammation, and pleurisy, likewise neuralgic and nervous affections. As regards fevers, the most prevalent at this season are the mucous, bilious, remittent (more or less dangerous), typhoid, and brain fevers. The third period comprises nearly the same diseases as the second; however, the yellow-fever and the cholera begin to decline, and gradually disappear; febrile disorders are somewhat aggravated in some years, those of a masked and pernicious character predominating; dysentery also is more common during this period, as also tetanus or locked jaw. Within a few years those cases of very acute consumption which sometimes destroy the patient in two months, are of very frequent occurrence. Notwithstanding that it has been stated by some writers that the climate of Cuba is unfavorable to human life, many and remarkable instances of longevity can be cited, among them those of several Indians who died during the last century at the age of 130 and 120 years, many persons (principally colored) who had attained the age of 119 years, and a great number that have died at over 90 years of age.*

Animals.—MAMMALIA.—The indigenous species still existing are the following: the almiquí, a carnivorous and nocturnal animal, feeding chiefly on insects, and having a long snout; the jutía, of which two kinds are known, viz.: the congo (called quemi by the Indians), easily domesticated, and having a conical tail; and the carabalí (known to the aborigines as guaminiquinar), inhabiting the mountains, and very untractable; its tail is long and bushy; and the corí, at present called curiel.† Besides these quadrupeds there existed, at the time of the

---

* In 1847 was published in the *Diario de la Marina* a relation of well-authenticated cases of unusual longevity. According to the official statistics of 1846 there were then in the island 29 persons over 100 years of age; viz., 4 of 101, 6 of 102, 1 of 103, 4 of 104, 4 of 105, 3 of 106, 1 of 107, 1 of 110, 3 of 111, 1 of 115, and 1 of 116. Our list of those now living includes a fisherman on the south coast who has completed his 112th year, and each of his two sons are over 80, and a distributer (!) of the *Faro* newspaper in 1851, who was more than 96 years old.

† The early historians mention also the following mammiferous animals: the aire and the mohi or mohui, which are not known at the present day, although the latter is supposed to be the agutí; also a mute-dog, supposed by some to be the species of dog

Conquest, both in this island and St. Domingo, other mammiferous animals, such as the bat, of which about 20 species are known, some of them of the vampyre genus; the whale, the dolphin, and the manatí or sea-cow, which frequents the coasts and bays affording sub-marine springs of fresh-water, as at Jagua. The domestic animals introduced by the Spaniards were the horse, ass, camel, ox, sheep, goat, hog, cat, house-dog, deer, the rabbit, and the rat. The horses of the island (generally of medium size, as descending from the Andalusian breed, which is of Arabian origin) are strong, spirited, and swift, but lack the intelligent expression of their forefathers. The paso or amble is the most usual gait, and is natural to all horses foaled on the island. The ass is not common in the island, the climate being apparently unfavorable to it; it is imported more for the purpose of breeding mules than for the increase of the legitimate race, mules being much used for carriage on all rural establishments. The camel, originally from Asia, has been introduced from the Canary Islands within a few years, but its usefulness, and probably its multiplication, is much impeded by the nigua or chigoe, an insect infesting its feet and almost preventing it from walking. The bovine race was introduced by Columbus on his second voyage; it is fine, strong, and corpulent.* The hog was taken to St. Domingo the year following the discovery; they increased so rapidly in that island, that it was found necessary to reduce their number, as they injured the sugar-cane plantations. The same was the case in Cuba, and Oviedo states that already, in his time, a vast number were running wild among the mountains. The hogs of Cuba have a wild appearance, doubtless in consequence of the roving life they lead on the plantations where they are bred. The *criollo* or yard-hog is distinguished from the *gallego*, or that bred on the petty farms. The former, which feeds chiefly on the berry of the palm, acorns (in some districts of the Vuelta-Abajo), and generally on wild fruit and maize, is small, active, and wild; its flesh is exceedingly palatable, and has a peculiar flavor, extending to the fat, which is very scarce, and resembles in color alone the bacon of Europe.† The other is larger, and better adapted for

---

called alco, or the washing-bear of Linnæus, called mapache in Mexico, and a species of canis, of the genera vulpes. At all events, these three species, together with the curiel, seem not to have been indigenous, but brought over from the continent before the discovery. Some modern writers mention another mammifer, under the name of tacuache, but Señor Poey, in his "Notes on the Natural History of the Island," denies that it ever existed.

* In the district of Guaimaro, on the heights called Gaguita, is a pigmy breed of oxen without tails, which are of very strange appearance, and supposed to be very ancient.

† It is esteemed in Europe and the United States for these qualities.

fattening, for which purpose it is almost exclusively raised. It is said that the *criollo* breed may be distinguished from the *gallego* by the greater roundness of the ribs of the former. The difference in flavor is attributed to difference of race. In mountainous and unpeopled districts there are a considerable number of wild hogs, called *orejános*. Sheep do not prosper much in Cuba. The race introduced by the colonists was the common or coarse-wooled In consequence of the wool being neglected, no use being made of it in so warm a climate, it has been observed that, when the animal has attained its full growth, it loses its wool, shedding it in crusts, when it is succeeded by a sleek coat of hair, like that of the goat; a change which also takes place in South America. Its flesh is not generally used, except in Havana and Cuba, and on some of the larger plantations, where the consumption is considerable. Its milk is used in some parts of the western department for making cheese. The goat is exceedingly useful, and the breed known as isleña (from the Canaries) yields abundance of milk, which is availed of for children, and in some cases medicinally. The breed of goats, like that of hogs, is supposed to be a distinct race from that of Europe. It was introduced from the Canary Islands. The house-dog has multiplied exceedingly; some have become wild, and do much damage to cattle. Many varieties have been introduced within the present century. Deer have been introduced within the century; at first in the vicinity of Bahia-Honda, and afterward in Cuba, where the number is sufficient to supply the market daily. Rabbits were brought to America at a very remote period; they do not multiply much, in consequence of the rats which destroy many of them. Rats (originally from Hindostan), introduced soon after the Conquest, have multiplied extraordinarily throughout city and country, doing great damage to the sugar-cane and the corn in the warehouses. The cat is of the European breed, and some have become wild.

BIRDS.—The island contains a great number of species, over 240 having been enumerated.* Among the birds of prey are found the aura tiñosa, belonging to the buzzard family, and which is so useful to public health; the cernículo or kestrel, a veritable falcon, although small; the caraira or Brazilian eagle; and the well-known nocturnal birds of prey, the owl, the sijú, and the siguapa. The order of smaller birds is still more abundant in species, and comprises the sinsonte, styled by naturalists polyglot orpheus, for its faculty of imitating all other animals; the pitirre or robin, whose persecution of the aura is so well

---

* See the works published by D. Ramon de la Sagra, D. Juan Lembeye, and D. Andrés and Don Felipe Poey.

known. Many species of fringillæ, among which are distinguished the negrito, the azulejo, the tomeguin, and others remarkable for the beautiful colors of their plumage;* the cao, representative of the crow family, and many others. There are also swallows, which spend the winter here and the summer in North Carolina; the chotacabras or goatsucker, also called guaraiba, a nocturnal bird, with the bill cleft to the ears, rendering it the largest-mouthed of all birds. Finally, we should mention the pedorrera, beautiful for the multitude of its colors, and the martin-pescador (king-fisher) or zabullidor, both very common in the vicinity of the coasts. Of the colibri or trochilus family there are several, which vary in size, the smallest being little more than an inch in length. There are also several carpenter-birds (including the royal); the tocororo, a splendid bird, brightly and variously colored; the arriero; the judía; the cotorra or parrot; the paroquet (periquito), etc., form the group of climbing-birds. Of gallinaceous birds are the common turkey, the cock or rooster, with its numerous varieties, the Guineafowl, and a multitude of pigeons, among which are distinguished the tojosita, the torcaz, and that improperly called perdiz or partridge, which is blue-headed. Wading or long-legged birds are numerous about the coasts, rivers, and lakes; and we notice the frailecillo, called vociferus by naturalists for its loud cries; the sevilla, with a spatular-shaped-bill; the cocos, one of which is of the ibis kind; various kinds of cranes and herons; the flamingo, of a purple red; and, lastly, the gallito, with great spurs on its wings, the widgeon, and the gallinuela. There are many species of aquatic birds: the saramagullon, remarkable for its upright position; the pelican; the corúa or sea-crow; the rabiahorcado or frigate-pelican; the rabijunco; the sea-gull; the pampero, and many more. Besides the goose should be mentioned many kinds of ducks, among which are distinguished the yaguaza or wild-duck, and the huyuyo, of various and finely-colored plumage. Of the above mentioned the common fowl or rooster and the goose were introduced into America from Europe.

REPTILES.—There are found in the island species of every order: there are turtles or tortoises, which sometimes attain a great size; the caguama; the caréy or shell-tortoise, abounding on the north coast, and formerly the object of a profitable fishery; and the jicotea or mud-turtle. Of the saurian family are two species of crocodiles, one of which (acutus) is vulgarly miscalled caiman or alligator; the other (rhom-

---

* In 1850 a number of sparrows, brought from Spain, were set loose in the garden of one of the convents in the capital, and it is observed that they are multiplying rapidly.

biferus) has only been found on the southern coast, especially on the island of Pinos and its neighborhood. Many species of lizards are also to be met with, of various form and size, among others that vulgarly called chamelion, although not belonging to that kind. There are two species of iguanas; one small, about a foot in length, which is found in the vicinity of Havana, at the foot of the Loma del Castillo del Principe; and the other, sometimes two yards long, abounds on the north coast and among the keys. Among the ophidians may be noticed the majá (boa angulifer), and about twelve species of jubos, none of which are venomous. Several species of frogs and toads of great size, and a few other batrachians, complete the list of Cuban reptiles.

FISH.—Among those of bony structure, which are exceedingly abundant in the island, the principal ones are the pargo, the rabirubia, the atun or tunny-fish (very rare), the aguja de paladar, the dorado, the masejuelo, the cherna or ruffle, and many others, comprising some that are dangerous to eat on account of the ciguatera or sickness that they cause; of these the most dangerous are the picuda,* the jurel, the morena-verde, the coronado, etc., although they are not all unwholesome, nor at all seasons. Among those of cartilaginous structure are many species of sharks: the shark proper is very dangerous and abundant; the female is called tintorera, and the cub, cazon; they have also been found fossilized, and teeth of the largest species known.† There are also the cornuda, the gata, the alecrin, provided with formidable teeth, and the saw-fish, so called from the form of the weapon it bears, although it is also improperly termed sword-fish.‡ The cornuda has a short and very broad head, comparable to a hammer, which name is therefore vulgarly applied to it.

INSECTS.—The species common to Cuba, although not so fine and brilliant as those of the Brazils and East Indies, are very numerous. Among them we notice the cocuyo or fire-fly, which abounds in May and June; a small insect (anobium bibliothecarium) which destroys books, and another that eats dry tobacco; the native bee, which produces dark-colored wax, and has no sting; the Spanish or stinging-bee, brought from Florida in 1764, and producing white wax as fine as that of Venice. There are many species of ants; among them the bibijagua, destructive to plants, and the common species introduced from Europe; the come-

---

* There are three species of picuda: the picuda, the picudilla, and the guaguanche; the last two are not considered unwholesome.

† (Squalus carcharias.) We have seen two of these fossils: one found in digging a well in Guamutas, and the other in the neighborhood of Jaruco.

‡ The true sword-fish is of the Mediterranean, and is rarely met with on these coasts, where neither the cod, the pollock, nor the bream are found.

jen or thermes, greatly destructive to wood; the bed-bug (an exotic insect) has been introduced into the island as everywhere; the nigua or chigoe, of the flea kind, which is also termed penetrans, from its habit of introducing itself under the skin of animals and frequently doing much injury; the louse, and the flea; a species of coccus, vulgarly termed guagua, introduced about 1833 : it has done very considerable damage to the orange, lime, and other trees. There are over 300 kinds of butterfly (chiefly indigenous), among which are remarkable the urania fernandina, most brilliantly colored, and commonly found at Cojímar; the caterpillar develops itself on the nut-tree, called avellano de costa; the palomilla, which attacks the sugar-cane, is a nocturnal butterfly of the genera crambus. There are some 300 species of fly, some adorned with metallic spots; one kind is improperly termed cantharide by the natives on account of its color, which is metallic, and very similar to the true cantharide or Spanish fly, which is a coleopterus; more than 12 kinds of mosquitoes, comprising the corasí, the zancudo or common musquito, the jagüey, the jejen, the guasasa, and the rodador. Of the spider family we notice the araña peluda or hairy spider, very venomous, but not mortally so. There are two kinds of scorpions, neither mortally venomous; ticks abound in the country, and are very annoying to cattle. There is a species of centipede, and another of mancaperro or dog-maimer. The moth, which destroys paper, is indigenous, and belongs to the genera lepisma. Of crustacea there are several species, the most notable being the ajae, found at some distance from the coast; the cangrejo moro or Moorish crab; the gallo crab; the jaiba or soft crab; there are also large lobsters, and both salt and freshwater shrimps. Among molluscs are the pulpo or cuttle-fish, and calamar or sea-sleeve, of many kinds. There are many testacea, both univalve and bivalve (commonly called shells and conches), the longoron being distinguished among the latter; two kinds of clams, and the oyster, which is small but finely flavored. At the mouth of the Miel River (Baracoa) are found mother-of-pearl shells. Sigua is the name of a univalve mollusc of the genera turbus; it is very indigestible. Among zoophites are many herizos or urchins, and star-fish; aguamares (vulgarly aguamalas), which comprise the medusa abounding in the harbor of Havana; many polypi, living congregated in polypedes, and exuding a calcareous matter the same as the gorgoneas which form the sea-fan and sea-broom. There are corals of commercial importance, and many sponges on the northern keys. The rivers contain several species of the leech.

Vegetables.—The following are arranged in the order of their most general application :

PHYSICAL, POLITICAL, AND INDUSTRIAL.   41

PRECIOUS WOODS.—Mahogany,* caobilla, cedar, lignum vitæ or guayacan, ebony (royal and coal), white and black cúrbano, caréy, granadillo, hayajabíco, naranjo, yaití, and café.
BUILDING TIMBER.—Acana, jijon (resembling mahogany), almendro or almond-tree, quiebra-hacha, carne de doncella, chicharron, jaimiquí, jiquí, tengue, maboa, frijolillo, sabina, guao, yaba, yaya, black and white oak, pitch-pine, evergreen oak (only in Vuelta-Abajo), jocúma, ocuje, moruro, sciba (for canoes), royal palm (for boards), majagua, strong and elastic; barza, guiro, etc.
PLANTS FOR OTHER USEFUL PURPOSES.—Dagáme, yagruma, ateje, brasilete, fustic or dyewood (largely exported from the east of the island), mangrove, jiquilete (yielding a blue dye), cavalonga, bambú or bamboo, also called wild cane; güin, aguedita, febrífuga, almácigo or mastich, algarrobo or locust, jaboncillo, daguilla, copal, black pepper, cinnamon, drago (dragon-tree), mulberry, grape, many sorts of palm, comprising the royal palm (one of the most beautiful and useful trees in the island), the cocoanut palm (growing wild at Baracoa), the corozo, the manaca, the cana, the yarei, the palma-barrigona or big-bellied-palm, the jata, the miraguano, and the exotic date-palm.
MEDICINAL PLANTS.—Ateje comun, cedar, arraigan, caicimon, yerbahedionda, aguedita, escoba-amarga, malva (mallows), malva blanca, sabia-cimarrona (wild sage), ocuje, rabo de zorra, guaguasí, mancei, ají-guaguao (green pepper), bija (anatto), yagruma hembra, picapica (cow-itch), apasote (basil), gramas (panic-grass), leñatero, almacigo (mastich), pimienta (black pepper), guira cimarrona, yedra (ivy), bledo (strawberry-blite) comun y carbonero, sanguinaria (knot-grass), yerbabuena cimarrona (wild mint), sandoval, verdolaga (purslain), caimito, romerillo blanco (white rosemary), zarzaparilla, raiz de China (China-root), calaguala, etc.
POISONOUS PLANTS.—Manzanilla, piñí-piñí, yaba, cabo de hacha, jabacaná; camagüey and prieto (vines); yuca agria (when not subjected to fire), the seed of the poma rosa, and tobacco.
FRUITS.—Among those indigenous to the island are distinguished the delicious pine-apple, the sweet and aromatic anón, the níspero or messapple, also called zapote; the ácana, very similar to the preceding; the caimito, caimitillo, ciruela or plum, guanábana or sour-sop, mamey colorado, mamoncillo, papaya (papaw), guayaba cotorrera (guava), of

---

* The mahogany tree is exceedingly abundant in the island, and in the eastern part the wood is of as fine a quality as that of Hayti. In 1808 one was cut down at Jagua for the Principé de la Paz which measured over 10 feet in diameter, and in 1850 the author saw one at Hanábana measuring 3¼ Cuban *varas* in diameter. Several cedars have also been found of nearly the same dimensions.

the kind most suitable for preserves; mamon, marañon, uva caleta (a grape), mora (mulberry), plátano (plantain), agua-cate (alligator-pear), hicaco (cocoa-plum), zapote de culebra, sour orange, lime, jobo, mamey amarillo or de St. Domingo, etc. Among the exotic fruit are the watermelon, the musk-melon, fig, strawberry, the Spanish grape (there being a native species, but very small and sour), the Peruvian guava, canistel, pomegranate, sweet or China orange, and cajel orange; toronjas or shaddocks, lima or sweet lemon, the French lemon, gooseberry, date, corojo, cautel, etc.

Minerals.[*]—METALLIC SUBSTANCES.—*Gold* has been found in the district of Pinar del Rio; at las Minas, in Bacuranao district; at Canasí; in the rivers Damují and Caonao, which empty into Jagua Bay; in those of Sagua la Grande and Agabáma, near the Escambray Mountain; in the mines of San Fernando (worked by the early inhabitants); in the mountains of Trinidad; in the Saramaguacan; in the hato of Monacos, and those of Holguin, Bayamo, and Nipe; in the Mayarí River (of 18 to 20 carats)[†] and in the Caney River. *Silver:* according to history and the investigations of Don José Escalante, silver has been found in the mines of San Fernando, in the Escambray Mountains; it is also to be found at Pinar del Rio, Canasí, and Yumurí. *Copper* of superior quality abounds in all the island, being one of the chief exports from Santiago de Cuba. *Iron* is abundant at Vuelta-Abajo; in the Trinidad and Escambray Mountains; very abundant in the mountains of the Pinar, south of Mayarí, and generally throughout the island, but no mine is worked. *Lead-mines* have been found in several places but not explored.

STONY SUBSTANCES.—*Amianthus* (silicate) abounds in the mountains between Trinidad and Cienfuegos; in those of Escambray it is of fine quality; also in the Guanabacoa Mountains. *Loadstone*, or magnetic oxide of iron, found in Guanabacoa; among the mountains of Trinidad

---

[*] The author is indebted for the greater part of the matter of this article to his learned friends Messrs. Velazquez, Auber, Poey, Lembeye, Lanier, and especially to Dr. Cayetano Aguilera, Professor of Chemistry of the Royal University, who has made excursions through the western department of the island, with the sole purpose of studying its geological constitution, and to collect minerals. In the Guia de Forasteros of the present year, 1853, have been published some notes on the mines registered by the royal treasury in 1852.

[†] In the *Memorias de la Real Sociedad Económica* for 1839 (page 354), is a note on the situation of a gold-mine at Mayarí. With regard to the amount of gold exported from the island by the discoverers, we refer to Sr. Sagra's work, wherein he says, "From these simple notes there results a total of $260,000 worth of gold received from the Island of Cuba from 1515 to 1834, but as the records of a great many other remittances are wanting, this sum can only be considered a minimum." We recommend the perusal of Sr. Sagra's article on Geology and Mineralogy, which affords all the information that can be had on those subjects.

is one composed of this mineral; in the Jaragua Mountains, and in all those of the eastern part of the island, there being a great quarry of it near the Caney. *Coal:* at Consolacion del Norte, Mantua, Bahia-Honda, Bacuranao, Guanabo, Canasí, Camarioca, Matanzas, Cárdenas, Palmarejo, etc. *Crystallized chalcedony:* at Guanabacoa; and in the district of Cienfuegos rock crystal (hyaline quartz) abounds. *Marble* is found in several parts of the island, but abundantly, and in greater variety, in the island of Pinos, at Trinidad, San Antonio, San Diego de los Baños, Bahia-Honda, Guane,* and Bajá, comprising statuary marble of superior quality, but scarce; also stalactite, snow-white, and so fine and transparent that it is equal to alabaster. *Granite:* in the mountains of Vuelta-Abajo; in the vicinity of Havana; in the mountains of Trinidad, Escambray, and Baracoa, and in the island of Pinos; also near Santiago, where it is similar to that of the Escorial. *Rock crystal* (hyaline quartz) abounds throughout the island. *Limestone:* very plenty, and frequently found crystallized as spar. *Gypsum* is found of bad quality; although at a place called Cayo de los Perros, in the district of San Juan de los Remedios, it is compact and sufficiently pure. *Carbonated lime:* there is a fine bank of it, about three leagues wide and six long, at the origin of the Güines River. *Sand* and *refractory clay:* the town of Cano is founded on a bank of this mineral; it is a species of pumice-stone, in transition to yellow sand, and serves exceedingly well for the manufacture of fire-brick. *Slate* or *schist* is found throughout the island, especially on the Guacamayas River, district of Las Pozas, where it is of the best quality. The town of Caney is founded on a rock of white schist. *Sulphate of Baryta* or *heavy spar:* to be found in the eastern department. *Serpentine:* in Guanabacoa and the eastern department, where there are both kinds. The town of Las Pozas rests on a bank of serpentine.

INFLAMMABLE MINERALS.—*Asphaltum* (called *chapapote*) is very abundant, especially at Guanabacoa, Mariel, and Bahia-Honda, between the Haciendas la Barbara and Maniabon, 14 leagues from Holguin, also on the Hacienda San Antonio, 8 leagues from Nuevitas. *Rocksalt:* there is a mine of it in Bacunayagua.†

MINERAL WATERS.—Cuba possesses many of the finest in the world, but, unfortunately, the majority have not been analyzed. Among the most interesting, are those of San Diego de los Baños, which are sul-

---

* At this place and its vicinity are found almost all varieties of fine marble; and also beautiful grottos containing gigantic stalactites of the most fanciful forms.

† Sr. Aguilera has found in the vicinity of Las Pozas blood-red jasper, cornelian, agate, feldspar, quartzose sand, magnetic pyrites, lignite or fossil coal, compact graphite, foliaceous antimony, and bismuth and tellurium.

44   CUBA:

phurous, as analyzed by Messrs. Estevez, Casaseca, and Sanchez ;* San Juan de Contreras, sulphurous; Charco-Azul, sulphurous; Copey, nitrous; Almendares (see analysis in the sequel) ; Guanabacoa, of many kinds; Santa Maria del Rosario ; Madruga, similar to those of San Diego, but imperfectly analyzed ; San Miguel, at the foot of Loma de San Juan, similar to those of San Diego ; San Pedro and Santa Ana; Ciego Montero, six leagues from Cienfuegos, sulphuro-gaseous; Baños de la Bija, eight and a half leagues from Cienfuegos; Mayajígua; Guadalupe; Camujiro; Dumañuceos; and Brazo-fuerte; and in Pinos island those of Santa Fé.† In the hamlet of Cantarrana there is a well of mineral water highly recommended for dropsy and other diseases.

POLITICAL AND INDUSTRIAL GEOGRAPHY.

Population.—The *absolute* population of the island appears to be 1,050,000,‡ of which 1,009.060 are stationary, and the rest transitory. Of the former, 501,988 are white, 176,647 free-colored, and 330,425 slaves ; and supposing the 40,940 constituting the floating population to be white, we have a total of 542,928 white and 507,072 colored. The former comprise about 90,000 from Spain, 25,000 from the Canary Islands, 3,000 French, 1,000 English, and 3,000 Americans and of other nations, so that the number of native whites is over 400,000. With regard to the *relative* population, as the island, together with its adjacent territories, has an area of 3,973 square leagues, the proportion is 254 inhabitants per square league, or 29 per square mile. Consequently, the Island of Cuba is more thickly populated than 20 of the 31 United States of North America (Florida has but one inhabitant per square mile); than each one of the Spanish-American States; than the Brazils; and than Sweden and Norway.

Religion.—The Roman Catholic and Apostolic is the only form of worship tolerated in the island.

Territorial Divisions.—They may be reduced to four classes, viz., *natural*, *topographical*, *vulgar*, and *administrative*.

---

* See the Memoria on these baths, published by Sr. Sanchez, Havana, 1851.

† According to the analysis made by Sr. Caro, and published in the "Revista de la Havana," the waters of these baths belong to the order of *saline excitants*, and must, therefore, possess important therapeutical properties. That gentleman is occupied in analyzing other waters in the island.

‡ Besides the causes that in all countries oppose statistical perfection, there are others peculiar to those where slavery exists, for which reason no one can doubt that the population of the island is 1,500,000, and that of Havana 180,000.

PHYSICAL, POLITICAL, AND INDUSTRIAL. 45

THE NATURAL or PHYSICO-GEOGRAPHICAL are two : *continent,* as the island is usually termed ; and *adjacent keys,* which comprises the islands and keys belonging to the Island of Cuba and surrounding it. When the island is spoken of in a general sense, the adjacent islands and keys are also included.

TOPOGRAPHICALLY, the island is divided into cities, villas, towns, villages, hamlets, and *rancherias,* or hut-groups ; and besides, into private possessions, severally classified as *hatos, corrales, potreros, ingenios, cafetales,* and *sitios de labor* or *estancias,* the description of which will be found under the head of *Agriculture.* At the present day are styled *cities,*[*] Havana, Cuba, Matanzas, Puerto Principe, Trinidad, Bayamo, Holguin, Baracoa, Santiago or St. Jago, Bejucál, Jaruco, Santa Maria del Rosario, Nuevitas, and Nueva Paz (the two last without *ayuntamientos* or corporations). *Villas,* are Guanabacoa, Güines, Santo Espiritu, San Juan de los Remedios, Villa Clara, Cienfuegos, and San Antonio de los Baños, while measures are being taken to obtain the same title for Pinar del Rio, San Cristóbal or Candelaria, and Cárdenas.

Navigators divide the island into Windward and Leeward, or east and west of the meridian wherever any one may be, but especially that of Havana.

VULGAR DIVISIONS.—In the first place are the well-known divisions of Vuelta-Arriba and Vuelta-Abajo, generic terms applied to the territory on the east or west of the person using the term wherever he may be. Thus, for instance, the jurisdiction of Santo Espiritu is in the Vuelta-Abajo as regards the resident of Puerto Principe, but contrarywise, or in the Vuelta-Arriba, relatively to the resident of Havana. However, in speaking of the island in general, by Vuelta-Abajo is understood the territory comprised between the rivers Sierra Morena and

---

[*] At the present day the distinction between the terms City and Villa may be deemed a purely honorary one ; but formerly, the first was applied to those communities, usually large, which, by their importance, historical associations, or especial services, obtained privileges or supremacy over the rest. The Villas also enjoyed marked preeminences (though not as many as the cities), among which was the privilege of having their own proper boundaries and jurisdictions. Seignories or manors were also held in the island by the founders of the villas of Bejucál, Santa Maria del Rosario, Jaruco, and San Antonio de los Baños, but were suppressed in 1811, although some continued in fact until a few years ago. *Pueblos,* or towns, are termed all communities of 50 houses and upward, which do not possess the title of either villa or city; *aldeas,* or villages, assemblages of 12 to 50 houses ; *caserios,* or hamlets, such as fall short of 12 houses : and *rancherias,* those places where there are *ranchos,* or huts, especially those of fishermen on the coasts or runaways in their haunts.. As these classifications in this island depend more on the number of houses than of inhabitants, it is well to state that all houses within 500 metres of the main group are considered as belonging to it.

Hanábana as far as Cape San Antonio; but in speaking of that territory alone, the term Vuelta-Abajo is applied to that part lying east of the meridian of Havana. As applied to distinguish a certain class of tobacco, the term especially comprises the territory between the San Diego river and Cape San Antonio, producing the best tobacco in the world, universally known as of the Vuelta-Abajo. Partidos de afuera (outer districts), or Los Partidos, is applied to the territory between the meridians of Havana and San Cristóbal; and Partidos de adentro (inner districts) to that comprised between the meridian of San Cristóbal and Cape San Antonio.* Partidos de los Llanos (districts of the plains) is the denomination sometimes given to the territory comprised between the jurisdictions of Cárdenas, Sagua la Grande, Cienfuegos, Villa Clara, and southern part of Matanzas. Tierra-adentro (meaning the interior country) is another expression commonly used in Havana to designate the territory comprised between the jurisdiction of Cienfuegos and those of Puerto Principe and Nuevitas, both inclusive, and even at times extended farther east unto the territories of the jurisdictions of Tunas, Holguin, Manzanillo, and Bayamo, although some persons, more properly, exclude the sea-ports.† Territorio de las cuatro Villas.—Under this name used to be comprised the territory corresponding to the jurisdictions of Trinidad, Santo Espiritu, Remedios, and Santa Clara, but since the last has been divided into the jurisdictions of Cienfuegos and Sagua la Grande, such a denomination is improper, particularly as Cienfuegos now ranks as a villa and Trinidad as a city.

ADMINISTRATIVE DIVISION.—The six principal branches of administrative science have in the island their determinate territorial divisions, but without suitable unity; however, measures are being taken to secure this end, which is the basis of all good administration.

Political Division.—The political territorial division is as follows. The entire territory of the island constitutes a single province, under the command of a superior political governor and vice-royal patron, and is subdivided into three governments, viz., that of Havana, in charge of the superior political governor, that of Matanzas, and that of Cuba, which also has annexed the vice-royal patronate, without dependence in this branch on that of Havana. The dividing line of the government of Matanzas extends from the port of Canasí to the confluence of the rivers Negro and Gonzalo with the Hatiguaníco River, then following the course of the Gonzalo till near the lagoon of Tesoro, whence it runs

---

* Noda :—notes published in the "Guia de Forasteros" (Stranger's Guide) for 1841 and '42. Notes on the Tobacco of the Island of Cuba, 1852.
† See the excellent Dictionary of Cuban phrases by Don Esteban Pichardo.

toward the north with various windings as far as Point Camacho, leaving the town of Corral-Falso in the jurisdiction of Cárdenas, and that of Aguacate in the jurisdiction of Jarúco. The dividing line between the governments of Havana and Cuba is the same that divides the archbishopric and the bishopric, and the military departments and intendancies.* The governments are divided into petty or inferior districts, although when of great extent, like those of Havana and Cuba, they are subdivided into lieutenant-governorships, comprising several petty districts. The *civil* and *rural* wards and the *petty districts* are subdivided into *quarters*. The civil wards are in charge of *celadores*, or commissaries of police; the rural wards and petty districts are commanded by district-captains, and the quarters by patrol-corporals. There are, besides, four small districts styled *colonies*, subject to the immediate command of a military officer called director, but dependent on the government in whose territory they are situated, viz., the colonies of Reina Amalia or Nueva Gerona (on the island of Pinos), of Santo Domingo, and of Caibarien, dependent on the government of Havana, and that of Moa on the government of Cuba.† The government of Havana has in immediate dependency the districts or lieutenant-governorships of Pinar del Rio, San Cristóbal, Bahia-Honda, Mariel, San Antonio, Santiago de las Vegas, Bejucál, Guanabacoa, Santa Maria del Rosario, Güines, Jarúco, Cárdenas, Sagua la Grande, Cienfuegos, Santa Clara or Villa Clara, Trinidad, San Juan de los Remedios, and Santo Espiritu.‡ The government of Matanzas has dependent on it, politically, no lieutenant-governorship, but, militarily, it has the lieutenant-governorship of Cárdenas. On the government of Cuba depend the jurisdictions or lieutenant-governorships of Puerto Principe, Nuevitas, Tunas, Bayamo, Manzanillo, Holguin, Jiguaní, Guantánamo, and Baracoa.

Ecclesiastical Division.—The ecclesiastical administration of the island is divided between two dioceses—the archbishopric of Cuba and the bishopric of Havana.|| The boundary line extends from the mouth of the river Yana, opposite the eastern extremity of Turiguanó island, to within a mile and a half east of Sabana-la-mar embarking-place, on the south coast, dividing the island nearly through its centre. Both dioceses are divided into *outer vicarages* and *curacies*, and the arch-

---

* See the royal decree of 21 October, 1853.
† This last has no existence in fact, as it contains but two inhabitants.
‡ The island of Pinos is a colony and district of the jurisdiction of Havana.
|| Subject to the archbishopric, besides the bishopric of Havana, is that of Porto Rico.

bishopric and bishopric are respectively superior one to the other in cases of appeal.

Judicial Division.—The judicial branch of affairs is subject to a court of judicature residing at Havana, and styled *Real Audiencia Pretorial de la Habana.**

Military Division.—The territory of the island constitutes a captain-generalship, and is subdivided (since 1851) into two departments—the western and eastern.† Each department is under the authority of a commandant-general, and is subdivided into sections and commandancies of arms; each section is in charge of a chief, and in every commandancy of arms there is a subaltern judge with limited faculties. The boundary line of both departments is the same ecclesiastical boundary between the two dioceses. With the title of *General Commandant of the Cantons*, there is a chief in the jurisdictions of Trinidad, Villa Clara, Remedios, Santo Espiritu, Cienfuegos, and Sagua la Grande, with casual exercise of authority, and immediately dependent on the captain-general. There is also one of the same class in the Mariel.

Treasury Division.—With regard to the royal treasury, the island constitutes a delegated general superintendency, and is subdivided into two intendancies, viz., that of Havana and that of Cuba, each subject to an intendant under the direction of the superintendent-general, and with the character and attributes of an intendant of the army. The two intendancies are subdivided into delegations and administrations, and these into receptories. The lieutenant-governors are delegates of the districts.

Maritime Division.—The Havana constitutes a naval station, the jurisdiction of which extends to the island of Porto Rico. It is subject to a superior commandant, who is the captain-general, and a general commandant, whose authority is vested in an officer of high rank. The maritime division of the island was established about the end of 1828,

---

* There was another at Puerto Principe, but by royal decree of 21 October, 1853, it was suppressed, and the territory, affairs, and archives were incorporated with that of Havana. The said *Audiencia*, or judiciary court of Puerto Principe, is the same that was established in 1511 at Santo Domingo, and in consequence of the revolution in that island, was transferred hither in 1800. The *Real Audiencia Pretorial* of Havana was installed in 1839.

† From 1826 to September, 1851, the island was divided into three military departments, the western, central, and eastern, the dividing line between the first two being the eastern limits of the lieutenant-governorships of Sagua la Grande and Cienfuegos, and between the last two the eastern limits of the lieutenant-governorships of Nuevitas and Puerto Principe. In said month of September, 1851, was established, *ad interim*, the present division into two departments, and sanctioned by her majesty by royal decree of October 21, 1853.

dividing the territory and adjacent islands into five provinces, viz., Havana, Trinidad, San Juan de los Remedios, Nuevitas, and Cuba, whose capitals are the towns of those names. The provinces are subdivided into districts, and these into adjutancies, subdelegations, and " alcaldias de mar." The province of Havana is under the immediate authority of the commandant-general of the station, and the other provinces are in charge of commandants or graduated officers. The districts are commanded by adjutants, and the subdelegations by alcaldes de mar. The province of Havana comprises all the territory, islands, and shoals lying west of a line that may be supposed to run along the following points: Canal del Pargo, Rio de la Palma, Artemisal, Punta Don Cristóbal, and Canal del Rosario, and is divided into the districts of Havana, Regla, Matanzas, Cárdenas, Batabanó, Pinar del Rio, Mariel, Bahia-Honda, and Mántua. The limits of the province of San Juan de los Remedios are the following: Canal del Pargo, Rio de la Palma, Artemisal, the central highway toward the east, passing by Alvarez, Esperanza, Villa Clara, Santo Espiritu, Jicotea, and Ciego de Avila, whence it proceeds in a straight line to Punta Curiana, and thence between the islands called Cayo Coco and Cayo Romano (the latter falling to Nuevitas). It is divided into the two districts of Remedios and Sagua la Grande. The limit of the province of Trinidad is a line supposed to run along the following places: Canal del Rosario, Punta Don Cristóbal, Artemisal, the central highway from that point to Puerto Principe, thence in a right line as far as Estero del Junco, and thence beyond Canal de Cuatro Reales. It is divided into the districts of Trinidad, Santa Cruz, and Jagua. The boundary line of Nuevitas passes by the following points: the channel between the islands of Cayo Coco and Cayo Romano, Punta Curiana, San Gerónimo, the high road running by Puerto Principe, Las Tunas, Bayamo, and Jiguaní; thence it proceeds to Santo Cristo, Cayo del Rey and Mayarí, and issues through the mouth of the Port of Nipe. It is divided into the districts of Nuevitas, Guanája, and Jibára. The province of Cuba comprises the remainder of the island, and is divided into the districts of Cuba, Baracoa, and Manzanillo. The island of Porto Rico is another province of the naval station of Havana.

Government.—The Island of Cuba is subject, in all branches of the administration, to the authority of a president of the royal court of judicature (*real audiencia*), who is also the superior civil governor, captain-general, superior commandant of marine, superintendent of the treasury, vice-royal patron, and vice-royal protector of public instruction; although the ecclesiastical, naval, judicial, and financial departments also have especial chiefs of high rank, as has been stated under the head of *Territorial Division*.

LAWS.—By the additional article of the constitution of the Spanish monarchy of 1887, the Island of Cuba is subject to especial laws, pending the formation of which are in force the laws, royal decrees, regulations, and orders dictated by the supreme government of the nation, and communicated to the island. Next in order, as regards political and judicial affairs, are the especial resolutions circumscribed to determinate localities, such as the municipal regulations or statutes of the corporations, the resolutions of the courts of judicature, and the government edicts (Bandos de Buen-Gobierno), especial regulations, etc. Then come the " Ordenanzas de Intendentes de Nueva España" (published in 1786, and reformed in 1803), commanded to be complied with in this island *as far as adaptable;* several articles of which are in force, particularly those relating to the treasury department. Then succeed in authority the body of laws entitled, " Recopilacion de las Leyes de Indias" published in 1681. In the military department, the ordinances of the army of the Peninsula succeed the most recent sovereign dispositions. As regards commerce, the " Codigo de Comercio" is followed, with laws, modifications, and the *ley de enjuiciamiento* for mercantile transactions. For the ecclesiastical department, is the " Sinodo diocesano de Cuba," approved in 1682, and which has recently been republished with additions. In the naval department are in force the " Ordenanzas Generales de Marina" for 1748 and 1793, and the " Ordenanza de Matriculas." After the last sovereign dispositions, and those of the before-mentioned legal bodies, the codes promulgated for the Peninsula exercise force of law in the following order: Novísima Recopilacion, Nueva Recopilacion, Leyes de Toro, Ordenamiento de Alcalá, Fuero Juzgo, and lastly, the celebrated Leyes de las Partidas.

Ethnography.—The races of inhabitants peopling the island are the Caucasian, the African, the copper-colored or American, and the Mongolian. The *Caucasian* proceeds from Europe, and although represented by a less number than the African, it surpasses, as everywhere, all the others in intelligence and civilization. As the island has belonged to Spain from its discovery (for its possession by the English was almost limited to the district of Havana, and lasted but one year), the races inhabiting the Peninsula naturally have been, and continue to be, those constituting the white population of the colony; besides, the system of commercial monopoly that existed until the end of the last century has contributed not a little to prevent the settlement of other branches of the Caucasian race of Europe. History assures, that at the commencement of the Conquest none but Castilians were allowed to come to America; but at present, the industrious Catalans or Catalonians, and the hard-working Isleños (islanders of the Canaries), are found to preponderate throughout the island. As regards foreigners, the rural districts of the jurisdiction of Cuba, of Saltadero, Güines, San Antonio, and the south of Mariel were, at the beginning of the present century, peopled by industrious and intelligent Frenchmen, refugees from the revolution in St. Domingo, who gave a powerful impetus to agriculture, especially the cultivation of coffee. The *Anglo-Saxon* race has somewhat extended itself in Matanzas, Cárdenas, and Nuevitas and Bagá, which they colonized. Next in order are the Germans, who apply themselves entirely to commerce by wholesale, and next, the Italians, in small number. The *African* or Ethiopian race was introduced in 1524, shortly after the conquest of the island, to serve as slaves. Notwithstanding the humane treatment that it has received, its propagation has not corresponded to the analogy of the climate with that of its own country; so that, in spite of considerable and constant importations until a few years back, the present number of the race does not appear to amount to much more than half a million. Those coming from Africa are termed *bozales* until they acquire the language of the island, and *ladinos* when they speak it; and such of them as are born in the island are called *criollos*.* The latter are distinguished, also, as being born in the towns, or as being born in the country, these latter being termed *criollos de campo*, and are more rustic in language and manners than the former, who are remarkable for aptness, and particularly for native musical composition. The *American* race, which exists in very small number, is the aboriginal, as, although subsequently to the discovery, several Indians were introduced from the continent, chiefly into the western department, and, on the separation of Florida from the Spanish dominion, some of them would occasionally come over to

---

* The African nations from which the negroes are derived are as follows: the *Mandingas*, who occupy the greater part of Senegambia, and are divided in *Mandingas proper*, *Yolofs*, and *Fulahs;* the latter are the most intelligent, perhaps from partaking of Arabian civilization, as the majority that have come to the island even know how to write, and possess industrial qualifications that render them more desirable; the *Gangás*, inhabiting the coast of Cape Palmas, south of the Kong chain of mountains, and distinguished as *Longovás*, *Manís*, *Fités*, *Kisís*, *Feés*, *Golás*, etc., are well conditioned; the *Minas*, from the Gold Coast; the *Lucumís*, brought from the Slave Coast, but apparently proceeding from Soudan, constitute the majority, and are distinguished by the stripes stained on their cheeks: they are strong for labor, but indomitable and inclined to suicide by hanging; the *Carabalís*, of the kingdom of Benin or the Carabalí coast, are distinguished as *Suamos*, *Bibís*, *Brícanos*, *Bruses*, etc., and have their teeth lanceolated, and are enemies of the *Congos;* the *Congos*, as their name indicates, proceed from the equinoctial or Congo line, and are distinguished as *Royal Congos* (those of Angola), *Motembos*, *Musundís*, *Mondongos*, *Mombasas*, *Mayombes*, etc. The *Macuas* are principally from the interior of the Mozambique.

Havana, we are not aware that they left any descendants. About the settlements of Carey, Santa Rosa, Tiguabos, Ti-Arriba, and Jiguaní, and in the environs of Holguin, are still found a few remnants of the primitive inhabitants, but the majority are crossed with mulattos. The privileges accorded to them by the Leyes de Indias were continued until 1845. Since 1847, Yucatecos or Yucatan Indians have begun to be introduced. The *Mongolian* race was rarely represented by occasionally a member of the crews of vessels visiting the island, until 1847, when Coolies began to be introduced from Emûi, in China. Up to the present time about 6,000 have arrived, and only 20 or 30 returned. They are employed by contract, generally for agricultural labor, or as common servants. They are intelligent and industrious, and soon learn the language. Of *mixed races*, the mulattos, resulting from the union of the whites and negroes, are the most numerous. The mulatto and the negro produce the *Chino*, which name confounds them with the Coolies or Asiatics, who are also so-called, although, in judicial proceedings, the term *Asiatics* is adopted. The mulattos generally employ themselves as carpenters, tailors, musicians, coach-builders, and painters, in which branches they usually excel.

Idiom.—The language used throughout the island is the Castilian, which is spoken more correctly than in those provinces of Spain where dialects are used, as in Galicia, Biscay, Catalonia, and Valencia. However, although in making the comparison we set aside certain provincialisms,* we are far from pretending that our language is as pure and genuine as that used by persons of refinement in Castile or Leon. Besides certain corrupt phrases, the Cuban, generally, does not correctly pronounce the syllables za, ze, zi, zo, zu, ce, ci, but pronounces them as if written sa, se, si, so, su, and se and si (exactly the reverse of the Andalusian), and he frequently confounds the *l* with the *r*, saying, for instance, *cualter, sordado*, instead of *cuartel* and *soldado;* but this defect (also peculiar to Andalusia) is rare among persons of any education. It is somewhat strange that, although constantly hearing the soft dialect of the African, only two or three of his words have been adopted by the Cuban, and that no one should have perfectly acquired any of those dialects.†

Character, Habits, and Customs.—The Cubans are well formed, and

---

* We say that we set them aside, because the true provincialisms (not corruptions) really increase the rich, sonorous, and majestic language of Castile. With what Castilian terms could we possibly designate so many indigenous productions bearing only indigenous names, and unknown in Europe ? See on this point the Dictionary of Cuban Phrases by Sr. Pichardo.

† In 1838 we had prepared for publication a Manual (useful in other times) of the Lucumí, Gangá, and Congo tongues, to facilitate communication with the new negroes.

possess a clear understanding; they are fond of poetry, dancing, and music. They are accused of liking to make a false show, of disinclination for mechanical pursuits, and a strong tendency to litigation. Those bred in the rural districts, constituting the peasantry, and distinguished by the name of *guajiros*, are of strong constitution, and although quick-witted, are indolent and given to routine. In the jurisdiction of the government of Cuba they wear jackets in the European style, but throughout the rest of the island their costume consists merely of shirt and trowsers, with a cutlass or *machete* belted round the waist, a handkerchief loosely circling the throat, and a hat of *guano de yarei* leaf or *jipijapa* straw, and none of them fail to possess a horse on which to ride. The Cuban women are handsome, delicate, intelligent, and well-mannered, and exceedingly fond of music and dancing. The immoral and pernicious game of *monte*, and the sanguinary exhibitions of cock-fights and duck-races in the country towns, are, unfortunately, a favorite passion of Cubans in general, although the first is persecuted by government with a laudable zeal, and the latter allowed only on Sundays, and in certain towns.* It is the custom to spend the summer out of the large cities, resorting chiefly to country seats or towns affording salutary baths. On such occasions the Cuban manifests his proverbial disinterestedness and hospitality, inviting, welcoming, and regaling all his friends and acquaintances. It is also the custom for planters to reside on their estates during crop-time. The active trade and the heat of the climate excuse the common propensity to use carriages, and the *quitrin* is one of the most peculiar, as well as most necessary, appendages to a household of any in the island.

Public Instruction.—INTELLECTUAL CULTURE.—Education has made great progress in the island, especially since the establishment of the Royal Economical Societies of Havana and Cuba, and above all since

---

* It has been *boasted* that the town of Consolacion del Sur possesses *two cock-pits !* In consequence of the new Plaza de Toros, or square for bull-baiting, at Havana, a taste is becoming diffused for another spectacle, no less bloody than that of cock-fighting, and the worst of it is that it is termed *national,* when all the enlightened men of the nation (who should certainly constitute the votes) condemn it in their writings. "The Spanish people (says the wise Sr. Monlan, in his Treatise on Hygienics), with all their temperance, have certain instincts which they should curb. We believe that government, far from fostering the taste for bull-fights for instance, should restrain it, and prepare for the advent of the time in which an exhibition so justly reprobated by all who possess any ideas of administration and government shall disappear. Instead of arenas for bull-fights, there should be gymnasiums for the youth of the country; and those communities that erect new circuses to amuse themselves by awakening and mocking the ire of a useful, animal would employ their money better in establishing scientific professorships or agricultural colonies, or in improving the condition of the public prisons."

1842, when an extraordinary change was made in the public schools, subjecting them to a board of inspection, which, as regards primary instruction, has been subdivided into provincial, local, and auxiliary committees. The capital contains a well-organized royal university, with a rector and thirty professors.* There is a seminary college in Havana, and another in Cuba, which are subject to especial regulations, and where the branches of ecclesiastical studies, philology, and philosophy are taught.

At present are published in Havana four daily papers, a monthly, with the title of *Anales*, etc., two illustrated semi-monthlies (the *Revista de la Habana* and *El Almendares*), and there occasionally circulate besides a few literary and scientific publications, chiefly edited by young Cubans, who, with laudable perseverance, have applied themselves to the cultivation of letters. In Matanzas the *Aurora* is published daily, and from time to time some other publication makes its appearance. Cárdenas, Sagua, Cienfuegos, and Remedios issue an *Hoja Económica* (economical sheet). In Trinidad is published the *Correo*, in Santo Espiritu the *Fenix*, in Puerto Principe the *Fanal*, and in Cuba the *Orden*, the *Redactor*, and *Memorias de la Real Sociedad Económica*. Pinar del Rio, Bayamo, and Holguin are the only large towns in the island wanting in an element which affords so good a proof of the culture of a community.

The branches of literature most affected by the natives are poetry, history, and novels; little having been published in regard to the exact sciences, and that only of the most elementary nature for the use of schools. In poetry, Zequeira Rubalcaba, Heredia, Blanchié, and Milanés† have shone conspicuously; the majority in descriptive and lyrical compositions, and some as dramatical writers. Among these Milanés has excelled in his tragedy of *El Conde Alarcos*. The Countess of Merlin has distinguished herself as a novelist. As historians, Arrate, Urrutia, Valdés, and Heredia; as a grammarian, Vidal; and the learned Presbyter Varela in philosophy; in jurisprudence, Ayala, Hechavarría, Ponce de Leon, Escovedo, Armas, and Govantes; and in medicine, the celebrated Romay. Among the most prominent Cubans have been the following: Don Luis M. de Peñalver y Cárdenas, archbishop of Guatemala; Bishops Palma and Hechavarría; Don Juan Bernardo de O'Gavan, dean and governor of the bishopric of Havana; Don Ramon José Mendi-

---

* There is now in course of erection at Havana, on account of the State, a fine edifice for educational purposes, under the title of Real Colegio de la Habana, and it is intended to establish a similar one at Puerto Principe.

† We include this poet in the number of departed authors, as the unfortunate state of his health renders him lost to the world of letters.

ola, magistrate of Puerto Principe and Porto Rico; Don José Domingo Benitez, minister of the Supreme Tribunal of War and Marine; Don Rafael Rodriguez, sole assessor of Havana, and honorary counsellor of state; Don Fernando O'Reilly, honorary judge and chief justice of Havana; Don Antonio Maria de la Torre y Cárdenas, political secretary from 1821 to 1841; the memorable statesmen and counsellors of state, Don Francisco Arango y Parreño, superintendent, and Count Villanueva, superintendent of Havana, senator, and grandee of Spain of the first class; General Don Gonzalo O'Farrill and Don Jorge Maria de la Torre ministers of War; Generals Don Francisco Diaz Pimienta, Count Revillagigedo, viceroy of Mexico, Count Mopox y de Jaruco, Don Carlos de Urrutia, Don José de Zayas, Don Vicente Genaro de Quesada, Don José Moscoso, Don Gabriel, and Don Domingo Aristizabal, Don Juan Montalvo, and the Marquis de San Felipe y Santiago; and Colonel Don José Maria de la Torre, who was governor of Florida.

Manufactures and Arts.—The island of Cuba does not at present rank as a manufacturing nor artistic country. However, the production of sugar (which is a manufacture) is more advanced than in many other cane-growing countries, as is proved by the preference and higher price which it obtains in foreign markets. Besides sugar and rum, in the rural districts are manufactured starch, *casabe* or yuca-bread, and pottery, also hats of the *yarei* palm,* and, at the western side of the island, mats, baskets, seroons, cocoa-nut oil, etc. A great number of persons are employed in manufacturing cigars, and on the coasts many are engaged in ship-building.† At Havana are good founderies, where entire steam-engines are cast. At Guanabacoa are manufactories of cutlass blades of excellent quality. There are also in the island manufactories of perfumery, pickles, nails, friction matches, felt hats, stearine candles, soap, superior composition metal, carriages (rivaling the best foreign), refined sugar, and others. In 1851 a large paper factory of all kinds was destroyed by fire at Puentes-Grandes.

Agriculture.—" The agricultural industry of the island may be considered as divided into two great systems, which in Europe are advantageously combined, but that here have continued separate since the

---

* This manufacture has greatly decreased since 1839, when hats of *jipijapa* straw began to come into general use.

† It is known that from 1724 to 1797 there were built at Havana 6 three-deck ships, 21 of 70 to 80 guns, 26 of 50 to 60 guns, 14 frigates of 30 to 40, and 58 smaller vessels; total 125, two of which mounting 120 guns. Subsequently there have been built several other vessels of war, and many merchantmen, including several steamers. The steamer "Sagua la Grande" was built at the place of that name, and two steamers at Havana, one for war.

earliest period of the settlement, viz., the breeding of cattle and the cultivation of the soil. The first is quite independent of tillage, and consequently employs no utensils nor manures, nor any thing tending to vegetable production. The second represents agriculture in its infancy, as much by the imperfection of the instruments used, as by the paucity of principles that constitute the husbandman's art; principles that, with few exceptions, may be reduced to the simple ones of sowing and reaping, leaving all the rest to the fruitfulness of the soil and the excellence of the climate." (Sagra, History of Cuba.*) Of the 916,571 *caballerias* of land† constituting the surface of the island and its adjacent territory, 48,572 are cultivated, 20,341 used for artificial pasturage, 149,248 for natural pasturage, 377,003 are mountainous or uncleared, and 321,407 of barren lands, mines, etc. There are consequently 68,913 *caballerias* under cultivation and 526,251 uncultivated, besides the 321,407 of barren lands, mines, etc. The statistics for 1827 state that in said year there were 91,819 *caballerias* registered for cultivation, and, according to Sr. Sagra (History of Cuba), the island numbered 66,441 *caballerias* under cultivation in 1840. Now no one that is aware of the extraordinary impulse received by the agricultural industry of the island since 1840, can doubt that the extent of land then under cultivation has at least been doubled, and, consequently, either the data from which the statistics of 1827 were formed, and on which Sr. Sagra's statement was founded, were greatly exaggerated, or, as is more likely, those constituting the basis of the last statistical returns are exceedingly underrated. It will, however, be observed that the said statistics of 1827 only give the number of *registered* " *caballerias*," including natural pasturages, woods, etc., which we have stated separately. The chief agricultural products are the sugar-cane, tobacco, coffee, cotton, fruit, and vegetables. Rice, sago, maize, and even cocoa, are cultivated on a small scale, not enough to supply the consumption of the interior. Wheat,‡

---

* Since the voyage made by the author to the United States in 1848 and 1849, commissioned by the Junta de Fomento for scientific and industrial information, a change is taking place both in the instruments used and in the system of various branches of cultivation, and also by the adoption of new methods, as is proved by the immense subsequent importation of instruments, animals, and seed.

† The maritime league of one-twentieth of an equatorial degree is equal to 5565.329 *metres* according to Humboldt, which is equivalent to 6562.89 Cuban *varas*. Therefore the maritime square league is equal to 43.071.40 square Cuban *varas*, or 230.7 *caballerias* of land: and 8,973 square maritime leagues equal to 916,571 *caballerias*, or 12,301.527 *hectares*.

‡ We can not conceive what has given rise to the idea that the cultivation of wheat was prohibited in the island, when, on the contrary, government has made several attempts to foster it. The true cause of its neglect is its small yield as compared with that of any other article.

indigo, and even the mulberry and nopal trees (for breeding the silk-worm and the cochineal insect) have been almost entirely abandoned. Sugar, rum, wax, and other petty manufactures, and the breeding of cattle, complete the list of agricultural labors in the island. The tenements where the preceding are cultivated and manufactured are classified in the island as follows: *Hato*, a circular space of land, with a radius of two Cuban leagues.* *Corral*, also a circular space, of one Cuban league radius. *Potrero*, an inclosed estate of less extent than either of the two preceding, but with more abundant pasturage. These three classes are devoted to raising live-stock of all kinds, but the first especially to horned cattle; the second to sheep, goats, and swine, and the third to grazing horned cattle and breeding horses. The number of cattle that the *hatos* and *corrales* may maintain depends on the nature of the land, since if it contains more meadow than thickets or woods it will be susceptible of raising more horned cattle, and *vice versa*. In the *potreros*, if well managed, may be raised and pastured on the average 25 oxen and horses for each *caballeria* of land. *Ingenio* is an agricultural and manufacturing estate, generally of greater extent than the *cafetal*, and where the sugar-cane is cultivated, and sugar and rum manufactured. It is the largest establishment in the island. The lands of Cuba are recognized as superior to those of the other Antilles for the cultivation of the sugar-cane. The produce of the cane is exceedingly irregular, depending as it does on the quality of the soil, the weather, the class and age of the plant, and especially on the apparatus used in the manufacture. In regard to the last, the island is in the highest stage of advancement, as is proved by its large crops and the quality of the commodity, which commands a decided preference in all the markets of the world.† A *caballeria* of land under favorable circumstances produces

---

* There are some *hatos* of three and of five leagues radius, like that of Hanábana, but the majority, the same as the *corrales*, are incomplete. As these two classes of estates are of great extent, and as from their apportionment most of the others have originated, the knowledge of them is important and necessary, especially to avoid confounding the administrative division, as the comprehensive extent of said cattle estates is vulgarly termed *partido* or district. Thus we frequently hear of *partidos* de la Bija, de las Virtudas, and even *province* of Barajagua, though such *partidos* or province have no existence.

† There are in the island many *ingenios* that produce 8,000 to 9,000 boxes of sugar. *La Ponina*, estate of Sr. Diago, produces 12,000, and the *Alava* of Sr. Zulueta 15,000, and there are two in process of establishment that will produce 16,000 and 80,000 respectively. (See the Editorial of the Diario de la Marina of 1st January, 1852.) A great manufactory of beet-root sugar in Belgium, with all the recent improvements, requires for its machinery and buildings (that is to say for its boiling-house) an outlay of $40,000, exclusive of the current expenses of manufacture, and will produce at the utmost three tons of sugar a day, equal to about 15 boxes. This becomes insignificant when compared with an *ingenio* in the island whose daily production is 125 boxes.

8,000 to 4,000 *arrobas* by the ordinary apparatus, and even double that quantity if the Derosne apparatus is used. *Cafetal* is a coffee plantation. Coffee, introduced into the island in 1748, did not begin to figure among the exports until toward the end of the last century; and became at the commencement of the present century the second staple in importance; but, unable to withstand the competition of Brazil, Java, and Ceylon,* it has, since 1832, retrograded to such a degree that it is apprehended that in the course of a very few years it will only be cultivated for domestic consumption. A *caballeria* of land produces on the average 800 *arrobas*, and in the eastern part of the island it is estimated at 1,600 *arrobas*. There are many plantations where a pound of coffee per plant is harvested. That grown in the jurisdiction of Cuba and Saltadero, equal to the Santo Domingo coffee, is still much esteemed in foreign markets. *Vega* is a plantation devoted to tobacco, and generally consists of a small space of land, in most instances situated on the banks of the rivers. Respecting the product of tobacco, a proper estimate can scarcely be formed, for on appropriate soil and with favorable weather the half million of plants that a *caballeria* of land may contain yield 120 to 150 *cargas*, at the rate of eight *arrobas* the *carga*, while the same space of land under unfavorable weather will only produce 30 or 40 *cargas*. "It is well known that the lands west of the meridian of Havana, and distinguished as Vuelta-Abajo, produce the finest tobacco in the world, in richness of color and fragrance, softness of leaf, and readiness of combustion. But it must not be imagined that all the western territory of the island enjoys the same privilege. The best lands for this plant (which are paid at the rate of $1,000 and a bonus of $100 or six doubloons) are comprised in an irregular oblong square, whose boundaries are, on the east the Rio Hondo or Consolacion del Sur River, on the west the Cuyaguateje or Mantua River, on the north the Sierra de los Organos, and on the south the belt of *barrigona* palms, that runs in a parallel direction to the coast. This oblong square is 28 leagues long and 7 wide. Out of it, toward the meridian of Havana, the tobacco is of fine color but less fragrant, and the first of these qualities gives it the preference with foreigners. From Consolacion to San Cristóbal the tobacco is of high *quality*, as the *veguero* terms it, but harsh and strong, and from San Cristóbal to Guanajay (excepting the district of Las Virtudas) the tobacco is inferior, and continues so eastward as far as Hol-

---

* The coffee of the island is incomparably superior to that of the countries named, and the decline in the production may be attributed to the differential duties imposed in the United States on imports from Cuba, in retaliation for our high impost on their flour taken in their vessels to the Brazilian markets.— *Vide* Torrente and Arboleya. [Coffee is at present admitted free of duty into the United States.—*Editor.*]

guin and Cuba, where it again becomes of good quality. The fertile valley of Güines produces bad smoking tobacco, but excellent for snuff, which used to be manufactured in large quantity for account of the factory. Among the same lands of the Vuelta-Abajo are some of superior kind, such as the Vegas de la Leña and Del Corojo, on the margin of the River San Sebastian, where the best tobacco in the island is gathered. There are also excellent *vegas* at Mayarí, on the eastern side. The Tobacco Board having determined in 1792 on the settlement and cultivation of that district, proposed that the 18 leagues of land composing it should be purchased by the treasury, and repaid by the colonists with five per cent. of the product of the tobacco, proving the preference given it. There are several other regions adapted to the cultivation of this leaf. The district of Guantánamo alone produced about six years ago 1,200 *arrobas*."* (Sagra's History.) *Algodonal* is a cotton plantation. Only in the eastern department are there estates exclusively devoted to this product, yielding 6,000 pounds of excellent quality per *caballeria*. In the avenues between the plants are cultivated maize and pulse.† *Cacagual* or *cacaotal* is a cocoa plantation. Only in San Juan de los Remedios are there properties of this description, as in other parts of the island cocoa, like cotton, constitutes but a part of the cultivation. 5,000 cocoa-trees may be raised on a *caballeria*, and as the product of each tree is estimated at five pounds, the average yield may be set down as 250 quintals. It is of good quality, and would be better if the seed, instead of having been introduced from Maracaibo, were that of Chuav, Choroní, or Ocumare (near Porto Cabello), or of Soconuco, in Guatemala, which produce

---

* In the five years of 1847 to 1852 the jurisdiction of Pinar del Rio and the district of Consolacion del Norte have produced an average of 150,000 *tercios* of tobacco, which, at the rate of 110 pounds each, amount to 16,500,000 pounds. In 1848 the average price was $25 a *tercio*, and in 1852, $27. The *vegas* of this district comprise 2,000 *caballerias* of land. (*Memoria Sobre el Cultivo del Tabaco, por un Amigo del Pais*, 1852.) See also another work by Sr. Salazar, and *El Tabaco Habano*, by Sr. Rodriguez-Ferrer; also some interesting notes on the same subject by the author's great-grandfather, Col. Don Antonio Maria de la Torre, his grandfather, Col. Don José Maria, and his father, government inspector of tobacco, some of which have been published in the *Memorias de la Real Sociedad Economica*.

† One of the chief objects of the author's mission to the United States in 1848 was to collect the best cotton seed, and learn the best method for its cultivation, being persuaded that it would be the best substitute for the retrograding production of coffee. He obtained five excellent kinds, including the *prolific promenate*, that had just been introduced there from Mexico, and which afforded a most satisfactory result in the trial made by Sr. Bonany. Having taken to Spain samples and seed of this cotton produced in the island, it drew the attention of several enlightened agriculturists; and such was the astonishment of the learned Sr. Olivan at so fine a product, that he presented the author to the Ministro de Fomento, who immediately sent some of the seed to Andalusia, where endeavors are now being made to acclimate the plant,

the best in the world.* *Estancia* is a small farm in the neighborhood of towns, where vegetables, fruit, etc., are raised; when not in the immediate vicinity of towns, it is termed *sitio de labor;* and, when exclusively belonging to a larger plantation, *sitio de viandas.* On the *estancias* poultry and cows are raised; and the *sitios de labor* produce cheese, *casabe,* and starch. *Tejar* is a place where pottery and bricks are manufactured. *Colmenar* is the place where bee-hives are kept. There are few tenements exclusively devoted to this branch, Puerto Principe being the most productive district. The wax of the island is of superior quality, and is exported to the markets within the Mexican gulf, and even to the Spanish peninsula.† *Quinta* is a country seat or summer resort, generally situated near the large towns. Maize, rice, sago, pulse, *yuca*, the *boniato* or sweet potato, plantains, and fruit are not grown on determinate possessions, but on nearly all, and especially on those termed *sitios de labor.* Maize is very variable in its crops, but the average yield of a *caballeria* of land, at the rate of 140 to 200 fold, is estimated at 200 *fanegas* or quintals of grain. Each *mazorca* or ear usually contains as many as 500 grains. It produces two crops a year. Rice yields 150 to 200 fold, and the average product of a *caballeria* may be estimated at 2,000 *arrobas,* or 3,000 on new and fruitful lands.‡ Mustard,

---

* The author intends publishing the notes written by his father in 1831 for the Minister Count Ofalia on the cultivation of cocoa, and recommends the work on the same subject by Don Pedro Santacilla, Puerto Principe, 1849, in which is the following passage: " Humboldt and Codazzi attribute to the extreme fertility of the soil that power of vegetable life which causes cocoa to produce in *five years* at the place called Rio Negro. Well, now, at the cafetal *La Union,* situate eight leagues from this city, there are cocoa-trees that have produced in *three years.* This precocious growth proves how favorable the climate is in general to this production, and, with good seed, we could doubtless have as good cocoa plantations as the best in South America."

† The breeding of bees and the production of wax are exceedingly interesting branches of rural industry, if we consider the great advantages afforded by the climate the constant vegetation of the island, the trifling outlay that is necessary, the abundance of suitable timber, the use of which is permitted to the bee-keepers, and the certain advantage of preference commanded by the superior quality of the product throughout the markets of the Mexican gulf. (For the raising of bees, etc., in the island, see the notes of Don Tomas Romay, 1796, and Don Pedro Boloix in 1815.)

‡ As will be seen in the Appendix, the author has introduced into the island various excellent kinds of maize, rice, and other seed, especially grasses for pasturage. It is a shame that although rice yields surprisingly, not only has its cultivation not been extended, but there is not an establishment with proper machinery for cleaning it, particularly in the beautiful and fruitful valley of Güines, whose river might be so advantageously availed of for water-power. Those persons who, like ourselves, have been desiring the establishment of a model *hacienda,* will soon have the pleasure of noticing a step toward it in the erection of a building in the present botanical garden, which is to contain a meteorological observatory, a professorship of botany, etc.

which is produced of superior quality, and of so much demand in England and the United States, is scarcely cultivated. The gutta-percha and caoutchouc or India-rubber trees have hardly been acclimated yet. Sago, little cultivated, though worthy of attention, has produced at San Antonio at the rate of 160 *quintals* of flour per *caballeria*, and in other places 6,400 *arrobas* of the root per *caballeria*. As regards pasturages, it is only in the central part of the island that meadows are formed of any considerable extent. Millet is abundantly raised, principally to feed horned cattle.

Navigation.—In 1851 there entered the several ports of the island 883 Spanish vessels, measuring 270,176 tons, and 2,982 foreign, measuring 727,814 tons. Total, 3,865 vessels, and 998,000 tons. The number of vessels cleared was 3,735, of which 793 were Spanish.*

COMMERCE.—The exterior trade of the island is in so prosperous a state that it equals in importance that of the metropolis.† In 1851 it amounted to $63,665,102.‡ The importation amounted to $32,315,745,|| of which (about $19,899,000)§ was in Spanish bottoms. The exportation amounted to $31,349,357,¶ whereof $6,204,653 under Spanish flag. The

---

* Throughout the entire Spanish peninsula, including its adjacent islands (Baleares and Canaries), the number of vessels entered in 1850 was 6,008, measuring 725,043 tons (3,164 Spanish, with 339,574 tons), and cleared 5,141, with 658,317 tons (2,490 Spanish, with 277,839 tons). As regards amount of tonnage, it will hence be seen that the shipping trade of the Island of Cuba exceeds that of Spain. It is very generally supposed that the distance between Havana and Cadiz is 1,600 maritime leagues, but we have carefully calculated it with intelligent naval officers, and find the directest route is no more than 1,382 maritime leagues. The quickest passages made from and to Havana have been the following: in 1829, from Havana to Cadiz, American ships Fabius and Teaplant, 21 days; 1833 (October), Spanish brig-of-war Jason, from Cadiz to Havana, 22 days; 1841 (September), French frigate Havre et Guadeloupe, to Havre, 21 days; 1843, Spanish brig Gallo de Oro, to Cadiz, 23 days; 1848, American steamer Crescent City, to New York, in 68 hours; 1853, Spanish steamer Fernando el Católico, to Vigo, in 17 days 7 hours.

† "But for the happy privileges of the port of Havana, Jamaica would have been the centre of all the mercantile operations with the neighboring continent."—*Humboldt, Political Essay on the Island of Cuba.* ‡ See Appendix No. 1.

| The average of 10 years (1840 to 1850) is $26,195,850. The chief imports in 1851 were as follows: liquids (such as wines, oils, etc.), $2,825,045; provisions, $1,985,423; spices, $86,442; fruits, $287,586; grain, $4,808,810; fish, $619,205; other provisions, $2,011,401; cottons, $3,021,009; linens, $3,528,084; woolens, $431,702; silks, $529,812; skins and furs, $589,457; wood and timber, $2,211,229; metals, $2,791,617; animals, $87,974; railway machinery and material, $634,429; ditto for sugar plantations, $506,862; other articles, $5,410,335.

§ In the original the sum is stated at $19,899, but it is evident that the final figures have been left out. In 1850 it was $18,445,072 in a total of $28,983,227.

¶ The average of 1841 to 1850 is $24,685,844. The chief exports in 1851 were as follows: principal productions of the island, $30,340,423; other, $87,962; wood and

order in which the countries trading with Cuba stand, according to the absolute value of their transactions, is as follows: United States, England, Spain, Germany, Spanish-American States, France, Russia, Belgium, Denmark, Holland, etc.; but in regard to importation only, the first in order is Spain, then the United States, England, Spanish-American States, Germany, France, Denmark, Belgium, Holland, Brazil, etc.; and in regard to exportation, the United States, England, Spain, Germany, Russia, France, Spanish-American States, Holland, Belgium, etc. The customs dues are in accordance with the tariff published in 1847, with the modifications made in 1852.

Revenue.—The revenues of the Island of Cuba are divided into *maritime* and *inland*, the first comprising customs and light-house dues, ship-visits, etc., and the second, various taxes and different tolls of an origin entirely distinct from that of imposts or contributions. Both sources are subdivided into *proper* and *alien* branches, that is to say, the portion of taxes immediately distributed by the Royal Treasury, and that which it collects for other account, applicable to special services, such as the Junta de Fomento (Board of Improvement), Beneficencia (Alms-house), etc. During the reign of the ruinous system of monopoly, the revenues of Cuba were so small, that, to cover her internal obligations and the many external ones imposed on her, it was found necessary to obtain assistance, which, under the name of *situado*,* was annually afforded by the treasury of Mexico. And who could have imagined that—thanks to free-trade—in a period of less than fifty years, the possession that received such aid would have a revenue one third greater than that of the opulent viceroyship which afforded it?† The total revenue of the island in 1851 amounted to $13,821,456, whereof $1,651,414 belonged to the "alien" branches.

---

timber, $398,811; re-exported articles, $514,485. The quantity of principal products exported was 1,539,994 boxes of sugar; 575,119 *arrobas* of coffee, 318,428 puncheons of molasses, 9,316,593 pounds of leaf tobacco, 270,313 thousands cigars. The average annual exportation for the five years ending with 1850 was as follows: 18,690,460 *arrobas* of sugar, 13,653 puncheons of rum,—240,155 puncheons molasses, 768,244 *arrobas* of coffee; 48,141 *arrobas* of wax, 291,347 *arrobas* of leaf tobacco, 896,008 thousands cigars, 598,647 quintals of copper. The average export of coffee for the five years ending with 1835, 1,995,882 *arrobas*; and between 1841 to '45, the average annual export of cigars was 941,467 thousands, and that of copper 1,023,838 quintals.

* It is not positively known at what time these *situados* began, but the receipt of one is recorded in 1584. From a published statement, it appears that, from 1766 to 1806, the treasury of Havana received $108,150,627, which is an average of $2,637,820 per annum. The external obligations imposed on the island were principally the building of vessels, the purchase of timber, tobacco, etc.

† The present annual revenue of Mexico is only about $8,000,000. (*See Catechism of Geography by General Almonte, Mexico*, 1852.)

Expenditure.—The total of expenses of the island during 1851 amounted to $11,969,750.*

Communication.—We shall divide this section into *Internal Communication*, or within the island, and *External Communication*, or with other countries.

INTERNAL COMMUNICATION.—The mediums of *land* communication are the common roads, causeways, railroads, and electric telegraphs; those of *maritime* intercourse are the coasting-trade and the lines of steamers and sailing packets between determinate points.

Common Roads.—Respecting these, it should be said that they require much improvement, being in a very bad condition, as much from their indirectness† as from their pavement, which, being natural, becomes so broken up, especially in the rainy season, as to be frequently impassable. A broad road runs through the centre of the island from Havana to Cuba, passing by Villa Clara, Santo Espiritu, Puerto Principe, and Bayamo, known as the Camino Real del Centro, or del interior. There are several other branch-roads to different towns and places on the coast.‡

Causeways.—There are at present—one ten and a half Cuban leagues in extent, from Havana (*puerta de tierra*) to Guanajay, with a toll-gate; another from Havana to Santiago de las Vegas, scarcely four leagues in length from the corner of Teja, also with a toll-gate; another, six leagues in length, from the corner of Tollo to Jamaica;|| another from Luyanó to the Gallega tavern (east of Guanabacoa, and soon to be continued as far as Guanabo, by Barrera), three and a quarter leagues in length; another from Casilda to Trinidad; and another from Batabanó to the beach, one league in length.

---

* As follows: collection, $809,971; justice, $169,002; ecclesiastical branch, $327,805; civil expenses, $1,044,697; military expenses, $5,985,963; naval expenses, $1,965,444; peninsular affairs, $1,590,130; legations and consulates of America, $76,788. Total, $11,969,750, and adding the expenses of "alien" branches, amounting to $1,327,456, the total expenditure is $13,297,206. In 1841 the amount, exclusive of the alien branches, was $10,112,533, and in 1850 $10,475,159, although from 1828 to 641 they did not exceed 3 to 4 millions of dollars annually.

† The road between Cuba and Baracoa is so winding, that at some places it runs seven leagues in an opposite direction to the one intended, besides crossing a single river (the Jojó) 11 times.

‡ The legal width of the highways is 24 *varas*, of the cross-roads 16, and of the bridle-roads 8 *varas*.

|| There are three leagues more contracted for from Jamaica to the Fuentes tavern, by Mount Candela; and the continuation of the Guanajay road as far as Candelaria, with 27 economical bridges, has just been approved. Stages run daily from Havana to Marianao and Guanajay; from Havana to Santiago (two lines); from Havana to San José de las Lajas; and from Regla to Guanabacoa, and as far as the Gallega tavern.

Electric Telegraphs.—The lines contracted for from Pinar del Rio to Cuba are already being constructed, with branches to the principal towns on the coast; and the section between Havana, Matanzas, Cárdenas, and Guanajay will soon be in operation, running along the line of railway on the western part of the island. Messages are already transmitted between Havana and Batabanó.

Railroads.—The Island of Cuba enjoys the glory of having forestalled many of the most civilized countries in the adoption of these rapid, commodious, and economical mediums of intercourse. After England and the United States, only Austria and France have preceded her—the first by three years, and the second by two. The railway opened in 1837 from Havana to Bejucál, and extended the following year as far as Güines, is not only the first in the Spanish monarchy,* but in all the Spanish-American countries. Their present extent is 351 miles, or 133½ Cuban leagues, distributed among the following lines: "Havana:" the Havana railroad consists of .108 miles, distributed as follows—Section from Havana to La Union, 77 4-5 miles, with the following stations, viz., Depósito de Villanueva (in Havana), Cienaga, Almendares, Aguada del Cura, Rincon, Bejucál, Quibican, San Felipe, Duran, Guara, Melena, Güines, San Nicolás, Los Vegas, Los Palos, Bermeja, and Union, where it connects with the Matanzas line; the branch-road from San Felipe to Batabanó, 9⅔ miles, with an intermediate station at Pozo-Redondo; branch from Rincon to Guanajay, 21 miles, with the intermediate stations of San Antonio, Seborucal, and La Seiba. "Regla to Guanabacoa," 4 miles. "Matanzas and Sabanilla road," 47⅜ miles from Matanzas to Isabel, with the following intermediate stations: Guanábana (where it connects with the Coliseo road), Cidra, La Sabanilla, Union, Bolondron, La Güira, Navajas (where it connects with the Cárdenas road), and Corral-Falso. The line is already surveyed for the branch that is to be built from La Isabel to connect with the Cienfuegos road at Las Cruces, touching at La Agüica. "Coliseo road," 16 miles (exclusive of the 7¾ between Matanzas and La Guanábana, connecting point), with the following stations: Guanábana, Ibarra, Caobas, Limonar, Sumidero, and Coliseo. The line that is to connect at this point with the Cárdenas road is already surveyed and will soon be commenced. "Cardenas road," 68¼ miles, distributed as follows: trunk-road from Cárdenas to Navajas, 29¼ miles,

---

* The railway from Mataró to Barcelona, the first on the peninsula of Spain, was opened in October, 1848; that from Madrid to Aranjuez in February, 1851; and to Tembleque in September, 1853. But although this proves how late Spain adopted this advantageous means of communication, it must also be acknowledged that few countries have evinced greater enthusiasm, patriotism, and decision in undertaking so many and extensive lines as are now being effected.

PHYSICAL, POLITICAL, AND INDUSTRIAL. 65

with the following stations: Contreras, Cimarrones, Bemba, Ranchuelo, Corral-Falso, Montalvo, and Navajas; branch from Bemba to La Macágua, 34 miles, with the following intermediate stations: Quintana, Perico, Tinguaro, Nueva Bermeja, and Agüica. "Júcaro road," 34 miles, distributed thus: trunk from Júcaro to Pijuan, 21 miles, with the stations of San Anton, Recreo, Artemisal, and Pijuan or Laguna Grande; branch of La Sabanilla de la Palma, 4 miles; branch of Banagüises, 9 miles. "Cienfuegos to Villa Clara," 19 miles completed, with the stations of Palmira and Las Cruces; and 23 miles in process of construction. "Mallorquin to Pijuan," in project. "Carahatas," half a league in the interior, in process of construction. "Sagua to Villa Clara," in process of construction. "Trinidad to Casilda and Santo Espiritu," in process of building. "Remedios to Caibarien," 6 miles built. "Remedios to Santo Espiritu," in project. "Santo Espiritu to Sasa," in project. "Puerto Principe to Nuevitas," 44 3-5 miles, with the following stations: San José (in Puerto Principe), Sabana-Nueva, Alcoy, Minas, Ramblazo, Buena-Vista, and Villa-Nueva (in Nuevitas). "Jibára to Holguin," in project. "Manzanillo to Bayamo," in project. "Cobre to Punta de Sal" (port of Cuba), 9 miles, of which 3 are on an inclined plane.

Lines of Steamers and Sailing-Packets.—Besides the sailing-vessels devoted to the coasting-trade,* the maritime intercourse of the island is performed by the following lines of steamers and sailing-packets, viz., between Havana, Matanzas, Cárdenas, and El Júcaro, steamers alternating every day, and reaching Matanzas in five hours; between Batabanó and Cuba, stopping at Cienfuegos, Trinidad, Santa Cruz, and Manzanillo, time, five days; between Batabanó and Bailen, stopping at Dayaniguas, Coloma, and Punta de Cartas, one day; between Batabanó and Pinos island, weekly, time, a few hours; between Havana and El Morrillo (Vuelta-Abajo, north coast); between Havana, Los Arroyos, and Bailen, Punta de Cartas, and Coloma. The foregoing are regular, but almost every month there are steamers that make voyages from Havana and Nuevitas, and even as far as Cuba, stopping at the principal inter-

---

* The coast-shipping of the Island of Cuba offers two highly satisfactory considerations. The first is its extraordinary increase within the last 10 years, both cause and effect of the growth of our internal trade; and the second is the excellence of the vessels and the variety of their motive power, there being in this regard no reason to fear a comparison with any other nation. The sailing-vessels employed in the coasting-trade are generally of sufficient capacity for the cargo that usually offers at the ports they frequent, and without neglecting solidity, they are in general fast sailers, thus combining three great advantages. In corroboration of this statement, witness those fine schooners that cover the waters of the harbor, some of them exceeding in burden many of the ocean vessels; and it is also worthy of note that very few of them are lost.

mediate ports. A steamer of 1,000 tons is expected from New York for the coasting-trade of the island, and others have been ordered.

EXTERNAL COMMUNICATION.—The intercourse of this island with other countries is as yet only by means of vessels; although it appears that the project of a submarine telegraph between the island and the American continent by the coast of Florida is likely to be realized. * The enviable position of Cuba, as the "Key of the New World, renders it exceedingly favorable as a stopping-place of all the navigation lines that are being established between Europe and America, and even those running between the different ports of the latter continent. There are, in fact (besides the very numerous sailing-vessels), the following lines of trans-Atlantic steamers: between Havana and Cadiz, monthly; time, 20 to 24 days. Between Key West, Savannah, Charleston, and Havana, the American steamer Isabel, making two trips a month. Between New York, Havana, and Mobile, steamer Black Warrior, making two trips a month. Between New York, Havana, and New Orleans, steamers Crescent City, Philadelphia, Empire City, United States, etc., twice a month. Between Southampton and Havana, monthly, English line. Between Havana and Buenos-Ayres, touching at Brazil, a new English line.

Coat of Arms.—In 1516 it was granted to Cuba to use " an escutcheon divided into two quarters, the upper emblazoned with the Assumption of Our Lady, mantled in purple and gold, and resting on a crescent, with four azure angels and clouds; and in the lower the image of Santiago in a green field, with rocks and trees in the distance; at the top the letter F, an I at the right and C at the left, being the initials of Fernando, Isabel, and Carlos; at the sides, a yoke and arrows; and beneath these figures, and pendant from the base, a lamb; showing that Cuba's distinctive and most honorable emblem is, Mary, the Holy Mother of God."

Measures.*—LONG MEASURE.—The Cuban *vara* contains 848 *millimetres*, and is divided into three *tercias* or four *cuartas;* it is half an inch longer than the Castilian, or, more properly, that of Burgos; therefore, by deducting from it 6 17-100 lines, we have the Castilian *vara;* by adding to it (*say*) 6¼ Cuban inches we have the *metre;* and adding 2 10-12 inches it becomes the English yard. It is not customary to call the third part of the *vara* " foot," but *tercia*, or " third."† The

---

* It is ordered, that after 1854 the metrical system shall be adopted in the dependencies of the State.

† This *vara*, known as the Cuban, provincial, De Flores, or surveyor's, is used throughout the island, except at Havana, where, for trade and surveying, the *vara Habanera*, or commercial, is made use of, and contains 845 metres. Whenever, in this chapter, the term *vara* alone is expressed, the Cuban *vara* is meant.

Cuban or provincial league contains 5,000 Cuban *varas*, or 4,240 French *metres*, while the Castilian is 6,571¼ Cuban, or 6,666⅔ Castilian *varas*.

SURVEYOR'S MEASURE.—The *cordel* of 24 *varas* (formerly 25); the *vara de tarea* (used in clearings and *chapeos*) is a pole of 6 *varas* in length (in Cuba, 4 Castilian *varas*); the *tendido de soga*, 25 *brazas* or fathoms (formerly 32, which it actually measures in Cuba); the *caballeria* of land is a square of 18 *cordeles*, or 432 *varas* on each side, or 324 square *cordeles*, or 186,624 square *varas*; the *solar*, or "lot," varies in different towns : in Havana it is 27 Habana *varas* front and 40 deep, in Matanzas it is 30 Cuban *varas* front and 40 deep, in Guanabacoa 20 by 30 *varas*, San Juan de los Remedios 30 by 40, etc.; the *caró* (*carreau*, French measure, adopted in the jurisdiction of Cuba), is the tenth part of a *caballeria* of land; the *mesana* (*besama*) is a space of land for tillage bounded by four furrows, one on every side, of an extent adapted to rest the oxen at the turn; the *tarea* (used in the *chapeos* or clearings) is a surface of 25 *varas de tarea* in length, and 1 in breadth, equal to 900 square *varas*; the *legua corralera* (which is understood whenever a superficial league of *hato* and *corral* is indicated) consists of 105¼ *caballerias*: the radius of an *hato*, or estate for large cattle, is 10,000 *varas* or 2 Cuban leagues, its circuit (a polygon of 72 sides) 12 leagues, its surface 12½ square leagues or 1,684¼ *caballerias* of land; the radius of a *corral*, or estate for small cattle, is 5,000 *varas*, or one Cuban league, its circuit (a polygon of 72 sides) 6 2-10 leagues, and area 3 square leagues, or 421 1-9 *caballerias*;* a *corte de ingenio* contains 30 to 40 *caballerias* of land; *cafetales*, *potreros*, tobacco *vegas estancias* are of various extent, but commonly contain from 6 to 12 *caballerias* the first, 6 to 40 the second, and ½ to 6 the last.

DRY MEASURE.—The box of sugar is 5 *cuartas* (quarters of a *vara*) long, 2 high, and 3 wide, and contains from 16 to 22 *arrobas* net of white sugar.† The hogshead, or *bocoy*, used for Muscovado sugar, is of three sizes, containing from 40 to 60 *arrobas* net. The bag of coffee is 5 *cuartas* long and 3½ in diameter, and contains 6 to 8 *arrobas* of coffee. The *saca*, or sack, of coal is equal to the coffee-bag; the *saco*, or bag, of coal is half a *saca*. The *carga*, or load, of tobacco is 2 *tercios*, or bales; the *tercio* is 1 *vara* long, ⅔ wide, and ½ high, and contains 70 *manojos* of *libra* tobacco (which is the finest quality) weighing

---

* There are very few complete *hatos* and *corrales*.

† When it contains less than 16 *arrobas* it is called *estuche*, or case, and is not admitted in trade. The tare (weight of the cask, leather straps, and the hooks for weighing) is graduated as 57 pounds. The tare of a hogshead of Muscovado sugar, 110 to 120 pounds; of a bag of coffee, 2 pounds; and of a *tercio* of tobacco, 12 pounds.

5 to 7 *arrobas*, and of other qualities, 80 *manojos*, weighing 4 to 8 *arrobas*; each *manojo* contains 4 *gavillas*, and each *gavilla* 25 leaves if *libra* tobacco; 30, if injured first quality; 35, if second quality; 40, if third; 45, if fourth. The term *gavilla* is also applied to that portion of tobacco which may be contained in the ring formed by the thumb and forefinger, used in the case of injured fifth or sixth quality tobacco, or cuttings to serve for filling. The *marqueta* of wax is $\frac{1}{2}$ *vara* long, $\frac{1}{3}$ wide, and $\frac{1}{3}$ high, and varies in weight. The *fanega* of maize, or Indian corn, contains, in the western part of the island, 1,000 ears, or 8 *arrobas* when off the husk; in Trinidad, Villa Clara, and Santo Espiritu, 366 ears (*mazorcas*); in Puerto Principe, where it is termed *seron* instead of *fanega*, 300 ears; in Cuba it is sold off the husk by the barrel, which contains 1,000 to 1,200 ears, or 180 pounds. A *seron* or *caballo* (horse-load) of plantains contains 60 *manos*, and each *mano* 5 to 7 plantains if *machos*, or large, or 10 to 12 if *hembras*, or small ones; in Cuba they are sold by the hundred, each *carga* or load containing 275 large, or 325 small plantains. The *tarea* of wood is 3 *varas* long, 1 wide, and 2 high, equal to 10 *caballos*; the *cuerda*, or cord, of wood is $2\frac{3}{4}$ *varas* long, 1 *vara* 16 inches wide, and 1 *vara* 16 inches high; the *caballo* (horse-load) of wood contains 40 billets or splits. The legal load (for a long distance) of a *carreta*, or ox-cart, is 120 *arrobas*; of a *carreton*, or dray, 40; and of a horse, 8. In Cuba, sugar, tobacco, and cocoa are sold by the *quintal*, or hundred pounds; cotton, by the *paca*, or bale, of 2 *varas* long, $1\frac{1}{4}$ wide, and $\frac{3}{4}$ high; and *frijoles*, or pulse, by the barrel of 180 pounds.

LIQUID MEASURE.—The *caneca*, $6\frac{2}{3}$ gallons, or 10 *frascos*; the *frasco*, $2\frac{1}{2}$ litres; the *frasco* of gin, $1\frac{1}{2}$ bottles; the *cuartillo*, or quart, of the corporation of Havana, 86 centilitres; the bottle (commonly used for Catalan wine and ale), 725 millilitres; the *pipa*, or pipe, of Catalan wine, 24 *garrafones*, or 600 bottles; the *cuarterola* of the same, 5 *garrafones*; the *barrica* of French wine, 11 *garrafones*, or 280 French bottles; the *bocoy*, or puncheon, is used for molasses, and contains 25 to 30 American barrels of $5\frac{1}{2}$ gallons;* the molasses cask, termed *bocoy de playa*, commonly contains 18 barrels; the *cuarterola* of molasses is half a *bocoy*; the *pipa* of rum, 180 *frascos*; the barrel of wine, 4 *arrobas*, or 80 bottles; the barrel termed *de conduccion*, or transportation-barrel, contains 10 *frascos*; the *contrata*, or contract-barrel, for molasses, contains 7 gallons at Havana, and $5\frac{1}{2}$ at Matanzas; the American, or *del comercio* barrel, $5\frac{1}{2}$ gallons; the rum-barrel, 45

---

* At present they are to be found as large as 180 gallons. The American gallon, which is used in such cases, is equal to $5\frac{1}{4}$ bottles: and the English gallon, $6\frac{1}{4}$ bottles.

PHYSICAL, POLITICAL, AND INDUSTRIAL. 69

bottles; the flour or corn-meal barrel, 7½ to 8 *arrobas*, or 8½ American bushels; the *garrafon*, or demijohn, 24 to 26 bottles; the *botija*, or jar, of oil, 6½ to 7 litres, or ⅓ *arroba*. The *pluma de agua*, or water-pipe, or conduit laid in Havana, is 4½ Castilian *lineas* in interior diameter, the *linea* being 1-12 of the Castilian inch.

Weights—Are the same used in Spain. The *tonelada* or ton=20 quintals. The *quintal*=4 arrobas=100 libras: equivalent to 46 kilogrammes or 101.4 pounds avoirdupois. The *libra* or pound=2 marcos= 16 commercial onzas or ounces=256 adarmes=768 tomes=9,216 granos or grains. The *pesante* (in weighing silk)=½ adarme. The *arrelde* (in weighing fresh beef)=4 libras or pounds. In Spain it is 4 to 10 libras. Gold and silver are weighed by the Castilian marco or mark=50 castellanos=400 tomines=4,800 grains. Apothecaries' weight is the Castilian ounce divided into 8 drachmas=24 scruples=576 grains.

Currency.—Accounts are kept in the gold and silver coins of the Peninsula, but not the *reales de vellon*, nor copper money; and with the difference that the Spanish ounce of gold, or doubloon, is worth $17 instead of $16, and its aliquot parts in proportion. The *peso*, or dollar, is equal to 4 *pesetas*, either pillared or of the Spanish-American stamp, or 5 Sevillian or simple *pesetas*; a pillared or Spanish-American *peseta* is equal to 2 *reales fuertes*, or 5 *reales de vellon*; a *real fuerte* is equal to 2 *medios fuertes*; a *peseta sencilla* (simple) is equal to 2 *reales sencillos*, or 4 *reales de vellon*; a *real sencillo*, 2 *medios sencillos*. The *maravedi*, of 34 to the *real fuerte*, is only used in the accounts of the intendancy and militia. •In trade, the *real fuerte* is divided into 4 *cuartillos*, or 8 *octavos, fuertes*, which only in the taverns is admitted in regard to the *real sencillo*, as *chicos*. The *ducado* is understood as 11 *reales fuertes*.

Forces.*—The army of the Island of Cuba is in the highest state of training, discipline, and equipment, and consists of 16 regiments of infantry of 1,000 men each; 2 companies of merit, with 125 men; a staff of officers for replacement; 2 regiments of lancers, composed of 4 squadrons each, with a force of 602 men and 500 horses, besides 4 extra squadrons, each of 151 men and 125 horses; a regiment of 8 batteries of foot artillery; a company of artillery-workmen; a brigade of 5 batteries (4 for mountain service, and 1 mounted); and a company of engineer-workmen; making a total of veteran troops, of 17,500 infantry; 1,808 cavalry, with 1,500 horses; 1,500 artillery, with 190 horses and mules; and 130 engineer-workmen; together, 20,938 men and 1,690

---

* Both the army and navy have been greatly strengthened by additions from the peninsular forces, and also by the enrollment of the militia.—EDITOR.

horses, exclusive of the civil guard, which also belong to the veteran corps. Besides, there are—a regiment of militia infantry; a regiment of disciplined militia cavalry, with 781 horses; 8 squadrons of rural troops, of 2 companies each, and 100 horses to each company; 600 horse of the civil companies, and 140 more of the civil companies of Puerto Principe and Cuba: being a total of over 3,500 men and horses; and, in case of need, the firemen, watchmen, safe-guards (foot and mounted), and carbineers of the customs of the island.

The squadron on service at the station is composed of a frigate, with 44 guns; 7 brigs, with 104 guns; 11 steamers, with 54 guns; 4 schooners, with 11 guns; 2 boats, with 6 guns; 2 transports; a pontoon and a ship, both dismantled: total, 25 vessels, with 219 guns and over 3,000 men.

There are also being built in the Peninsula 2 steamships for this station. The personal and material force of the island belonging to its marine enrollment is as follows: 2,052 effective men; 495 on service; 487 ineffective; 7 vessels of over 400 tons; 30 from 200 to 400 tons; 99 from 80 to 200 tons; 295 from 20 to 80 tons; 208 less than 20 tons; of foreign construction, 389; steamers, 20; minor vessels, such as boats, etc., 2,454.

PHYSICAL, POLITICAL, AND INDUSTRIAL. 71

ADJACENT ISLANDS.
ISLA DE PINOS, CAYO-ROMANO, GUAJABA, CAYO-COCO, AND TURIGUANO.

Isla de Pinos (called Evanjelista by Columbus, who discovered it in 1494) is situated 18 maritime leagues south of Batabanó.* Its greatest extent is 12 Cuban leagues from north to south, and 16 from east to west, with an area of 68 square maritime leagues, or 615⅓ square miles, and its least distance from Cuba is 16¾ Cuban leagues from Punta de los Barcos to Punta Carraguao. The climate is acknowledged to be one of the most salubrious, for which reason a multitude of invalids annually resort to it, especially consumptives, who frequently regain their health, which in a great measure is due to the soft and beneficial nature of its waters. The aspect of the island is most diversified and picturesque, presenting lofty mountains, extensive plains, a multitude of streams, and a notable swamp, dividing it into two unequal parts, one on the north and the other on the south. At the north are the bays of Columbo and Bibijágua; at the west, the bay of Los Barcos, and the vast one of La Siguanea; and at the south several coves, among which is the remarkable one of Carapachivey, whose mouth is over a quarter of a league in width. The principal capes and points are—Cabo Francés and Punta de Columbo, at the north; Punta Buenavista and Punta de Barcos, at the west; Puntas de Fuera, De Piedra, and Cayo del Este, at the east; and Punta Cocodrilos, on the south. The most remarkable mountains are—Sierra de la Cañada, 551 Castilian *varas* above the level of the sea, and flanked by natural walls as high as 50 *varas*; the Daguilla ridge, 492 *varas* above the level of the sea: it is shaped like a cone, clothed at the base with thick forests, and at the top only with pasturage: its summit commands a view of the whole island; the Sierra de Caballos (358 *varas* in height) and that of Casas, half a league distant from one another, are of marble of all kinds and colors, the white statuary marble being as fine as that of Carrara; the Cerros of Bacunagua, Malpais, and San José; the Cerro de Cristales is not lofty, but

---

* Between 21° 27′ 15″ and 21° 58′ 17″ north lat. and 76° 11′ 11″ and 76° 52′ 6″ west long. of Cadiz. Several interesting works have been published on this island by Messrs. Tirry, Delgado, Lanier, Piña, Serrano, and Poey. The best, as regards the geography of the island, is that of Sr. Lanier, who was commissioned by government to survey it in 1831. Although in the great chart of the island its area is stated at 810 square miles, only about 614 square miles are assigned to it by Sr. Lanier.

is distinguished for the abundance of true rock-crystal found at its base, and which might become an object of speculation. The principal rivers are—Las Nuevas, which empties on the north, and is the largest in the island: it is formed by the streams of Callejon, Cisternas, Piedras, and El Medio: it is prevented from being navigable by a bar at its mouth allowing a draught of only four palms; the Santa Fé, whose waters are mineral, passes by the hamlet of that name, and empties at the east: it is navigable as far as the embarcadero de Balandras, distant one and a half leagues from the mouth, affording 10 to 13 palms draft; the Rio Sierra de Casas, passing near Nueva Gerona, is navigable for vessels drawing five and a quarter feet, which is the depth at its mouth, although farther up it is two fathoms deep for the space of a league: it is 140 *varas* wide at the mouth, and 70 at Nueva Gerona. There are besides, the rivers Piedra, Guayabo, Jagua, San Pedro, Siguanea, De los Indios, etc.; the lagoon De las Guanábanas, south of Sierra de Caballos, and the notable swamp receiving the waters of the Siguanea, San Pedro, and Jagua, and dividing the island into two unequal portions, one on the north and the other on the south, the only communication being by a very narrow neck called Cayo de Piedras: the south part presenting great keys on low, bushy, or marshy land, covered with mangroves and *yana* so entangled as to be impassable, and containing many lagoons full of terrapins, alligators, etc., and through the gaps, some of which are 100 *varas* wide, is heard the noise of interior currents of water. The northern section, which is the most interesting, and extends over a surface of 74 square Cuban leagues, contains the spacious savannas and the mountains and rivers already mentioned. The island is a dependency of Havana, and is under the immediate rule of a military and political commandant, who is at the same time Director of the Colony, which, under the name of Colonia de la Reina Amalia, was founded in 1828, and consists of five square Cuban leagues. Nueva Gerona, the head of the colony is an interior port, picturesquely situated at a distance of three quarters of a league from the mouth, and on the left bank, of the Rio Casas, which there has a depth of two fathoms, although at its mouth the presence of a bar only affords a draft of five and a quarter feet. The land on which the town lies is a plain between the sierras de Caballos and Casas. It contains at present four wide and straight streets, running north-west and south-east, and north-east and south-west, which is the most convenient direction in these latitudes; there are 109 houses in 32 blocks, and 157 lots for distribution; two public walks, a church, barracks, hospital, and free-school. Besides two fine sailing-packets, there is a steamer running weekly from Batabanó to the head of the island in seven or eight hours.

PHYSICAL, POLITICAL, AND INDUSTRIAL.

The town of Santa Fé, which was entirely destroyed in the hurricane of 1846, has begun to rise again within the last eight months, already containing 20 houses, and several in course of building. Its excellent mineral waters will cause it to flourish very soon. The population of the island in 1797 was 76, in 1828, 427, and at present is 1,400, of which 160 are colored, and the rest white. The productions are cattle, small, but affording excellent beef, which is salted and exported as jerked beef, to the extent of about 150 *arrobas;* a little tobacco is grown, but of the best quality. There is an abundance of two kinds of pine trees (whence the name of the island), mahogany, cedar, and other valuable trees; marble of all sorts and colors, rock-crystal, sulphur, black sand, etc.; also mines of silver, iron, and even quicksilver (which was assayed by Don Esteban Sabá, who discovered the silver). The inhabitants are chiefly employed in raising cattle and salting beef, quarrying marble, gathering tar and pitch, making spirits of turpentine, and especially in an extensive turtle-fishery, etc.

Cayo-Romano is a long and narrow island, divided by a channel about half a mile wide. It is over 16 maritime leagues in length, and two at its broadest part, and contains 172 square miles. It is flat, the only prominences being the not lofty mountain of Silla de Cayo-Romano, seen at a distance of 24 miles, and the Loma de Ají. It lies north-west and south-east, and contains a cattle estate abounding in horned cattle and horses. The *jerked beef* produced here is greatly prized throughout the island. There are, also, some timber, fine pastures, and productive salt-ponds, but no streams. It belongs to the district of Guanaja, jurisdiction of Puerto Principe.

Guajaba.—This island is situated between Cayo-Romano and Punta del Sabinal; is 30 maritime miles long, about 1½ wide, and 15 square miles in area; contains three cattle estates, well watered and fertile soil, and productive salt-ponds. It belongs also to the district of Guanaja, in the jurisdiction of Puerto Principe.

Cayo-Cocos.—This island has an area of 28 square miles, and abounds in fisheries.

Turiguano.—This island has an area of 38 square miles, and runs into the coast, with which it forms the Laguna de Moron. Under the denomination of islands should also be placed the keys, so-called, of Ensenachos, with an area of 19 square miles; Cruz, 59 square miles; and Cayo Largo, east of Pinos, 32 square miles.

DESCRIPTION OF THE JURISDICTIONS.

Pinar del Rio, or Nueva Filipina.*—BOUNDARIES.—North-east, the jurisdiction of Bahia-Honda.; east, the jurisdiction of San Cristóbal; and on other sides, the sea.

CAPITAL.—Pinar del Rio, a town and curacy of 350 houses and 1,500 inhabitants, and having a municipal corporation; situated on a rising in the vast and beautiful savanna south of the Sierra de los Organos; distant 45 leagues from Havana, whence the transit may be performed in one day by the steamer that arrives about 8 P.M. at La Coloma, only six leagues distant. The water of the rivulet Yagruma (affluent of the Guamá), which supplies the town, is excellent, coming, as it does, from pine-bearing land. The climate is so salubrious that in the year 1852, which was among the least satisfactory as regards health, the proportion of burials was only 153, to 569 christenings and 62 marriages. The inhabitants are styled *Pinarienses*.

PETTY DISTRICTS.—Pinar del Rio, Baja, Consolacion del Sur, Guane, Mantua, and San Juan y Martinez.

COMMUNITIES.—Baja, a hamlet of 12 houses and 42 inhabitants; a sub-curacy. Nombre de Dios (Baja district), a hamlet with 6 houses, 19 inhabitants, and many *vegas* scattered around. Mantua, a village of 40 houses and 100 inhabitants, and a sub-curacy; it is a "dry port" of considerable trade, the shipping of which is at the bay of the same name, and that of Los Arroyos, three leagues distant, the latter being a stopping-place for the "Veguero" steamer; it is the most westerly settlement in the island, being sixty-six leagues from Havana. Montezuelo (Mantua district), a hamlet of 8 houses and 40 inhabitants. Lazaro (Mantua district), a hamlet of 7 houses and 25 inhabitants. Guane, a village and sub-curacy of 24 houses and 120 inhabitants; it was formerly called Filipina, and was the capital of the jurisdiction. Paso-Real de Guane (Guane district), village; 25 houses, 70 inhabitants. El Sábalo (Guane district), hamlet; 11 houses, 40 inhabitants. Garay, or Bailen (Guane district), hamlet; 4 houses, 20 inhabitants; it is a stopping-place for steamers, and has a tobacco trade. San Juan y Martinez, village, sub-curacy; 31 houses, 170 inhabitants, and surrounded by incomparable tobacco *vegas*. Noda, or Bahia Galafre (San Juan y Martinez district), hamlet; 5 houses, 50 inhabitants. Punta de Cartas (district as above), two warehouses; a stopping-place for steamers. San

---

* So called because the district was first settled at Guane, under the name of Filipina.

Luis, a village (district as before); 33 houses, 140 inhabitants. Coloma (Pinar del Rio district), hamlet, with 6 houses and 30 inhabitants, and a port of much trade, at the mouth of the river of that name; six leagues distant from Pinar del Rio; steamers stop here from Batabanó, at 8 P.M. Colon (Pinar del Rio district), warehouses and port on the Coloma River, five and one-fourth leagues from Pinar del Rio. Consolacion Sur, an old town and sub-curacy of 76 houses and 120 inhabitants, producing in its environs the best tobacco in the world. Santa Clara, village; 16 houses, 20 inhabitants. Herradura, village; 10 houses, 40 inhabitants. Rio Hondo, hamlet; 6 houses, 30 inhabitants. These three last are in the district of Consolacion del Sur.

PRODUCTIONS.—The chief is tobacco, of a quality unrivaled in the world; it also exports cattle and some timber, likewise mangrove bark for tanning. It is the district that most abounds in pitch-pine trees and oaks, whence arises the peculiar flavor of its pork. On its coasts and keys, both north and south, are plenty of turtle (including the tortoise-shell kind), *caguamas*, sea-cows, and sponges; and iguanas and flamingoes abound; there are numerous birds for game, including parrots, cranes, macaws, and *carpinteros reales*, which overrun the district; there are also nightingales, *aparecidos*, and a greater number of migratory birds than in the eastern districts, owing to greater proximity to the continent. The climate among the mountains is the most salubrious on the island, and the waters of the rivulets, irrigating pine lands, are soft and excellent. There are no coffee plantations, but there are marble quarries, and mines of gold, silver, copper, coal, arsenic, and other substances.

PECULIARITIES.—Many caves in the Guaniguanico Mountains, and the remarkable arcades on the Cuyaguateje River. *Longevity.*—In the hamlet of Baja there lived, in 1847, Don José Hernandez, aged 110, and the negro Juan Crisostomo de Consolacion, aged 115. At San Juan y Martinez died Doña Lorenza Rubi, at the age of 108. The creole Negro Jorje Sierra, at present aged 96, has his mother living.

San Cristobal.—BOUNDARIES.—North, Bahia-Honda and Mariel; east, San Antonio; south, the sea; and west, Pinar del Rio.

CAPITAL—San Cristóbal, sub-curacy (removed from Santa Cruz de los Pinos) and town, with 50 houses and 270 inhabitants, and a municipal corporation, 24 leagues south-west from Havana and 5 from the south coast, and crossed by the river of the same name, of excellent water. The climate is of the best, the land being elevated and dry.

PETTY DISTRICTS.—San Cristóbal, Candelaria, Los Palacios, San Diego de los Baños, and San Marcos, or Las Mangas.

COMMUNITIES.—Santa Cruz de los Pinos (San Cristóbal district), a hamlet, whence was transferred the church, in 1816, to San Cristóbal. Santa Cruz (San Cristóbal district), hamlet; three leagues east of San Cristóbal, with 4 houses and 20 inhabitants. Candelaria, a curacy and town in a picturesque and salubrious situation, containing 54 houses and 360 inhabitants. Bayate (Candelaria district), a village, with 13 houses and 70 inhabitants. Las Mangas de Rio Grande (head of the district of San Marcos), a village of 19 houses and 100 inhabitants. Mojanga (San Marcos district), a hamlet; 6 houses, 130 inhabitants. Guanacaje, a hamlet and sub-curacy (San Marcos district). Palacios, town and sub-curacy, on the river of that name, 31 leagues from Havana, with 67 houses and 320 inhabitants. La Isabela (Palacios district), hamlet; 5 houses, 20 inhabitants. San Diego de los Baños, or de las Galeras, a town of 50 houses and 130 inhabitants, permanent population, for during the bathing season (February to May) there are over 2,500 visitors;* it is intended to build a church here. Paso Real de San Diego (above district), 50 houses and 240 inhabitants.

PRODUCTIONS.—Tobacco, cattle, coffee, a little sugar, and wood of the finest descriptions, which is not exported because of the difficulty of transportation. On the keys at the south are found turtle, tortoiseshell, *caguamas*, flamingoes, etc.

PECULIARITIES.—The celebrated baths of San Diego. In the mountains are found lithographic stone, agate, and other precious stones; and the Cusco Mountain is the haunt of runaway negroes.

Bahia-Honda.—BOUNDARIES.—North, the sea; east, the jurisdiction of Mariel; south-east, that of San Cristóbal; and south and west, that of Pinar del Rio.

CAPITAL.—Bahia-Honda, a town with a municipal corporation, 78 houses and 570 inhabitants, situated half a league from the bottom of the port of that name, and 25 leagues from Havana. Nearly all the houses are built of palm, which gives the town an unfavorable appearance.

PETTY DISTRICTS.—Bahia-Honda, Consolacion del Norte, Las Pozas, and San Diego de Nuñez.

COMMUNITIES.—San Diego de Nuñez, town and curacy, with 70 houses and 271 inhabitants. Las Pozas, or Cacarajicaras, a village and sub-curacy, 29 leagues from Havana, with 25 houses and 98 inhabitants. El Morrillo, hamlet and embarking-place, with 5 houses and 13 inhabitants. La Mulata, hamlet of 12 houses and 36 inhabitants, and stopping-place of the steamers of the north coast. La Vega de Ferral, hamlet, near the preceding, with 4 houses and 16 inhabitants. The last three are in the district of Las Pozas.

---

* See the description of these baths by Dr. Isidro Sanchez, 1851.

PHYSICAL, POLITICAL, AND INDUSTRIAL. 77

PRODUCTIONS.—Sugar, cattle, copper, coffee, coal (mineral and vegetable); and on the keys at the north, turtle, *caguamas*, sea-cows, sponges, etc.

PECULIARITIES.—Mineral waters in the Aguacate, and copper mines in the district of Consolacion del Norte. The territory is hilly, and some of its loftiest summits (such as the Guajaibón and Cajálbana) are extinct volcanoes. On Cayo-Blanco lives a fisherman 114 years old, whose son, aged over 80, is employed on the Regla steamers.

Mariel.—BOUNDARIES.—On the north, the sea; east, the jurisdictions of Santiago and San Antonio; south, that of San Cristóbal; and west, that of Bahia-Honda.

CAPITAL.—Guanajay, a curacy and town with municipal assembly, situated two and one-half leagues from the port of Mariel, and at the junction of the northern and southern roads of Vuelta-Abajo, and surrounded by valuable properties which have influenced to render it one of the most commercial districts in the island. The town is regularly built; the situation is cheerful, and the climate cool and salutary. It contains a barracks, hospital, schools, and good hotels, among the best of which is that of the Five Nations. The distance from Havana is ten and one-half leagues by the causeway, and 21 English miles by the railroad, of which it is the western extremity. It contains 485 houses and 3,000 inhabitants.

PETTY DISTRICTS.—Mariel, Cabañas, Cayajabos, Guanajay, Guayabal, and Puerta de la Güira, Quiebra-Hacha, and Seiba del Agua.

COMMUNITIES.—Mariel, or Muelle de Tablas, a curacy, port, and town of 175 houses and 1,296 inhabitants. It lies 14 leagues west of Havana, and 2½ from Guanajay, the terminus of the railroad of that name, to which place a causeway is being built. It was an authorized port and the capital of the jurisdiction until the 1st of January, 1854. Santa Cristo de la Sabana (Mariel district), with 4 houses and 20 inhabitants. Cabañas, a curacy, without a church since 1835,* and town, situated a short distance east of the bottom of the port of the same name, with 106 houses and 500 inhabitants. Amiot, a bay at the bottom of Port Mariel, with a hamlet (in the district and port of Cabañas), containing 10 houses and 50 inhabitants. Cayajabos, a curacy and town of 49 houses and 300 inhabitants. Puerta de la Güira, a curacy and village of 20 houses and 130 inhabitants. Artemisa (in the preceding district), a curacy and town of 54 houses and 280 inhabitants. When coffee commanded good prices, this district was appropriately styled the

---

* There is a temporary oratory in one of the houses, pending the erection of the new church.

Garden of Cuba, for the beautiful coffee plantations that it contained.* Las Cañas, in the same district, a hamlet of 11 houses and 100 inhabitants. Quiebra-Hacha, a curacy and village of 24 houses (including the hotel of the Five Nations) and 160 inhabitants. San Luis de la Seiba, or Seiba del Agua, a curacy and town of 60 houses and 330 inhabitants. Virtudes and Capellanias, both in the preceding districts, hamlets; the first with 4 houses and 13 inhabitants, and the second 30 houses and 130 inhabitants. Guayabal, curacy and village with 20 houses and 60 inhabitants. Banes, a town in the preceding district, with 60 houses and 270 inhabitants, and resorted to for sea-bathing.

PRODUCTIONS.—Sugar, coffee, wax, tobacco, coal, cattle, and pottery.

PECULIARITIES.—Mineral waters at Charco-Azul. In the district of Seiba del Agua died Don Francisco de Castañeda, aged 119 years.

San Antonio.—BOUNDARIES.—North, the jurisdiction of Santiago, east, that of Bejucál; west, those of Mariel and San Cristóbal; and south, the sea.

CAPITAL.—San Antonio Abad, or de Los Baños, a villa, or chartered town, since 1795. Situated south-west of Havana, on dry and rocky land. It is planned in the best manner, with right-lined streets, 690 well-built houses, 2,890 inhabitants, a theatre, philharmonic society, schools, cavalry barracks, etc. The bread made here is of so excellent a quality that it is supplied to Havana. The river of the same name, after crossing the town, disappears in a cavity at the root of a remarkable *seiba* tree south of the town, constituting one of its greatest curiosities. The distance from Havana is eight and a-half leagues by the directest common road, and eight by the railroad, the train of which arrives at 8½ o'clock and leaves at 11.

PETTY DISTRICTS.—Alquizar, Güira de Melena, and Vereda Nueva.

COMMUNITIES.—Alquizar, a sub-curacy and town, 10 leagues from Havana, with 108 houses and 562 inhabitants. The environs, like those of Puerta de la Güira, contained such charming coffee estates at the time when the berry commanded a good price, that, like Artemisa (in the Mariel), it also was called the Garden of Cuba. Palenque, or Guaibacoa (Alquizar district), a village of 14 houses and 50 inhabitants. Guanimar (Playa de), an embarking-place and hamlet (Alquizar district), of 8 houses and 42 inhabitants. Güira de Melena, a sub-curacy and town of 146 houses and 496 inhabitants. Cajío (Baños de), in the preceding district, a hamlet of huts on the beach. Govea, a hamlet of 5 houses and 26 inhabitants. Vereda Nueva, a curacy and town of 158 houses and 606 inhabitants. Caimito and Tumba-cuatro, in the preceding dis-

---

* See our modern illustrated map of the island.

trict; the first a town of 46 houses and 203 inhabitants, and the second a hamlet of 7 houses and 24 inhabitants.

PECULIARITIES.—The territory is among the most level and fertile of the island, although of the number least favored in regard to rivers.

Havana.—BOUNDARIES.—North, the sea; east, the jurisdiction of Guanabacoa and Santa Maria del Rosario; south and west, that of Santiago.

CAPITAL.—Habana (San Cristóbal de), the capital city of the island,* situated on the margin of the fine port of its name, on a peninsula of level and calcareous soil. It is a fortified place of the first order, divided into two parts—the *intramural*, or walled, and the *extramural*—and is surrounded by imposing forts, among which that of la Cabaña is one of the largest in the world. The streets, although generally right-lined, are mostly narrow, with the exception of the principal ones, which are paved with granite; the rest suffer from the great and active trade, coupled with the deluging rains of the tropics. The principal ones are lighted with gas. It contains a cathedral (where the remains of Christopher Columbus are deposited) and several other churches; a court of judicature; university; seminary; college; lyceum; a splendid theatre, capable of accommodating 6,000 persons, and where Italian opera companies of the first order have performed; charitable asylums; squares; beautiful shaded walks and spacious saloons for recreation, and a fine military band plays every evening. The picturesque environs of the city are embellished by beautiful country-seats and extensive walks, affording a most agreeable picture, enlivened during the fine tropical evenings by a multitude of promenaders in fine carriages. There are 15 typographical printing and eight lithographic establishments, at present issuing four daily and three or four monthly and semi-monthly publications. Besides the principal extramural wards which form the compact part, are included those of Atarés, Pilar, Villanueva, Jesus del Monte, and Cerro, which are commodiously and economically communicated with by means of omnibuses continually circulating among them. Havana likewise comprises the towns of Regla and Casa-Blanca on the opposite side of the port, communicating with the first by means of steam ferry-boats that start from each side every five minutes. Havana contains within its walls 3,810 houses, and without, in the chief wards, 8,542; together, 12,352 houses, and a population of 108,083, exclusive of the troops, transient residents, etc. The populated parts of the wards of Pilar, Atarés, Villanueva, Jesus del Monte, Cerro, and Arroyo-Polo contain

---

* See our illustrated map of the city and environs, to be had of all booksellers in Havana, together with the ancient and modern map of the island, new edition, also illustrated.

2,004 houses and 17,832 inhabitants. It comprises within the walls a peopled area of 12 *caballerias* of land; and without the walls, as far as Chavez bridge, including the peopled part of San Lazaro and Pueblo-Nuevo, 25 *caballerias;* and adding thereto the 14¼ *caballerias* comprised by the wards of Villanueva, Atarés, Pilar, Jesus del Monte, Arroyo-Polo, and Vibora, and 6½ by that of Cerro, which are all united to the city, the total is 57¼ *caballerias* of land.* The port of Havana is one of the safest, most picturesque, and best frequented in the world, the arrivals in the month of March frequently amounting to 22 vessels in one day. It is considered the sixth in order of commercial importance.† The climate is as healthy as any in the island, and would be rendered still more so by filling up a small swamp in the eastern part of the port, from which direction the breeze blows upon the city. The community is supplied with water from the Almendares River by means of pipes and a trench, which serve to irrigate the land in its course, and also to work several machines.‡ This city gave birth to the historians Urrutia, Arrate, and Valdez; the distinguished writer Countess de

---

* Though in the last statistical returns it is stated that Havana and its suburbs, as far as Chavez bridge, only comprises 17 *caballerias* of land, Don Mariano Carles (surveyor) and the author have found 6,730,000 square Cuban *varas* including as far as Chavez bridge and the populated part of San Lazaro and Pueblo-Nuevo; 2,760,000 the populated area of Horeón, Jesus del Monte, and La Vibora; and 1,200,000 square *varas Cubanas* the area of Cerro. The populated area of Madrid contains 86¼ Cuban *caballerias;* of Sevilla, 16¼ *caballerias;* Barcelona, 17¼; New York, 158; Philadelphia, 65; Baltimore, 42; New Orleans, 72; Boston, 81.

† The only ports that exceed Havana in commercial importance are London, Liverpool, New York, Marseilles, and New Orleans; and it is superior to Rio Janeiro, Boston, Havre, Philadelphia, Newcastle, Hamburg, St. Petersburg, Cowes. Bordeaux, Constantinople, etc. The revenue from maritime customs at the port of Marseilles in 1851 was 30,677,000 francs; that of Havre, 26,164,000 francs; Paris, 11,570,000; Bordeaux, 10,460,000; Havana, $5,797,476, or 28,987,380 francs; and Barcelona (in 1852, which was the most satisfactory year), $2,000,000. Although in the following comparison of arrivals and clearances for several of the United States ports in 1850, and Havana in 1851, it would appear that New Orleans was inferior to Havana in the amount of shipping, such is not the case when we add the coasting-trade of the former with the depôts of New York, Boston, etc., the total then being, 2,266 vessels arrived, with a tonnage of 910,853:

VESSELS INWARD AND OUTWARD, EXCEPT COASTWISE.

	Inward.	Tonnage.	Outward.	Tonnage.
New York	3,162	1,145,381	2,609	982,473
Boston	2,872	478,859	2,839	437,760
Philadelphia	537	132,370	479	111,616
New Orleans	896	349,949	843	369,987
Baltimore	438	99,583	521	126,819
Havana	1,749	591,572	1,692	not recorded.

‡ It is intended to bring the water from a spring at Vento, near the Almendares

PHYSICAL, POLITICAL, AND INDUSTRIAL. 81

Merlin; the philosopher Varela; the eloquent and erudite theologian Don Augustin Caballero; the rhetorical Mendoza; the enlightened physician Romay; the poets Zequeira, Blanchié, and Foxá; the jurisconsults Urrutias, Ayala, Sans, Gonzalez, Gato, Ponce de Leon, Escovedo, Santos-Suarez, Govantes, and Bermudez; the archbishop Don Luis Peñalver y Cárdenas; the statesmen Don Francisco Arango and Don Claudio M. Pinillos; the witty comedian Covarrubias; the generals Count de Revillagigedo, Diaz-Pimienta, Count Mopox y de Jaruco, Urrutia (Don Carlos), O'Farrill, Quesada, Aristizabal, Zayas, Moscoso, Castillo (Marquis of San Felipe y Santiago), Montalvo (Don Juan); of Don Jorge Maria de la Torre, Counsellor of State and Minister of War; and Don Antonio Caro, Counsellor of State. The inhabitants are termed *Habaneros*, although those residing without the walls are vulgarly called *hueseros*.

PETTY DISTRICTS.—Puentes-Grandes, Quemados, Arroyo-Naranjo, Calvario, and Pinos Island.

COMMUNITIES.—Pescante, a village between the Morro and Cabaña castles (Casa-Blanca district); with 22 houses and 60 inhabitants. Casa-Blanca, a town (ecclesiastically dependent on the cathedral of Havana), situated on the northern margin of the port of Havana, and containing 244 houses and 1,070 inhabitants. Regla, a town and subcuracy, with 1,278 houses and 7,240 inhabitants, situated on the eastern margin of the port of Havana, with which city it communicates every five minutes by steamers. It contains a large foundry, fine warehouses,

River; and the following analysis has been made by Sr. Casaseca, Director of the Institute for Chemical Investigation:

	ALMENDARES.	VENTO.	SEINE.
	Water from the Aqueduct.	Water from the Springs.	Water taken below Paris.
Carbonic acid gas............(centilitres)	56.2	48.9	12.5
Residue on evaporation.........(grammes)	4.492	3.956	2.608
Sulphate of lime	.172	.416	.295
Carbonate of lime	2.917	1.920	1.940
Carbonate of magnesia	.321	.385	—
Carbonated oxide of iron	.116	.080	—
Silicate of iron	.048	.080	—
Chloride of sodium	.733	1.000	—
Deliquescent salts	—	—	.373
Organic extractive matter	.185	.075	

From this comparison it appears that the Vento waters contain rather less carbonate of lime than those of the Seine, and in that respect are better. It is true that those of Vento contain nearly one third more of salenate or sulphate of lime than those of the Seine, but on the other hand, the chloride of sodium and carbonate of magnesia held by the former should render them more digestive. According to recent analyses the Seine water does contain common salt.

4*

and a good careening-place. Both Casa-Blanca and Regla are wards of Havana. Calvario, a town and sub-curacy, 2½ leagues from Havana, with 114 houses and 500 inhabitants. Mantilla (Calvario district), a village, with 22 houses and 106 inhabitants. Chorrera del Sur (Calvario district), a hamlet, 14 houses and 49 inhabitants. La Chorrera (Puentes-Grandes district), a village at the mouth of the river Almendares, 2 leagues from Havana, with 28 houses and 180 inhabitants, and is a resort for rural recreation. Arroyo-Naranjo, a town, with 68 houses and 191 inhabitants. San Juan, in the preceding district, a hamlet of 9 houses and 24 inhabitants. El Puente, a hamlet, with 5 houses and 19 inhabitants. Arroyo-Polo (ward of Havana), a village of 23 houses and 110 inhabitants. Mordazo (Puentes-Grandes district), a curacy and town of 84 houses and 335 inhabitants. Puentes-Grandes, a town without a church, but united with Mordazo by a bridge, and containing 140 houses and 699 inhabitants; La Seiba (above district), a hamlet between the preceding town and Quemado Viejo, with 12 houses and 40 inhabitants. Quemado Viejo, or Curazao, a hamlet in Quemados district, with 8 houses and 112 inhabitants. Quemados, a curacy and town of 100 houses and 520 inhabitants. Marianao (Puentes-Grandes district), a town, 3 leagues east of Havana, on the fine causeway of Guanajay, with bathing establishments and a medicinal spring. It is a place of resort from May to September, and contains a grove arranged for balls, etc. Population, 540, in 126 houses. La Playa de Marianao (Quemados district), a village, with 37 houses and 118 inhabitants. Uribazo (Quemados district), a hamlet near Marianao. Luyanó, a village, with 14 houses and 90 inhabitants. San Antonio Chiquito, a town of the rural ward Del Principe (Havana), with 87 houses and 509 inhabitants. Nueva Gerona and Baños de Santa Fé (see Island of Pinos).

PRODUCTIONS.—The peculiar productions of the jurisdiction of Havana are excellent fruit, garden vegetables from the very fertile and well-cultivated lands in the vicinity, and lime; and in the island of Pinos (belonging to the jurisdiction), those already enumerated in the description of that island.

PECULIARITIES.—In the mountains near Luyanó copper ore is found; calcareous and schistose rock abounds, and there are also quarries of granite.

Santiago.—BOUNDARIES.—On the north, the sea and part of the jurisdiction of Havana; east, that of Santa Maria del Rosario; south, those of Bejucál and San Antonio; and west, that of Mariel.

CAPITAL.—Santiago de las Vegas, a curacy and city, situated on level land of a reddish color and fertile, five leagues south of Havana, one from Bejucál, and half a league from the Rincon station. It is regularly planned with right-lined streets,* and contains 425 houses and 2,274 inhabitants. The climate is very wholesome, being the only town among those surrounded by the cholera that has escaped that epidemic. It contains a theatre and a philharmonic society, and a barracks is being built for climatization. The inhabitants are called *Santiagueros*.

RURAL DISTRICTS.—Rancho-Boyeros, Calabazar, Santa Maria, and Rincon de Calabazas

PETTY DISTRICTS.—Arroyo Arenas, Cano, Guatao, Bauta, and Ubajay, or Guajay.

COMMUNITIES.—Nueva Cristína, or Calabazar, a village with 28 houses and 102 inhabitants. El Rincon de Calabazas, a village with 16 houses and 68 inhabitants. Rancho de Boyeros, a village with 36 houses and 140 inhabitants. Ubajai, or Guajai, a curacy and town with 69 houses and 221 inhabitants. Guatao, sub-curacy and town, five leagues from Havana, with 108 houses and 574 inhabitants. Cruz de Piedra, or Camino Real (Guatao district), a village of 17 houses and 113 inhabitants. Cangrejeras (Guatao district), a village with 28 houses and 114 inhabitants. Santa Ana (Guatao district), a village on the beach of that name, with 44 houses and 49 inhabitants. El Cano, a curacy and town, four and three-fourth leagues from Havana, with 178 houses and 791 inhabitants. La Liza (Cano district), a village with 13 houses and 57 inhabitants. Arroyo Arenas, a town with church, four leagues from Havana, with 69 houses and 301 inhabitants. Cuatro Caminos, a hamlet with 10 houses and 32 inhabitants. Cantarranas, a village with 15 houses (on but one side of the road) and 66 inhabitants. Jaimanitas, a village with 21 houses and 68 inhabitants. Santo Domingo, a hamlet with 8 houses and 22 inhabitants. (The last four are in Arroyo Arenas district.) Hoyo Colorado (Bauta district), a town seven leagues from Havana, with 91 houses and 505 inhabitants. Corralillo (Bauta district), a town with 37 houses and 136 inhabitants.

PRODUCTIONS.—Sugar, coffee, fruit, yuca bread, or *casabe*, starch, garden vegetables, and pottery.

PECULIARITIES.—The coast is bordered with lagoons. There is excellent clay for pottery. ·

Bejucál.—BOUNDARIES.—North, the jurisdictions of Santiago and Santa Maria del Rosario; east, that of Güines; south, the sea; and west, the jurisdiction of San Antonio.

CAPITAL.—Bejucál (San Felipe y Santiago), a sub-curacy and city, founded in 1704, on level but high land (100 Castilian *varas*), at the

---

* See the map of this city, its jurisdiction, and the most of its towns, about to be published by Sr. Carles.

foot of the Sierra de Bejucál, and containing 438 houses and 2,264 inhabitants. The city is regularly laid out, and the climate so salubrious that it affords instances of greater longevity than any other town in the island, as may be shown by the following examples, viz.: Felipe, an Indian, died at the age of 130; Doña Dorotea Toledo, at 125; Don Pedro Acosta, at 116; Don Juan de Matos, at 108; Doña Teodora Dominguez and Doña Juana Martinez, at 104; Don José Marrero, at 112. The distance from Havana is six leagues, and eight from the roadstead of Batabanó, and is the station of the principal trunk of the Havana railroad, whose passenger-train arrives at 7½ o'clock, and returns to Havana at 3 o'clock.

PETTY DISTRICTS.—Batabanó, Gabriel, Quibican, and San Antonio de las Vegas.

COMMUNITIES.—La Salud (Santa Cristo de la), or Gabriel, a curacy and village, with 31 houses and 214 inhabitants. Güiro de Boñigal (preceding district), a hamlet with 19 houses and 92 inhabitants. Quibican, sub-curacy and town, half a league from the Havana railroad, with 166 houses and 592 inhabitants. Buenaventura (Quibican district), a village with 18 houses and 108 inhabitants. San Felipe (Quibican district), a hamlet and railroad-station, with 7 houses and 32 inhabitants. Güiro Marrero, a village with 18 houses and 108 inhabitants. San Antonio de las Vegas a curacy and town with 114 houses and 610 inhabitants. Batabanó, a curacy and town, situated one league from the roadstead of that name, with 143 houses and 898 inhabitants. La Playa, a town, and southern terminus of the Havana railroad, and which, being situated on the Batabanó roadstead, is generally known by that name; it contains 54 houses and 222 inhabitants.

PRODUCTIONS.—Coffee, sugar, yuca bread, starch, maize, garden vegetables, fruit, and poultry, hogs, etc. Timber is scarce. The soil is fruitful, but probably least watered of any in the island.

PECULIARITIES.—All the coast is swampy. Besides the cases of longevity already cited in Bejucál, Quibican district affords that of the negress Maria Nicolasa Perez, who died at the age of 110 years.

Uanabacoa.—BOUNDARIES.—North, the sea; east, the jurisdictions of Jaruco and Rosario; and west, that of Havana.

CAPITAL.—Guanabacoa (la Asuncion de), a curacy and villa since 1555, situated less than a league east of the port of Havana. It is irregularly laid out, and contains 29 streets, 1,777 houses (mostly of bad appearance), and 8,100 inhabitants.* It has a philharmonic society. The climate, though dry and salutary, is hot during the day, and cool

---

* See map of this town and jurisdiction, by Sr. Carles.

PHYSICAL, POLITICAL, AND INDUSTRIAL. 85

at night, even in summer. The medicinal virtues of the waters of the rivulets surrounding and running through the town, and the facilities of communication with Havana (by means of a railroad of four miles to Regla, and a causeway of half a league to the same town), attract many families during the bathing season, which extends from 1st May to 1st September. Notwithstanding the height of 80 *varas* on which the town is situated, the wells are of very little depth. The inhabitants are called *Guanabacoenses*, vulgarly *Cazueleros*.

PETTY DISTRICTS.—Bacuranao, Buenavista, Guanabo, Pepe-Antonio (formerly Peñalver), and San Miguel del Padron.

COMMUNITIES.—San Miguel del Padron, a curacy and village of 14 houses and 47 inhabitants. Jacomino and Luyanó, in the preceding district; the first, a hamlet of 5 houses and 24 inhabitants; the second, a village of 18 houses and 49 inhabitants. Dolores, or Bacuranao, a curacy and village of 32 houses and 149 inhabitants. La Playa, or Boca de Bacuranao, in the preceding district, a village of 25 houses and 88 inhabitants. Peñalver, or Guadalupe (Pepe-Antonio district), a curacy and village of 29 houses and 121 inhabitants. Guanabo, a curacy and village, seven leagues from Havana, with 44 houses and 212 inhabitants. La Boca de Guanabo (Guanabo district), a village of 8 houses and 54 inhabitants. Rincon de Sibarímar (Guanabo district), a village of 17 houses and 60 inhabitants. Jiquiabo (Guanabo district), a curacy and hamlet of 8 houses and 34 inhabitants. Boca de Jaruco (Guanabo district), a hamlet, situated on the western side of the mouth of Jaruco River, with 12 houses and 32 inhabitants. Cojímar (Buenavista district), a village and port with 86 houses and 137 inhabitants; it affords abundance of game and fishing, for which purpose it is resorted to.

PRODUCTIONS.—Excellent *casabe*, or yuca bread, coffee, sugar, garden vegetables, fruit, poultry, mineral coal, pottery, and very fine steel cutlass-blades of five *cuartas*.

PECULIARITIES.—Wells afford water at the depth of three feet, although the land of the whole jurisdiction is high. In the district of Buenavista died the negress Juliana, at the age of 115 years, and Doña Francisca Alvarez, at the age of 109; and in 1847 there lived in the district of Peñalver Don Anselmo Llerena, aged 114 years.

Santa Maria del Rosario.—BOUNDARIES.—North, the jurisdiction of Guanabacoa; east, that of Jaruco; south, those of Güines and Bejucál: and west, those of Santiago and Havana.

CAPITAL.—Santa Maria del Rosario, a city founded in 1733, situated on high land, two leagues south-east of Guanabacoa and four from Havana. It contains 7 streets, 110 houses, and 450 inhabitants.

PETTY DISTRICTS.—Santa Maria del Rosario, Managua, San José de las Lajas, Tapaste, and San Francisco de Paula (a dependency of the chief town).

COMMUNITIES.—San Francisco de Paula (dependency of the capital town), a village of 26 houses and 150 inhabitants. San José de las Lajas, a curacy and town of 164 houses and 1,050 inhabitants. Jamaica, in the preceding district, a hamlet of 18 houses and 150 inhabitants. Managua, a curacy and village, six leagues south of Havana, with 30 houses and 400 inhabitants. Nazareno (Managua district), a town of 57 houses and 300 inhabitants. Tapaste, a curacy and town of 100 houses and 900 inhabitants.

PRODUCTIONS.—Fruit, garden vegetables, maize, sugar, coffee, and tobacco.

PECULIARITIES.—This jurisdiction does not possess a single port. In Managua district died Doña Felipa Jorje, at the age of 120 years.

Guines.—BOUNDARIES—North, the jurisdiction of Jaruco; east, that of Matanzas; south, that of Cienfuegos and the sea; west, those of Bejucál and Santa Maria del Rosario.

CAPITAL.—San Julian de los Güines, a villa situated on level and exceedingly fertile land, with 541 houses and 3,542 inhabitants, a good church and barracks. The streets are pretty wide. The distance south-east from Havana, by a fine causeway, is 12 leagues, but by railroad, 45 miles.

COMMUNITIES.—Guara, a curacy and village near the railroad station, with 42 houses and 176 inhabitants. La Catalina, a curacy and town of 79 houses and 231 inhabitants. San Nicolás, a curacy and village with 22 houses and 88 inhabitants. El Jobo (S. Nicolás district), 6 houses and 27 inhabitants. Melena del Sur, a town with 72 houses and 309 inhabitants. Rosario, in preceding district, a hamlet and embarking-place, with 5 houses and 10 inhabitants. Madruga, a curacy and town of 159 houses and 767 inhabitants, and mineral waters. Pipian, a sub-curacy and village with 24 houses and 120 inhabitants, in Madruga district. Nueva Paz or Los Palos, a town with the title of city, 20 leagues from Havana, containing 112 houses, a church, and 655 inhabitants. La Jagua, in the preceding district, a hamlet of 10 houses and 48 inhabitants.

PRODUCTIONS.—Sugar, coffee, tobacco, wax, fruit, birds, and hogs. Deer abounds. There are marble quarries at Pipian, and hot baths at Madruga.

PECULIARITIES.—The Loma de la Candela, " whence the most magnificent view in the world may be enjoyed," as Humboldt remarked, in allusion to the splendid valley of Güines. In this jurisdiction alone has the advantageous system of irrigation been availed of. There are magnificent *ingenios*, or sugar plantations.

PHYSICAL, POLITICAL, AND INDUSTRIAL. 87

Jaruco.—BOUNDARIES.—North, the sea; east, the jurisdiction of Matanzas; south, that of Güines; and west, those of Santa Maria del Rosario and Guanabacoa.

CAPITAL.—Jaruco, a curacy and city since 1790, situated on the summit of a hill, well planned and paved. It contains an excellent barracks, and 105 houses with 611 inhabitants. The climate is as salubrious as at Holguin, Bejucál, and Pinos island. The water drank is very soft. The distance from Havana, 10 leagues, and 12 from Matanzas. The inhabitants are styled *Jaruqueños.*

PETTY DISTRICTS.—Aguacate, Bainoa, Rio Blanco del Sur or Casiguas, Jibacoa, and Rio Blanco del Norte.

COMMUNITIES.—Casiguas, a curacy and hamlet; head of the district of Rio Blanco del Sur, with 6 houses and 18 inhabitants. San Antonio de Rio Blanco del Norte, a curacy and town of 50 houses and 311 inhabitants. San Matias de Rio Blanco, in the preceding district, a curacy and village of 35 houses and 79 inhabitants, situated on the roadstead at the mouth of the Jaruco River. Rio Jaruco (belonging to the head of the jurisdiction), a hamlet of 11 houses and 28 inhabitants. Jibacoa, a curacy, "dry port," and town, 15 leagues from Havana, with 76 houses and 405 inhabitants. The port of Rutinel, which serves for its shipping trade, als· bears its name. Santa Cruz (Jibacoa district), a village of 21 houses and 75 inhabitants. Aguacate, a curacy and town, 15 leagues east of Havana, with an oratory, 33 houses, and 177 inhabitants. Caraballo (Bainoa district), a curacy and town of 55 houses and 361 inhabitants.

PECULIARITIES.—In 1847 there lived in the city of Jaruco, in good health and in a robust condition, Don Luis Garcia, Don Francisco Rodriguez, Don Gerónimo de los Santos, and Doña Maria de Regla Sanchez, all at the age of 103 years; and there died Don Felipe Gonzalez, aged 119, and Doña Antonia Jorje, aged 120.

Matanzas.—BOUNDARIES.—North, the sea; east, the jurisdiction of Cárdenas; south, that of Cienfuegos; and west, those of Jaruco and Güines.

CAPITAL.—Matanzas, a city, situated at the bottom of the angle of the harbor of that name; founded in 1693 on the Indian town of Yucayo; it is well built, and occupies an area of 22 *caballerias*, containing 4,000 houses and 26,000 inhabitants, including the bridge-connected wards of Versalles and Pueblo-Nuevo, separated from the city, the first by the Yumurí River, and the second by the San Juan. Matanzas is a curacy, and one of the best planned cities in the island: the streets, which run north to south and east to west, are somewhat wider than those of Havana, and the land is undulated in some places. Although it is watered by two rivers, the inhabitants are supplied, for drinking purposes, from a great distance by conduits, or by wells and cisterns. The climate is unhealthy. It contains two colleges, two printing establishments (one of which publishes the *Aurora*, a daily paper), and is divided into eight wards. The inhabitants are called *Matanceros*, and vulgarly, *Cangrejeros*. In regard to trade it is the second city of the island, although not as concerns population or buildings.*

COMMUNITIES.—Seiba-mocha, a curacy and village of 33 houses and 875 inhabitants. San Francisco de Paula, in the above district, a village of 26 houses and 144 inhabitants. Cabezas (San Antonio de las), a curacy and village with 48 houses and 317 inhabitants. Baños de San Augustin or Paso del Medio (Seiba-mocha district), a hamlet with 8 houses and 10 inhabitants. Santa Ana, a curacy and village of 30 houses and 187 inhabitants. La Guanabana (Santa Ana district), a hamlet of 5 houses and 24 inhabitants, at the junction of the Matanzas and Coliseo railroads. Alacranes,† a town and curacy of 75 houses and 527 inhabitants. Coliseo (Limonar district), a hamlet at the eastern extremity of the railroad of that name, with 10 houses and 32 inhabitants. Union or Reyes (Alacranes district), a village of 18 houses and 104 inhabitants, at the junction of the Havana and Matanzas railroads.‡ Bolondron (Alacranes district), a hamlet of 13 houses and 109 inhabitants; station of the railroad between Matanzas and Isabel. La Bermeja (Alacranes district), a hamlet and curacy of 10 houses and 72 inhabitants, and is a railroad station. Limonar, a town with a church, 30 houses, and 180 inhabitants, situated very near the Coliseo railroad. Baños de San Miguel (Limonar district), a hamlet of 27 houses and 18 inhabitants. Canímar or Tumbadero, an inland port and hamlet of 8 houses and 38 inhabitants. San Miguel de Camarioca (Canímar district), hamlet of 13 houses and 106 inhabitants. Boca de Camarioca (Canímar district), hamlet of 17 houses and 44 inhabitants. Corral-Nuevo, a village of 11 houses and 38 inhabitants. Canasí, in the preceding district, a village and curacy of 15 houses and 41 inhabitants. Surgidero de Canasí (Canasí district), a hamlet of 7 houses and 21 inhabitants. Sabanilla del Comendador, a curacy and town of 120 houses and 466 inhabitants, and station of the Matanzas railroad.

---

* See map of this city and jurisdiction by Sr. Pichardo.
† Twenty-seven leagues from Havana.
‡ In 1849 the author was commissioned to inform the government in regard to the transfer of the head of the district from Alacranes to Reyes, and recommends the perusal of his report published in the " Anales of the Junta de Fomento, etc.," to any one interested in founding settlements in the island, as an exhibit of the principles that should rule in the matter.

RURAL DISTRICTS.—Alacranes, Cabezas, Corral-Nuevo, Camarioca, Canímar, Limonar, Seiba-mocha, Sabanilla, and Santa Ana.
PRODUCTIONS.—Sugar, coffee, rum, molasses, tobacco, sweetmeats, garden vegetables, and fruit.
PECULIARITIES.—The land is hilly, fertile, and contains many valuable plantations. There are several caverns, the most remarkable of which is that of Yumurí, and the splendid valley of that name which has an entrance near the city. Near Corral-Falso, Don Juan Arcina died, aged 118 years; at Yumurí, Don Miguel Gonzales, aged 115; at Alacranes, Don Pedro Orozco, aged 105; at the same place, the Mexican Indian Juan Escalona, aged 124; and there lived at Sabanilla, in 1847, Don José Chinique, at the age of 106.

Cardenas.—BOUNDARIES.—On the north, the sea; east, the jurisdictions of Sagua la Grande and Cienfuegos; south, that of Cienfuegos; and west, that of Matanzas.

CAPITAL.—Cárdenas, a town with a municipal assembly, founded in 1828 on the bay and *hacienda* of that name, on level and marshy land. It is an authorized port since 1843, having increased greatly in importance since 1840, when the railroad was built, which was subsequently extended to unite it with Havana. After the fire which occurred on the north side in January, 1853, some fine buildings have been erected, giving a fine appearance to the town as seen from the port. The area built upon and laid out contains 15 *caballerias*; greatest length, 1,947 *varas*; width, 1,300 *varas*. The streets are 12 *varas* wide, except that of Isabel Segunda, which is 20 *varas*, and a few others yet wider. It contains 858 houses and 6,173 inhabitants. The distance from Havana is 30 leagues by the common road, and 121 miles by the railroad.*

PETTY DISTRICTS.—Cantel, Ceja de Pablo, Cimarrones, Guamutas, Hanábana, Lagunillas, Macurijes, and Palmillas. The town of Cárdenas constitutes a commissariat (which, however, also comprises several rural quarters) of the district of Lagunillas.

COMMUNITIES.—Cantel, a hamlet on a mountain, with 11 houses and 68 inhabitants. Guásimas, a village, dependent of Cantel, with 14 houses and 47 inhabitants. Lagunillas, a village with 27 houses and 390 inhabitants. El Jucaro (in above district), a hamlet on the beach with 10 houses and 177 inhabitants, and terminus of the Jucaro railroad. Cimarrones, a curacy (church in process of building) and village of 43 houses and 269 inhabitants. Bemba (Cimarrones district), a village of 43 houses and 486 inhabitants, and station of the Cárdenas railroad, where it connects with the Macagua branch. Guamutas, a curacy and

---

* See map of this town published by Sr. J. Lopez y Martinez.

village of 23 houses and 269 inhabitants. Roque, a village of 36 houses and 276 inhabitants. Hato-Nuevo, a village of 16 houses and 211 inhabitants. Vergara or Alava, a hamlet of 6 houses and 58 inhabitants, and containing large warehouses perfectly stocked. Pijuan, a hamlet of 11 houses and 194 inhabitants. (The last four places are in Guamutas district.) Palmillas, a curacy and village of 39 houses and 218 inhabitants. Nueva Bermeja (Palmillas district), a village of 49 houses and 408 inhabitants. Sierra Morena (Ceja de Pablo district), a village of 15 houses and 96 inhabitants. Corralillo, or Felipe (above district), a village of 19 houses and 157 inhabitants. Macurijes, a curacy, without population. Isabel (Macurijes district), a hamlet of 5 houses and 24 inhabitants. Corral-Falso (above district), a town of 55 houses and 335 inhabitants, surrounded by valuable plantations, and is a railroad station. Navajas (above district), a hamlet of 9 houses and 34 inhabitants. Hanábana, a curacy and hamlet of 6 houses and 22 inhabitants. Caimito (Hanábana district), a village of 25 houses and 151 inhabitants. Jagüey-Grande (Hanábana district), a hamlet of 9 houses and 69 inhabitants.

PRODUCTIONS AND PECULIARITIES.—The productions are sugar, coffee, cattle, coal, salt, and timber. The territory is level and exceedingly fertile, and filled with sugar and coffee plantations, and cattle estates; it is the most traversed by railroads of any in the island, an effect of its flourishing agricultural condition. The soil has produced sugar-canes of a truly astonishing length, thickness, and yield. In 1850 we saw cut down at Hanábana a mahogany tree of the first quality, that measured over one and one-fourth *varas* in diameter. The cabinet of the profound naturalist, Mr. Gumlach, is well worth visiting.

Sagua la Grande.—BOUNDARIES.—North, the sea; east, Villa Clara; south, Villa Clara and Cienfuegos; and west, Cárdenas.

CAPITAL.—Sagua la Grande, a town with a municipal assembly, situated on the left margin of the river of that name, on level and swampy land, and contains 400 houses and 2,200 inhabitants, an infantry barracks, and two schools. It is an inland and authorized port, seven leagues from the mouth of the river of the same name, half the distance being in the windings of the river, as in a straight line it is but three and one-half leagues. From Villa Clara, to which place a railroad is about being built, the distance is 12 leagues, and from Havana 76. The inhabitants are called *Sagüeños*.

PETTY DISTRICTS.—Amáro (the head of which is Cifuentes), Calabazar, Jumagua (formerly Egidos), Rancho-veloz, Santo Domingo (a colony), and Yabú.

COMMUNITIES.—Pueblo nuevo de San Juan (Jumagua district),

a village of 26 houses and 30 inhabitants. Jumagua, a hamlet of 6 houses and 19 inhabitants. Guatá de la Izquierda (Jumagua district), a hamlet of 6 houses and 23 inhabitants. Boca del Rio Sagua (Jumagua district), a hamlet of 7 houses and 32 inhabitants. San Francisco del Calabazar (Calabazar district), a village of 26 houses and 100 inhabitants. Viana (Calabazar district), a village of 22 houses and 160 inhabitants. San Narciso de Alvarez, a curacy and hamlet on the central highway, with 17 houses and 109 inhabitants. Jiquiabo (Alvarez district), a hamlet of 5 houses and 20 inhabitants. Cifuentes (Amáro district), a town with church, 50 houses, and 270 inhabitants. Quemado de Güines, a curacy and village of 47 houses and 170 inhabitants. Carahate, or Carahatas (preceding district), an embarking-place and hamlet of 14 houses and 40 inhabitants. Colonia de Santo Domingo, a village of 40 houses and 181 inhabitants. Playa de Sierra Morena (Rancho-véloz district), a hamlet of 4 houses and 18 inhabitants. Sierra Morena (Rancho-veloz district), a hamlet of 5 houses and 17 inhabitants.

PRODUCTIONS.—Sugar, cattle, timber, coal, and some wax.

Cienfuegos.—BOUNDARIES.—North, Sagua la Grande, Güines, Matanzas, and Cárdenas ; east, Villa Clara and Trinidad ; south and west, the sea.

CAPITAL.—Cienfuegos, a curacy and villa founded in 1819, the neatest and most regular of any in the island, situated on the small peninsula of Majagua, in the port of Jagua. the cleanest, safest, and most magnificent port probably in the world. The built surface is six *caballerias.* The appearance of the town is very fine ; the streets are wide and straight, and contain 950 well-built houses and 4,708 inhabitants ; a theatre that can accommodate 1,000 persons ; a school, and a printing establishment which publishes an *hoja economica* (economical sheet). The climate is very salubrious. It has the disadvantage of lacking good drinking water, being only supplied by the surrounding rivers. It is an authorized port, within 90 leagues of Havana, 23 of Villa Clara, and 21 of Trinidad. The inhabitants are termed *Cienfuegueños.**

PETTY DISTRICTS.— Camarones, Cumanayagua, Santa Isabel de las Lajas, Padre las Casas, and Yaguaramas.

COMMUNITIES.—Yaguaramas, a village and curacy of 80 houses and 190 inhabitants. In the district of that name are the hamlets Los Abreus, of 16 houses and 30 inhabitants ; Jibacoa, of 20 houses and 40 inhabitants ; and Bagasal, of 13 houses and 70 inhabitants. Camarones, a curacy and town of 80 houses and 400 inhabitants ; and in the same district, the villages Ciego-Alonso, of 14 houses and 150 inhabitants ;

---

* See the different plans and maps of this town and jurisdiction by Sr. Lanier.

and Ciego-Montero, of 42 houses and 290 inhabitants. Cumanayagua, a curacy and hamlet of 7 houses and 40 inhabitants; and, in the same district—Arimao, a village of 43 houses and 251 inhabitants; San Anton, a hamlet of 4 houses and 30 inhabitants; La Mandinga, a hamlet of 7 houses and 40 inhabitants; and La Sierra, a village of 18 houses and 110 inhabitants. Las Lajas (Santa Isabèl de), a town of 86 houses and 600 inhabitants; and in the same district the villages—Cartagena, of 18 houses and 130 inhabitants; Santiago, of 15 houses and 100 inhabitants; Salto, of 22 houses and 80 inhabitants; and Congojas, of 13 houses and 60 inhabitants. Nueva Palmira (Padre las Casas district), a village formerly called Ciego Abajo, with 40 houses and 210 inhabitants. Caonao (Padre las Casas district), a village of 28 houses and 150 inhabitants. El Salado, a hamlet of 7 houses and 20 inhabitants. Soledad, a village of 12 houses and 100 inhabitants. Santa Rosa, a hamlet of 7 houses and 25 inhabitants. Mordazo, a hamlet of 8 houses and 30 inhabitants. Medidas, a hamlet of 7 houses and 18 inhabitants.

PRODUCTIONS.—Sugar, wax, timber, cattle, grain, tobacco, and hides.

PECULIARITIES.*—The remarkable mahogany tree, four *varas* in diameter, cut down in 1808, and other subsequent ones. The fresh-water springs that arise in the sea on the coast.

Villa Clara.—BOUNDARIES—North, Sagua la Grande and the sea; east, San Juan de los Remedios; south-east, Trinidad; and south-west, Cienfuegos.

CAPITAL.—Villa Clara (Santa Clara), a curacy and villa, founded in 1683, between two rivulets, on sandy and somewhat hilly land, 136 *varas* above sea-level, and on the central road. It is a pretty town, and contains 1,090 houses and 6,604 inhabitants, a poor theatre, and a printing establishment that publishes the *Eco* thrice a week. The climate is of the most salubrious in the island, as is proved by the fact that in 1852 there were only 546 deaths against 1,077 births and 127 marriages. The Sagua la Grande and Cienfuegos railroads will soon connect at this point, and render it the centre of a great trade. The distance from Havana is 78 leagues, from Trinidad 24, from Cienfuegos 23, from Sagua 11, and 12 from Remedios. It is the birth-place of the

---

* In January, 1849. the author published in the *Diario de la Habana* some notes on the *Ingenios* of Cárdenas and Matanzas, indicating all their elements (even to the dimensions of the buildings), crops, soil, etc., those districts containing the largest in the island at that time; but at present there is one being established at Cienfuegos whose probable crop is estimated at 30,000 boxes of sugar! In this district, and at Cárdenas and Sagua la Grande, canes have been produced nine *varas* high and five inches thick, and some *caballerias* of land have yielded 120 to 150 hogsheads of muscovado sugar, being an average of 4,500 *arrobas*.

distinguished jurisconsult, Don Indalecio Santo-Suarez. The inhabitants are called *Villa-Clareros* or *Poblanos*.

PETTY DISTRICTS.—Anton-Diaz (formerly Egido), Baez, Esperanza, Manicaragua, Niguas (formerly San Diego), Pelo-Malo, San Lazaro del Granadillo, San Juan de los Lleras, or Yeras, and Seibabo.

COMMUNITIES.—Esperanza or Puerta de Golpe, a town and curacy of 180 houses and 1,580 inhabitants, situated on the central highway, and remarkable for the regularity of its buildings. El Salto (Lazaro district), a village of 15 houses and 220 inhabitants. Manicaragua, a town with church, 40 houses, 140 inhabitants, and 3 copper mines in the vicinity. San Fernando (above district), a hamlet of 9 houses and 30 inhabitants, near a copper-mine. San Diego (Niguas district), a hamlet of 15 houses and 70 inhabitants. San Juan de los Yeras, a village of 35 and 190 inhabitants. Yabú, a village of 13 houses and 27 inhabitants. Condado (Anton-Diaz district), a town of 80 houses and 460 inhabitants.

PRODUCTIONS.—Hogs, excellent draught horses, wax, cocoa, timber, copper, and some wheat and *yerenes*.

PECULIARITIES.—Three copper mines, one of which was worked at the time of the Conquest, and silver and gold extracted from it.

Trinidad.—BOUNDARIES.—North, Remedios; east, Santo Espiritu; south, the sea; and west, Cienfuegos and Villa Clara.

CAPITAL.—Trinidad, a curacy and city since 1815, situated one league north of the port of Casilda, forming an amphitheatre with Mount Vijía. The climate is so healthy that the deaths in 1852 were only 354, against 834 births and 79 marriages. The area built upon is 11 *caballerias* of land, nearly equal to that of Havana within the walls. It contains 2,270 houses and 14,119 inhabitants, and a printing-office publishing the *Correo* three times a week. The distance from Havana is 90 leagues. It is a "dry port," communicating with the coast by the port of Casilda, whither a railroad is to be built, and is the stopping-place of several steamers. It is the birth-place of Malibran, an unfortunate hero in the late civil struggle in Spain. The inhabitants are termed *Trinitarios*.*

PETTY DISTRICTS.—Cabajan, Casilda, Guaniguical, Güinía de Miranda, Palmarejo, Rio de Ay, San Juan, San Francisco, Sipiabo (formerly Jumento), and Táyaba.

COMMUNITIES.—Casilda, the chief port of Trinidad, and future terminus of a railroad, with 185 houses and 1,400 inhabitants. Güinía de Miranda, a town of 60 houses and 300 inhabitants. Cayaguani (above district), a hamlet of 4 houses and 18 inhabitants. San Pedro de Pal-

---

* See the map of this city by Don Rafael Rodriguez.

marejo, a curacy and village of 20 houses and 30 inhabitants. Caracusey (above district), a hamlet of 10 houses and 40 inhabitants. Rio de Ay, a curacy. Las Jiquimas, a hamlet of 6 houses and 30 inhabitants. Sipiabo, a hamlet of 5 houses and 15 inhabitants. Jumento, a hamlet of 8 houses and 20 inhabitants.

PRODUCTIONS.—Sugar, coffee, wax, mules, tobacco, marble, ox-horns, *yarei* palm leaf, and famous conserves and sweetmeats. On the coast are caught sea-cows, from the skin of which beautiful walking-canes and other articles are made.

PECULIARITIES.—The magnificent valley of Los Ingenios; the lofty mountain Pico del Potrerillo; and the copper mines called Los Pobres, near Cabayan River, and one of amianthus.

San Juan de los Remedios.—BOUNDARIES.—North, the sea; east, Santo Espiritu and Trinidad; and west, Villa Clara.

CAPITAL.—San Juan de los Remedios, a curacy and villa founded about 1545, and at present situated on level, low, and damp land, of reddish soil, rendering it unhealthy in the rainy season. Its appearance is fair; and it contains a good church, 890 houses, 5,270 inhabitants, and a printing establishment publishing the *Boletin* twice a week. It is an authorized " dry port," whose shipping is done by the port of Caibarien, with which it communicates by a railroad of five miles. The distance from Havana is 86 leagues.

PETTY DISTRICTS.—Caibarien, Egidos, Guadalupe, Guaracabuya, Mayajigua, Santa Fé, San Felipe, Santa Rosa, Taguayabon, Vega-Alta, Vega-Redonda, Yaguajay.

COMMUNITIES.—Las Vueltas (San Antonio de), a village in Vega-Alta district, of 31 houses and 230 inhabitants. Guaracabuya, or San Anastasio de Cupey, a curacy and village of 24 houses and 170 inhabitants. Nazareno (above district), a hamlet of 9 houses and 32 inhabitants. Yaguajay, a village of 12 houses and 110 inhabitants. Mayajigual, a curacy and village of 42 houses and 260 inhabitants. Vives, or Caibarien, a port and town in the colony of that name, with 194 houses and 780 inhabitants; it is a railroad terminus, and is having a church built.

PRODUCTIONS.—Sugar, wheat, tobacco, cattle, cocoa, *yerenes*, and timber.

PECULIARITIES.—The many and remarkable caves in the Sierras de Matacumbé. The cultivation of cocoa and wheat.

Santo Espiritu.—BOUNDARIES.—North, Remedios and the sea; east, Puerto Principe; south, the sea; and west, Trinidad.

CAPITAL.—Santo Espiritu, a curacy and villa founded in 1514, by Velasquez, and situated a short distance from the river Yayabo, over which is a fine bridge. It is regularly built, with 1,600 houses and 9,982 inhabitants, and contains a printing-office that publishes the *Fénix* twice a week. It is an authorized "dry port," shipping by the port of Sasa; a railroad is about to be built to Trinidad and Casilda, and there are projects of one to the embarking-place of Sasa, and another to San Juan de los Remedios. Distance 101 leagues from Havana, 18 from Trinidad, and 50 from Puerto Principe. The inhabitants are vulgarly called *Guayaberos*.

PETTY DISTRICTS.—Algodonal, Alicante, Banao, Cayaguasí (formerly Egidos), Ciego de Avila, Chambas, Iguará, Jíbaro, Jobosí, Minas, Neiba, Pueblo-Viejo, Rivera, Santa Lucia, and Yayabo.

COMMUNITIES.—Sasa (Algodonal district), a village of 13 houses and 60 inhabitants, and is the shipping-port of Santo Espiritu. Banao, a village of 25 houses and 110 inhabitants. Jicotea (district of Ciego de Avila), a village of 12 houses and 30 inhabitants. El Jibaro (San Antonio Abad de), a curacy and village of 28 houses and 450 inhabitants. Moron, a curacy and town of 222 houses and 1,200 inhabitants. Ciego de Avila, a village and curacy (known as San Eugenio de la Palma) with 40 houses and 300 inhabitants.

PRODUCTIONS.—Cattle, tobacco, wax, sugar, cocoa, *yarei*-palm, and famous lace.

PECULIARITIES.—It coasts the sea both on the north and south, thus rendering the maritime and civil divisions nearly alike. Near the capital town guava trees are very abundant

Puerto Principe.—BOUNDARIES.—North, the sea and Nuevitas; east, Las Tunas and Bayamo; south, the sea; and west, Santo Espiritu.

CAPITAL.—Puerto Principe (Santa Maria de), a city situated on a low and sandy plain, watered by the Tínima and Jatibonico streams. Its buildings, which afford nothing remarkable, occupy twelve and one-half *caballerias* of land, with winding streets, the most of which are narrow, and numbering 3,576 houses and 26,648 inhabitants. It contains a fine theatre, and a printing establishment issuing the *Fanal*. The Intendancy and Court of Judicature that resided here (the latter being the first court established in Spanish America) have recently been suppressed. Here were born the botanist Don Tomas Pio Betencourt; the orator Presbyter Fernandez (called Pico de Oro, or golden tongue); the priest Varona de la Vicenta (of historical and tragical memory); and the distinguished jurisconsult, Don Francisco de Armas. Distance from Havana 151 leagues, 12 from the port of La Guanaja, 22 from Santa Cruz, and 19 from Nuevitas, with which city it is connected by a railroad. Santa Cruz and La Guanaja, which belong to its jurisdiction, are authorized ports. The inhabitants are called *Camagüeyanos.**

PETTY DISTRICTS.—Sabana Grande, Guayabo, Zaragozano, Monte del Horno, Maraguan, Guananey, Jimaguaisí, Porcayo, Caonao, Caobabo, Cubita, Yaguajay, Padre Valencia (Concepcion), Najasa, Guaicanamar, San Pedro, Altamira, La Trinidad, San Gerónimo, Magorabomba, Jaramí, La Guanaja, Sibanicú, Cascorro, Monte-oscuro, Guaimaro, Guaimarillo, Yáguimo, Santa Cruz, Bioya (formerly San Juan), Curajaya, San Carlos, Vertientes, Mata-Recua, Corojó (formerly Cumanayagua), Yayabaco, Judas Grande, and Guanamaro

COMMUNITIES.—Banao, a village of 22 houses and 110 inhabitants. Cercado, a hamlet of 9 houses and 21 inhabitants. Tuabaquey, a hamlet of 5 houses and 14 inhabitants. La Entrada, a hamlet of 8 houses and 27 inhabitants. Limones, a hamlet of 5 houses and 9 inhabitants. Corojo, a hamlet of 8 houses and 23 inhabitants. Hermita-Vieja, a hamlet of 10 houses and 19 inhabitants. Cubita (to which district the preceding hamlets belong), a curacy and hamlet of 6 houses and 29 inhabitants. Zaragozano, a hamlet of 4 houses and 13 inhabitants. San Gerónimo, a curacy and hamlet of 5 houses and 34 inhabitants. La Guanaja, a village of 35 houses and 138 inhabitants. Sibaniyú, a curacy and town of 78 houses and 527 inhabitants. Cascorro, a village of 32 houses and 196 inhabitants. Guaimaro, a curacy and town of 82 houses and 450 inhabitants. Guayabal, a village of 13 houses and 54 inhabitants. Santa Cruz, a curacy and town of 116 houses and 552 inhabitants; is an authorized port, 22 leagues south of Puerto Principe, and the stopping-place of steamers bound for Cuba. Vertientes (San Pedro de), a curacy (just transferred to Santa Cruz) and hamlet of 4 houses and 21 inhabitants.

PRODUCTIONS.—Sugar, cattle and horses, candles, soap, pottery, excellent wax, horns, *yarei*-palm leaf, tobacco, copper, mats, cheese, jerked beef, and fine conserves and sweetmeats.

PECULIARITIES.—The Sierra de Cubita, with its remarkable entrance and its singular caves. The island of Cayo Romano belongs to this jurisdiction.

Nuevitas.—BOUNDARIES.—North, the sea; east, Las Tunas; south and west, Puerto Principe.

CAPITAL.—Nuevitas (San Fernando de) a curacy and city without a corporation, but having a municipal assembly, founded in 1819, on level but high land, on the margin of the fine port of that name, at a point called El Grincho, where Columbus planted a cross, and Velasquez

---

* See the map of this city by Sr. Lavallée.

of the Mayarí River, with 650 houses and 998 inhabitants. The district produces good tobacco, excellent wax, sugar, and cattle. Distant 21 leagues from Sagua de Tánamo, 32 from Cuba, and 25 from Holguin. Contiguous to it lies the hamlet of Braguetudos, and near by those of La Herradura, Chavaleta, Arroyo Hondo, Guayabo, Cubonico, Caguasal, and Barajágua. Sagua de Tánamo, a town and curacy, distant 30 leagues from Baracoa and 34 from Cuba, situated on a peninsula at the extremity of the hacienda Demajagua, and contains a barracks, 91 houses, and 224 inhabitants. Its district contains at present 22 cattle estates, 3 *ingenios*, 1 *potrero*, and 337 tobacco *vegas*. The chief production is tobacco, of which in fruitful years the crop amounts 14,000 or 15,000 quintals. El Cobre (Minas Santiago Real del Prado de), a villa without corporation, but with a municipal assembly, a curacy with a church, and a sanctuary containing the reverenced virgin Del Cobre; 460 houses and 2,069 inhabitants. Juan Diaz (S. de Tánamo district), hamlet of 9 houses and 15 inhabitants. Ti-Arriba (Concepcion de), a curacy and town of 74 houses and 126 inhabitants. Palma Soriano, a curacy and village of 45 houses and 185 inhabitants. Caney (San Luis_ del), a town with a sub-corporation and municipal assembly and curacy; contains 151 houses and 622 inhabitants, and is noted for its fairs. Socapa, a small hamlet at the entrance of the port of Cuba, with 11 houses and 28 inhabitants.

PRODUCTIONS.—Coffee, sugar, celebrated tobacco, pine-trees (at Mayarí and Sagua), cotton, cocoa, hides, fustic, ginger, vanilla, and wax. Deer is so abundant that the markets are daily supplied with venison.*

PECULIARITIES.—The coffee is as fine in quality as that of Santo Domingo or Porto Rico, for which reason it often commands double the price of that of Havana. The quality of the sugar, on the contrary, is not as good as that of the western department, probably because not well manufactured. This jurisdiction is the richest in copper ore† and in timber and precious woods, such as mahogany (as good as the Haytian), fustic, Brazil-wood, *ácana*, etc. The oppressive heat of Cuba contrasts singularly with the constantly cool temperature of the Sierra Maestra, three and a half leagues distant, where many European fruits are cultivated so successfully that artichokes, quinces, and strawberries are sold about the streets. Pinks grow wild in the *cafetales* of the Sierra Maestra. It is so cool on the heights around the city as to render extra bedclothes necessary at night, even in summer. There are a large num-

---

* We have observed recently that venison is to be had in the markets of Havana.

† The greatest depths of the principal mines which are being worked in this district are as follows—La Isabelita 308 Castilian *varas*, El Santuario and La Londeña 283, San José 264, San Andrés 218, etc.

ber of camels in this district for labor in the mines. The Sierra Maestra contains haunts of runaway negroes.

Guantanamo.—BOUNDARIES.—West and north, the jurisdiction of Cuba; east, that of Baracoa; and south, the sea.

CAPITAL.—Santa Catalina de Guaso, a town situated on level land near the Salto de Guaso, three leagues (by the highway) north of the harbor of Guantánamo, with barracks, 184 houses, and 863 inhabitants; distant 25 leagues from St. Jago de Cuba and 44 from Baracoa.

PETTY DISTRICTS.—Guaso, Guantánamo, Humboldt (formerly Ojo de Agua), Los Indios (formerly Santa Rosa), Monte Libano, Tiguabos, El Toro, Ulloa (formerly Filipina), and Yateras.

COMMUNITIES.—Tiguabos, a curacy and town of 51 houses and 155 inhabitants. Cerro Guayabo or Santa Rosa (Los Indios district), a hamlet of 10 houses and 82 inhabitants, where there are still a few of the primitive race.

PRODUCTIONS.—The lands of this district are the most fruitful in the island, but the greater part is uncultivated, although at present several large sugar and coffee estates are being established. The chief products are sugar, coffee, cotton, cattle, and timber and precious woods.

PECULIARITIES.—The mountainous nature of the territory affords the finest prospects, caves, etc., and perhaps mineral substances. This is the district that contains the greatest number of French agriculturists and aboriginal Indians.

Baracoa.—BOUNDARIES.—North, east, and south, the sea; and west, the jurisdictions of Cuba and Guantánamo.

CAPITAL.—Baracoa (La Asuncion de), the first settlement of the conquerors in the island, is a city situated at the bottom of a beautiful bay called Playa de Miel, at a height of five *varas* above the level of the sea, and seven leagues from Cabo Maisí. It was founded in 1512 with the title of villa, being one of the seven founded by Diego Velasquez. The streets are wide and level, and contain 34 tiled houses, 44 shingled, and 422 of *yarei*-palm, a primary school, and a permanent population of 2,400. The church contains the remarkable *cruz de parra* or vine cross. The climate is temperate even in summer, and would be the most salubrious in the island but for the lagoons that are formed in the rainy season. Water of excellent quality is supplied by the rivers Macaguanigua and Miel. It is an authorized port and well defended. Distance 69 leagues from Cuba and 44 from Santa Catalina de Guaso. The inhabitants are called *Baracoenses*.

PETTY DISTRICTS.—Cabacú, Cupey, Cagüeijabe, Duaba (San Pedro de), Guinea, Imias, Jauco, Jaimayabon, Jojó, Mabujabo, Maisí, Mata, San Salvador, and Velasquez.

COMMUNITIES.—There are none besides the capital, for the colony of Moa or Vives contains but two houses at present, the inhabitants having removed to Sagua de Tánamo.

PRODUCTIONS.—The land, though very hilly, is exceedingly fertile, producing all kinds of precious woods, timber, pine-trees, etc., also fruit, coffee, tobacco, cocoa, ginger, cattle, plantains, and abundance of cocoa-nuts of great size and fine flavor, most of the palms growing wild, and their oil constitutes one of the chief exports.

PECULIARITIES.—The strange custom of riding on oxen. Mother-of-pearl shells in the mouth of the Miel River.* The Yunque, an isolated mountain of a conical figure, with a lake on the summit, supposed to have been the crater of a volcano. On the hacienda Pueblo-Viejo, not far from Cabo Maisí, exists the foundation of a rectangular wall, 180 *varas* long and 85 wide, which is attributed to the primitive inhabitants, although what purpose it was built for is not known. There are many remarkable caves abounding in bones, benches, jars, etc., of the early race. On the hacienda Mariana is a palm-tree with 10 arms, and the air is so cold in winter that the river is covered with a slight crust of ice. There are yellow and even white parrots, walnut wood like that of Europe, and the jaragua tree.

---

* The author is indebted to Don Manuel Borges for many specimens of minerals of this district, several pearls, and a splendid opal two centimetres long and one and a half wide.

ANCIENT GEOGRAPHY.

UNDER this head are comprised the geographical notices that have been preserved both of the Indians, or primitive inhabitants, and of the first discoverers and conquerors of the island.

The cattle-estates, ports, and especially the rivers and mountains, chiefly retain the Indian names, and, as they are numerous, we shall only notice such as are mentioned in the historical records and documents of the time of the discovery and colonization in the fifteenth and sixteenth centuries.

Cuba was the name of the island among the natives, although Columbus called it Juana on his first voyage in compliment to the Prince Don Juan, son of their Catholic majesties, and Alpha and Omega on his second voyage, and soon after it received the several names of Fernandina, Santiago, Ave Maria, and San Salvador, and was termed by mariners Lengua de Pajaro. Its original appellation has prevailed.

Neighboring Land.—On the north Cautió (Florida), with the Cayos de Matacumbé (afterward de los Mártires, and at present known as the Florida reefs); the Organos islands (Banco) de los Roques; and the islands Yucayas or Lucayas, of which the most worthy of note are the Guanahani (now San Salvador or Gato—Cat Island), the first land discovered by Columbus in America; the group of Bimini or Buyoca, and the islands of Arenas, which name was given by Columbus to the Mūcaras shoal (which perhaps at that time protruded as islets or keys). On the east the island of Haytí, Quisqueya or Bohio, called Española by Columbus, and subsequently Isabela and St. Domingo, by which last it is best known.[*] On the south is the island of Jamaica, which Columbus called Santiago; the Tortugas (at present Little Caimans), and Great Caiman. On the south-west the peninsula of Yucatan.

Seas.—Columbus, on his first voyage, gave the name of Mar de Nuestra Señora to a tract of water which he traversed at the Jardines del Rey, and is supposed to lie on the north of the island of Cayo Romano. The bay of Cochinos[†] is also mentioned on the old charts.

---

[*] This island has on the north the islet of Tortuga, a celebrated haunt of pirates until a late period.

[†] Is it not likely that the name bestowed by the Spaniards on this bay was Conchillos, instead of Cochinos? The author infers it from the fact that Lope Conchillo was, at the time of the discovery and conquest, one of the most influential personages of the court, especially with regard to colonial affairs. (See the author's *Memoria justificativa del mapa antiguo.*)

founded the villa of Santa Maria del puerto del Principe. It contains 170 houses and 830 inhabitants, and is the terminus of the railroad to Puerto Principe.

PETTY DISTRICTS.—Mayanabo, Montalvan, Bayatabo, and Nuevas-Grandes.

COMMUNITIES.—Bagá, a village of 28 houses and 128 inhabitants, and sea-port, at the bottom of the harbor of Nuevitas, and contains an auxiliary church. San Miguel, a town of 56 houses and 291 inhabitants. Villa Nueva, a hamlet and railroad-depôt, containing 4 houses and 22 inhabitants. Itabos y Yamagual, a hamlet in Bayatabo district.

PRODUCTIONS, ETC.—Tortoise-shell, sponges, cattle, timber, and woods (among which is the *cúrbana*, whose bark is an inferior cinnamon), copper, etc. There are large crocodiles in the Saramaguacan River, and the coast is infested by a plague of mosquitoes, *jejenes*, and other insects, almost intolerable in the rainy season.

Tunas.—BOUNDARIES.—North, the sea; east, Holguin; south, Bayamo; and west, Puerto Principe and Nuevitas.

CAPITAL.—Tunas, a curacy and town, situated in the centre of the jurisdiction, with 289 houses and 2,004 inhabitants.

PETTY DISTRICTS.—Cabaniguan, Manati, Rompe, San Augustin, Unique, and Yariguá.

COMMUNITIES.—San Miguel de Manatí, a hamlet of 12 houses and 72 inhabitants. Yarey, a village of 35 houses and 96 inhabitants. Embarcadero, a hamlet of 8 houses and 28 inhabitants. Paso de Cauto, a hamlet of 5 houses and 20 inhabitants. Arenas, a small hamlet in Unique district.

PRODUCTIONS.—Cattle, *yarei*-leaf, wax, copper, and building timber.

PECULIARITIES.—The district is famous for the wildness and fierceness of its bulls, and contains extensive savannas.

Bayamo.*—BOUNDARIES.—North, Tunas; east, Jiguaní; south, Cuba and Manzanillo; west, the sea and Puerto Principe.

CAPITAL.—Bayamo (San Salvador de), a city founded, with the title of villa, in 1513, by Diego Velasquez, in a great plain, on the margin of the Bayamo River (an affluent of the Cauto). It occupies a space of four and one-half *caballerias* of land, and contains a theatre, college, four schools, a philharmonic society, 1,351 houses and 5,875 inhabitants. The climate is unwholesome from September to October, during which period intermittent fever prevails. It is the birth-place of Doctor Infante, and of the priest Montes de Oca. Distance from Havana 199 leagues, and 32 from Cuba Its shipping trade is done by Man-

---

* See the map published by Don Rafael Rodriguez.

zanillo and Cauto del Embarcadero. The inhabitants are called *Bayameses*.

PETTY DISTRICTS.—Barrancas, Caureje, Casibacoa, Cauto del Embarcadero, Dátil, Guabaranao, Guajacabo, Guiza, Tamayo (formerly El Horno), and Valenzuela.

COMMUNITIES.—Guiza, a village (with title of villa and corporation till 1845) and curacy of 48 houses and 241 inhabitants. · Dátil, a village one league south of Bayamo, containing a highly venerated sanctuary, 89 houses and 165 inhabitants, and is a pleasure resort of the *Bayamese*. Horno, San Pablo del (Tamayo district), a village of 16 houses and 91 inhabitants. Barrancas, a hamlet of 5 houses and 12 inhabitants. Cauto del Embarcadero, a town of 79 houses and 678 inhabitants.

PRODUCTIONS.—Sugar, tobacco, arrow-root, cattle, *yarei*-leaf, vanilla, *casabe*, woods (including fustic and pine wood), preserves, etc.

PECULIARITIES.—In the southern part pine trees abound. Its chief wealth is in cattle. The famous Cauto River traverses and disembogues in the jurisdiction. In the mountains is still to be found the indigenous animal called *andarás*.

Manzanillo.—BOUNDARIES.—North-east, Bayamos; east, Cuba; and south and west, the sea.

CAPITAL.—Manzanillo, a villa and curacy, a mile from the mouth of the Yara River. It is regularly built, with straight streets 14 or 15 *varas* wide, but not paved; and contains 595 houses and 3,050 inhabitants. The climate is rather unhealthy. It is an authorized port, and serves for the district of Bayamos, distant 14 leagues, whither a railroad is in project.

PETTY DISTRICTS.—Bicana, Guabeje (formerly Jibacoa), Portillo, Seiba, Yara, and Yaribacoa.

COMMUNITIES.—Yara-Abajo, a curacy and village with 40 houses and 377 inhabitants, and surrounded by *vegas* of excellent tobacco. Zarzal (Yara district), a village of 26 houses and 34 inhabitants. Bicana, a curacy and village of 34 houses and 291 inhabitants.

PRODUCTIONS.—Sugar, *yarei*-palm, cattle, precious woods and timber, wax, rushes, cocoa-nuts, dressed hides, the well-known Yara tobacco, turtle, tortoise-shell, and mullet roes.

PECULIARITIES.—There is an abundance of *yarei* and cocoa-nut palms, pitch-pine trees, and Tabasco pepper ; also copper, gypsum, ochre, and loadstone. In this district is the loftiest mountain-peak in the island, the Turquino, and also the Ojo de Toro, where there are lichens and pine forests, as well as on the Sierra Maestra, and the indigenous animal *guabiniquimar*, at present very rare in the island.

Holguin.—BOUNDARIES.—North, the old Bahama channel; east, the

PHYSICAL, POLITICAL, AND INDUSTRIAL. 99

..ea and the jurisdiction of Cuba; south, also Cuba and Jiguaní; and west, Las Tunas.

CAPITAL.—Holguin (San Ysidoro), a vicarage and beautiful city, founded in 1751 in a fine and fertile plain between the Jigue and Marañon rivulets. It covers seven and one-third *caballerias* of land, and is one of the most regularly built in the island, with right-lined streets, 693 houses, and 3,754 inhabitants. The climate is among the healthiest known. Distance 18 leagues from Tunas, and as much from Bayamo. The inhabitants are termed *Holguineses*.

PETTY DISTRICTS.—Auras, Banes, Bariay, Cacocum, Dehesa, Fray Benito, Guirabo y Pedernales, Guabasiabo (formerly San Andrés), Guairajal, Jibára, Majibacoa, Maniabon (formerly San Cristóbal), Santo Cristo, Sao-Arriba, Tocajó, Tacamara, Yayal, and Yareyal.

COMMUNITIES.—Punta de Yarey (Jibára district), a curacy and town on the western margin of the port of Jibára, seven leagues from Holguin, with a church, 257 houses, and 1,230 inhabitants. Auras, a hamlet of 18 houses (inhabitants not enumerated), and Velasco, a hamlet of 5 houses. Retrete, a curacy and hamlet of 4 houses and 11 inhabitants.

PRODUCTIONS.—The excellent pasturage of this district causes cattle to be the chief production, but there is also abundance of fine woods of all kinds, including fustic and *yarei*-palm. There is also gold, copper, amianthus, loadstone, etc. Sugar, honey, wax, tobacco, *casabe*, copper, and timber are produced.

PECULIARITIES.—This district contains the greatest number of fine ports. Cigar making is carried to great perfection, and the exportation is considerable. On the Banes estate are caves containing bones, instruments, utensils, etc., of the aboriginal inhabitants.

Jiguaní.—BOUNDARIES.—North, Holguin; east and south, Cuba; west, Bayamo.

CAPITAL.—Jiguaní (San Pablo de), a town with a sub-corporation, situated on the left margin of the River Jiguaní, on somewhat hilly land, on the highway from Bayamo to Cuba, and contains 251 houses and 950 inhabitants, an infantry barracks, and a school. Like Cuba, it is subject to frequent earthquakes. Distance 7 leagues from Bayamo, 14 from Holguin, and 25 from Cuba.

PETTY DISTRICTS.—Baire, Concepcion, Ojo de Agua, Yarey.

COMMUNITIES.—Baire, a village of 59 houses and 351 inhabitants. Santa Rita, a village of 15 houses and 140 inhabitants.

PRODUCTIONS.—Sugar, cattle, tobacco, vanilla, wax.

Cuba.—BOUNDARIES.—North, Bayamo and Jiguaní, Holguin, and the sea; east, Baracoa and Guantánamo; south, the sea; west, Manzanillo.

CAPITAL.—Cuba (Santiago de), a city, founded with the title of villa in 1514 by Diego Velasquez, on the eastern coast of the magnificent port of the same name, on clayey and hilly land, the highest part of which is 60 *varas* above the level of the sea. The streets are narrow and have a poor appearance, owing to the undulation of the land and the lowness of the houses, rendered necessary by the prevalence of earthquakes, and for the same reason they are built on piles. It contains 24,253 inhabitants, a fine metropolitan cathedral,* a seminary-college, an economical society, four printing establishments (publishing two dailies, the *Redactor* and the *Orden*†), theatre, public walk, a fine square, a philharmonic society. Also a walk on the margin of the port, two very pretty squares adorned with trees, and a theatre (de la Reina), of good architecture. Water is provided of good quality by an aqueduct from the Paso de la Virjen. The climate is exceedingly warm during the day, in consequence of the city lying in a hollow, but cool at night, even in summer. Several lagoons in the vicinity seem to induce a propensity to tertian ague, and it is certain that the black vomit exercises greater power here than in any town in the island. The greatest degree of heat observed with a centigrade thermometer is 30° to 31°, yet the summer season appears to be more healthy than the winter. The two memorable earthquakes experienced by this city in 1853 will prove to be the cause of its great decline. Distance from Havana 236 leagues, 32 from Bayamo, 32 from Mayarí, 25 from Santa Catalina, and 69 from Baracoa.

PETTY DISTRICTS.—Amistad, Andalusia, Armonia de Limones, Aserradero, Barajagua, Bolaños, Brazo de Cauto, Caimanes, Caney, Cauto-Abajo, Dajao, Demajagua, Demajayabo, Dos Bocas, Enramada, Guanicú, Hongo-Losongo, Juan Angola, Jutinicú, Lagunas, Mamey, Manantuaba, Maroto, Mayarí-Abajo, Mayari-Arriba, Nimanima, Palma Soriano, Paz de los Naranjos, Pilon, Piloto-Arriba, Purial, Ramon, Rio-Frio, Rio Seco, Rojas, Sagua de Tánamo, San Andrés, Sevilla, Ti-Arriba, Yaguas, and Zacatecas.

COMMUNITIES.—Moron, a curacy and hamlet (Jutinicú district) of 4 houses and 25 inhabitants. Mayarí-Abajo (San Gregorio de), a curacy, town, and inland port, three and a half leagues from the mouth

---

* In 1816, in building the foundations of this church, the sepulchre of Don Diego Velasquez was discovered. The breaking of the slab caused uncertainty regarding the year of his decease, but the documents published by Sr. Pezuela prove that it occurred in 1524.

† There is published besides a monthly periodical entitled *Memorias de la Real Sociedad Económica*, that nobly rivals the weekly issued at Havana under the name of *Anales y Memorias;* both containing very important information for the merchant and the man of science, and indispensable for the planter and the Cuban historian. The first is edited by Don Juan B. Sagarra and the second by Col. Don Jacobo de la Pezuela.

Capes and Points.—Cabo Guaniguanico, re-named San Anton, and at present San Antonio, doubtless by the famous pilot Anton de Alaminos (discoverer of the new Bahama channel), who doubled it several times, although the change of name should have been in honor of Sebastian de Ocampo, who first doubled it; Cabo Hicacos, which name continues; Punta Yucanaca, opposite the western point of Turiguanó island; Cabo Palmas, a name applied by Columbus to the most westerly discovered by him on his first voyage, and which is supposed to be the present Punta Yana; Cabo Cubaná, termed Campana by Columbus, and at present Lucrecia; Cabo Maisí, the eastern extremity of the island; Cabo Cruz, name bestowed by Columbus, and retained. Punta Don Cristóbal, mentioned in the oldest maps, and being better known than other more prominent ones, it was chosen as a boundary in the maritime division. Punta Serafin was the name given by Columbus to the present Punta-Gorda; and, lastly, Cabo Corrientes, mentioned in several old charts.

Islands, Keys, and Shoals.—Evangelista, name bestowed by Columbus on Pinos island, discovered on his second voyage, and whose Indian name is supposed to have been Siguanea; Guajaba island, still so called; Jardines del Rey, name bestowed by Columbus on a group of islands discovered on his first voyage, and which are supposed to be Cayo Romano and its adjacents; Jardines de la Reina, applied by Columbus on his second voyage to the Cayos de las Doce Leguas, of which he called Santa Marta, the one now known as Cayo Piedra, where he stopped; Camarreos or Canarreos, a name given by the natives to the Banco de los Jardines and Jardinillos, and even part of the keys north of Pinos island.

Ports.—Bahia-Honda* and Cabañas, are mentioned in the oldest maps; Marien, changed to Mariel, where the commissioners sent by Cortés from Mexico to Spain put in; Carenas, a name given the port of Havana because Sebastian de Ocampo there careened his ships with asphaltum, of which he found abundance. The present name of Habana is due to its being situated in the Indian province so called. Ports of Jaruco and Chipiona are mentioned in the old maps; Yucayo, changed to Matanzas by the conquerors on account of the slaughter (matanza) made by certain Indians of some Spaniards that had come from Urubá; Sabána is the name on the old maps for San Juan de los Remedios; Mares is the name given by Columbus to a port and river visited by him on his first voyage, and supposed to be Caonao-Grande; San Salvador, the name

---

* Probably Bayamon, from an abundance of the native tree of that name, since said inlet of the sea does not correspond to the appellation of Bahia-Honda, being neither a harbor nor deep to a sufficient degree to thus distinguish it. In Santo Domingo there is a port named Bayamon.

5*

given by the religious Columbus to the first port and river visited by him in the island the 28th of October, 1492, supposed to be the river Maximo.* Port of Santa Catalina, name given by Columbus to one visited by him on his first voyage, supposed to be the bay of Sabinal; Puerto Principe, the name bestowed by Columbus on the present port of Nuevitas; Ports Manatí, Padre, and Nipe, cited in old maps; Puerto Santo, name given by Columbus to the port of Baracoa, which he visited the 27th of November, 1492; Puerto-Escondido, mentioned in old maps; Puerto de Palmas, where Velasquez landed on coming to conquer the island, and which is the present bay of Palmas, between Guantánamo and Puerto-Escondido; Guantánamo, a great bay called Puerto-Grande by Columbus, when he visited it on his second voyage; Macaca, stopping-port of all the chief navigators of the south of the island; Guacanayabo, at present bay of Manzanillo; Vasco Porcayo de Figueroa, at present port of Santa Cruz; Jagua, port visited by Sebastian de Ocampo on his voyage round the island; Matamanó, bay entered by Columbus on his second voyage, and now called Batabanó; Guaníma, a bay cited in some old maps, at present called Guanímar.

Rivers.—Nearly all retain their aboriginal names. Those mentioned by history in the 16th century are as follows : Manimaní, now Maniman; Marien, now Mariel; Baní, now Banes; Casiguaguas, now Chorrera or Almendares; Yumurí, that disembogues in the port of Yucayo (Matanzas); Mares, name given by Columbus to the Caonao-Grande; Luna, name given by Columbus, it is supposed, to the Jigüey; San Salvador, name given by Columbus to the river at whose mouth he first landed in the island, supposed to be the Maximo; Toa, at present written Toar by some, disemboguing north-west of Baracoa; Macaguanigua, name retained by one of the rivers that empty into Baracoa; Yumurí, that disembogues near Cape Maisí; Yara, which retains its name; Jobabo,

---

* Don José G. de Arboleya, in his Manual de la Isla de Cuba, offers a dissertation on the courses that the distinguished writer, Washington Irving, aided by an able and practical navigator, supposes Columbus followed along the coasts of Cuba on his first voyage. We regret that the reasons opposed by him to the opinion of Irving (and others adopting it, like Humboldt, Sagra, and Navarrete) do not convince us, and that we have no time to refute at length Señor Arboleya's opinion. We shall merely allude to his statement that we have adopted, without discussion or examination, Mr. Irving's judgment in the ancient chart published by us. We could not only prove our careful examination of Irving's opinion by what we wrote in 1836, but also that, not satisfied with the statements of books and maps, we undertook a voyage solely with the object of confirming the course steered by Columbus on his first voyage, embarking for the purpose in a government schooner, commanded by the lieutenant-colonel of the navy, Don Antonio Montojo (now harbor-master of Trinidad), and the results of which, together with views, topographical descriptions, etc., we intend to publish.

on whose banks gold used to be gathered: and in its vicinity is a rich copper mine worked by the conquerors; Rio de la Misa, name given by Columbus to the river at whose mouth he caused to be said the first mass in the island the 6th of July, 1494, supposed to be the Jatibonico del Sur; Táyabo or Guaurabo, near Trinidad; Arimao, on whose banks gold was found, and at its origin was a rich mine of gold and silver (the San Fernando mine, which in modern times has only produced good copper); Onicajinal, the name which, according to Gomara, was that of the river on whose banks the villa of San Cristóbal (now Havana) was originally founded, and supposed to be the Mayabeque or Güines; Caiguanabo, now San Diego, and Cuyaguateje, which retains its name.

Provinces.*—The provinces of the aborigines, hitherto proved, and which are mentioned by the old historians, are as follows, commencing on the west of the island: Guanahacabibes, on the peninsula formed by Cape San Antonio, and whose inhabitants were the most rustic, according to Diego Velasquez and the historian B. Diaz, which is strange, as they were the nearest to the civilized Mexican empire;† Guaniguanico, where the hacienda of that name is situated, near the Guadiana inlet; Marien, now Mariel, where the hacienda of that name was situated; Habana, which, doubtless, comprised the harbor of Matanzas; Hanámana, where is at present the hato called Hanábana; Macoriges, where the hacienda Macurijes is situated; Cubanacan (which signifies centre of Cuba), where there were gold-mines; Sabána or Sabaneque, where at present are Carahatas and San Juan de los Remedios, which used to be called Sabána; Jagua, around the port of that name, where gold was gathered; Guamuhaya, about where Trinidad is situated; Magon, on the south coast, near the mouth of Sasa river; Ornofai, near the mouth

---

* Until the publication of the author's ancient map and *Memoria justificativa*, modern historians (even Herrera, Casas, and others) only mentioned nine provinces, and some of those erroneously named. In his said works the existence of thirty provinces is established—a number which, by a strange coincidence, corresponds to the jurisdictions into which the island is at present divided. "It is surely an error," says Señor Poey, "to believe that the Indians occupied only the provinces of which we have notice; especially if by province we understand a district governed by a cacique. We modern investigators are limited to the provinces mentioned in the primitive histories, remaining ignorant in regard to the rest, doubtless as numerous in the central and western parts of the island as in the eastern, which was the most known at the beginning of the 16th century."

† This circumstance, the paucity of reptiles in Yucatan of the same species as those of the island, and especially the great dissimilarity between the Maya language used on said peninsula, and the Siboney or Lucay spoken by the islanders (of the first of which the author has consulted grammars and dictionaries), should be borne in mind by any one attempting to determine the epoch at which Cuba was separated from the American continent.

of the river Jatibonico del Sur; Camagüey, about where Puerto Principe is situated; Guáimaro, toward the present hacienda and community of that name; Cayaguayo, supposed to have lain between the provinces of Camagüey, Cueibá, and Maniabon; Cueibá, about the present hacienda Cueibá; Guacanayabo, where at present is situated the villa of Manzanillo; Macaca, where is now the hacienda of that name; Maniabon, near the hacienda of that name: Maguanos, near the place of the present hacienda Maguanos-Viejos; Bayamo, the site of the city of that name; Maiyé (Maibío?) and Guaimaya, supposed to have been between those of Bayamo, Boyuca, Barajagua, and Maniabon; Baní, near the present hacienda and port of Banes (east); Barajagua, site of the hacienda of that name; Boyuca, toward the west of the port of Cuba; Sagua, site of Sagua de Tánamo; Bayaquitirí, where at present are the haciendas Baiquerí, Baiquirí, and the port of Bairiquerí; Baracoa, site of the city of that name; Maisí, about the cape so called.

Communities.—Guaniguaníco, a town near the hacienda of that name; Mayanabo, now Marianao; Matamanó, now Batabanó; Guanabacoa, at present a villa, then an Indian town, where in 1554 it was ordered that the natives who were roving about the neighborhood should be gathered; Tarraco, an Indian town near Guanabacoa. San Cristóbal, the seventh villa founded by Diego Velasquez, the 25th of July, 1515; it was situated at the mouth of the Onicaginal River (Mayabeque, five leagues from Güines), soon after transferred to the mouth of the Casiguaguas (Chorrera), the site being known some time subsequently as Pueblo-Viejo), and about 1519 it was removed to the port called Carenas by Sebastian de Ocampo; the name of Habana, added to that of said villa, arose from its being situated in the Indian province of Habana. Yucayo, an Indian town, where it is supposed that the city of Matanzas was founded; Hanámana, now Hanábana; Carahatas (written Carahate by Las Casas), an Indian town near the present hacienda and port of that name; Caonao, a town near the port of Jagua, retaining the name. Camarreo or Canarreo, a town where Father Las Casas and his friend Pedro de la Renteria settled when Diego Velasquez had designated the sites of the villas he intended to found; according to tradition, it was situated where at present is the hacienda Las Auras, where Señor Lanier has found ancient earthenware and other articles that seem to confirm it. Trinidad, the third of the villas founded by Velasquez, established in 1514, where now is Casilda, and soon after removed to its present site. Sabána, an Indian town, where in 1545 was founded the villa of San Juan de los Remedios, also called El Cayo, from having been situated on a key previous to its removal to the present site. Santa Espiritu, fourth of the seven villas founded by Velasquez, established in

1514 on the extremity of the hacienda Minas, at the place called Pueblo-Viejo, where is a spot named Cayo de la Iglesia, because it was the site of the church then existing. According to tradition, the removal to the present locality of Santo Espiritu took place in 1522. Santa Maria, the fifth of Velasquez's seven villas, was founded in 1514 in the port named Del Principe by Columbus (now Nuevitas), near the place now known as Pueblo-Viejo, or Chorro de Lazaro Pinto; it was afterward translated to an Indian town called Caonao, and soon again to another populous one, called Camagüey; for which reasons this city, the most distant from the coast of any in the island, is termed a port, and hence, also, are the inhabitants called *Camagüeyanos*. Guáimaro, a a town which retains the name and position; Cueibá, a town on the hacienda now called Cueibá; Maniabon, Baní, and Barajagua, towns near the haciendas so called; Guacanayábo, a town and port corresponding to the situation of Manzanillo; Bayamo, a town where Velasquez founded the second villa, which he named San Salvador, because he was there delivered from the cacique Hatuey, and hence the present city is called San Salvador de Bayamo; Macáca, a town and port near the site of the present hacienda of that name, and was a place of considerable trade in the early times of the Conquest; Manicanao, a town where the famous Hernan Cortés was *encomendero*. Santiago, the sixth villa, was founded by Velasquez in June, 1515, in the western part of the port now known as Cuba, at the mouth of the river Paradas, so as to be near the del Cobre mines (for it was founded with the object of establishing a foundry); afterward, in consequence of the plague of ants and other insects, it was found necessary (as in the case of nearly all the other villas) to remove it to its present site; in 1522 it received the title of city, and was known as Santiago de Cuba, the addition being doubtless to distinguish it in those times from Jamaica, which was also called Santiago. Caney, a town where still exist some of the aborigines, though not of as pure race as at Santa Rosa and Tiguabos; Tiguabos, a town yet containing some of the indigenous race; Bayatiquerí, an Indian town. Baracoa, a town where in 1512 Diego Velasquez founded the first of the seven villas established by him in the island, calling it La Asuncion. In 1518 it became a city and bishopric, and was considered as the capital of the island until 1522, when the distinction and the bishopric passed to Santiago de Cuba. Maisí, a town on the site of the present hacienda of that name, in whose vicinity are vestiges of great monuments, skeletons, utensils, etc., of the aborigines.

HISTORY OF THE ISLAND.*

THE history of Cuba is divided into five epochs: the *first*, entitled DISCOVERY, which comprehends the period from the landing of Christopher Columbus to the beginning of the Conquest, or from 1492 to 1511; the *second*, entitled COLONIZATION, which comprehends the period from the beginning of the Conquest to the division of the island into two governments, or from 1511 to 1607; the *third*, entitled ORGANIZATION, which comprehends the period from the division into two governments to the siege and capture of Havana by the English, or from 1607 to 1762; the *fourth*, entitled CIVILIZATION, which comprehends the period from the siege and capture of Havana to the declaration of free commerce, or from 1762 to 1801; and the *fifth*, entitled PROSPERITY, which comprehends the period from 1801, continued to the present time.

First Epoch.—DISCOVERY: 1492-1511. The island was discovered previously to Hayti or St. Domingo, by Christopher Columbus, in the evening of the 27th of October, 1492. He landed on the following day at the mouth of the River Maximo, which he named Port San Salvador, entering through the strait which no doubt is therefore called Boca de las Carabelas, north of the harbor of Sabinal. He afterward surveyed the coast westward as far as Punta Yana, which he named Cabo Palmas, and, returning to the mouth of the River Caonao-Grande, which he named Rio de Mares, sent an embassy to the cacique of Camagüey (Puerto Principe), supposing him to be the Grand Khan of Tartary. After passing along the keys which he named Jardines del Rey, on the north coast, he steered toward Cabo Maisí, visiting the port of Nuevitas (which he named Puerto del Principe), and that of Baracoa, which he named Puerto Santo, following on to the island of Hayti or St. Domingo, which he discovered the 5th of December following, and named Española.

Columbus revisited the island on his second and fourth voyages, but not on the third. On his second voyage, coming from San Nicolas (in St. Domingo), he reconnoitred Cabo Maisí; then visited Guantánamo (which he named Puerto-Grande), and Cuba; and, steering south, discovered Jamaica, then returning to this island, and landing in the port of Macáca, whence he determined to reconnoitre the island on the south.

---

* This division of the present volume is a translation from De la Torre's *Elem. de Geog. e Hist. de la Isla de Cuba.* Havana, 1855.

His object being to determine whether it was an island or not, when he had arrived at the bay of Cortés, where the land curves southward, he became persuaded that it was a continent, and caused a certificate to be made to that effect by the notary he had on board. On his fourth voyage he touched at Cayo Piedras, in the Laberinto de las doce Leguas, which he had already visited on his second voyage; and subsequently at Trinidad and Macáca. Columbus died at Valladolid, in Spain, the 20th of May, 1506, aged about 70, and his remains were deposited in the Carthusian monastery of Seville, whence they were conveyed to the island of St. Domingo, and, in consequence of the revolution in that island, finally brought to this island in 1796, and deposited in the cathedral. It is at present intended to erect a suitable monument to his memory. Columbus died in the belief that the island was the eastern extremity of Asia, and it was not known to be an island until 1508, when Sebastian de Ocampo sailed round it by order of Nicolás de Ovando, governor of St. Domingo.

The origin of the Indians of Cuba is doubtful, but it is generally believed that they came over from Florida and the Yucayas,* and very few from Yucatan. According to some writers they numbered 200,000† at the time of the discovery, but others suppose much less, as it is known that in 1532 there were only 4 or 5,000.

The inhabitants of the centre especially were peaceful, and even timid; those of the province of Guanahacabibes coarse and rude; and those of the eastern part of the island were warlike, owing probably to the necessity of defending themselves from the frequent attacks of the cannibal Caribs.

Their religion is described as a superstitious idolatry. Their divinities were called *Semi* or *Vaganiona;* the devil, *Mabúya;* and their priests or soothsayers, *Behíques.* However, to the great astonishment of Columbus and his companions, the cacique of Ornofay, after the first service of mass performed in the island, manifested a belief in a Supreme Creator, in the immortality of the soul, and rewards and punishments in a future life. Their amusements were the *ureitos*, or dancing and singing parties, and the game of *batos*, or bat and ball, for which there was one or more squares in every town. They employed themselves chiefly in fishing, hunting, and agriculture. In their *conucos* or gardens they raised cotton, sweet potatoes, yuca (which they called *aje*), plantains, maize, pulse, sweet potatoes, etc.

---

* Bahama Islands.
† The aboriginal population of Porto Rico (one ninth the area of Cuba) was estimated at 600,000!!—(*Translator.*)

The Indians were called Siboneyes, and each province was governed by a cacique whose government was patriarchal. The nobles were termed *naitanos*, and the lower orders *naborias*. The caciques had the title of *matuseri* or highness; the nobles, that of *bahari* or lordship; and the plebeians were addressed as *guaxoti*, or you or thou. Their houses were built of the palm-tree, suited to withstand the hurricanes, and similar to those now called *bohios*. Some were of an oval form like those at present in Cubitas; others coniform, and termed *caneyes*; while those inhabited by the caciques were called *cancies*. The roofs were adorned with flowers, *cobos*, and *sibas*, or stones. No house was without a *hamaca* or bed, and some were furnished with seats called *dujos* or *duchos*, made of a block of wood shaped like an animal with eyes and ears of gold;* but the most general custom of the aborigines was to squat on their hams. Their shipping was limited to *canoas* or *cayucos*, by which they communicated with the neighboring land.

Second Epoch.—CONQUEST AND COLONIZATION : 1511-1607. The island was conquered by Diego Velasquez, native of Cuellar (Segovia), who was sent by Don Diego Colon, son of the Admiral Columbus, and Governor of St. Domingo. He sailed from Salvatierra de la Sabana, in St. Domingo, at the end of November, 1511, with four ships and 300 men, and landed in the port of Palmas, between Guantánamo and Puerto-Escondido. He was opposed by the valiant Hatuey, the cacique of Guajabá in Hayti, who with some of his vassals had taken refuge in the island on the occupation of Hayti by the Spaniards, but soon defeated him and condemned him to death at Bayamo. Velasquez then proceeded to distribute the territory in *encomiendas* (commanderies), in aid of which measure he founded the villa of Asuncion on the site called Baracoa by the Indians. He afterward founded Bayamo, and in 1514 Trinidad, Santo Espiritu, Santa Maria at the port named del Principe by Columbus; in 1515 Santiago de Cuba, and the 25th of July, same year, the Havana, at the mouth of the Mayabeque River. Havana was afterward transferred to the mouth of the River Chorrera, and subsequently to its present site, where, in 1519, the first mass was celebrated under a seiba tree, where at present is the monument of the *Templete*, erected to commemorate that ceremony. The villa or town of Santa Maria was founded at the port called del Principe by Columbus (now Nuevitas), near the bay of Guincho, but in consequence of the abundance of insects, and piratical invasions, it was transferred to the Indian town of Caonao, and finally to that of Camagüey—for which

---

* In 1775 one of these seats was in the possession of Doña Concepcion Guerra, in Bayamo, having belonged to the cacique of that province.

PHYSICAL, POLITICAL, AND INDUSTRIAL. 117

The following sovereigns have reigned in Spain since the discovery of Cuba: Ferdinand of Aragon and Isabel of Castile, styled the *Catholic sovereigns*, the discovery having been made under the auspices of the latter in 1492; Philip I. and Jane, who ascended the throne in 1506; Charles I. of Spain and V. of Germany, in 1516; Philip II., in 1556; Philip III., in 1598; Philip IV., in 1621; Charles II., in 1659; Philip V. (first time), in 1700: Louis I., in 1724; Philip V. (second time), in 1725; Ferdinand VI., in 1746; Charles III., in 1759; Charles IV., in 1788; Ferdinand VII., in 1808; and Isabel II., in 1833.

The governors of the island who have distinguished themselves, previous to Tacón, whose successors are yet living, are the following: the Marquis de la Torre, who instituted the police, and many material and ornamental improvements. The memorable Don Luis de las Casas, to whom beneficence and literature owe so much. Sr. Someruelos, who sustained the island in the midst of the stormy events of the Peninsula in the years '8 to '12; and Sr. Vives, who, with prudent and wise policy, protecting the natives, saved the island from following in the footsteps of the other Spanish-American possessions.

Among other public functionaries, the following have distinguished themselves: Bishop Compostela, who established various country curacies and charitable institutions. The memorable Espada y Landa, distinguished as the Mecænas and the friend of humanity in Cuba. The superintendents Don Alexandro Ramirez, ever to be remembered for the immense benefits due him by the island, the confirmation of property in the lands granted as *mercedes*, freedom of forests, abolition of the tobacco monopoly, etc.; and Don Francisco Arango, who merited a statue for having promoted free trade and the freedom of tobacco, which he constantly strove for until he obtained them; and Count Villanueva, whose enlightened financial administration has contributed to the aggrandizement of the island. The following individuals also deserve honorable mention: Don Martin Calvo de Arrieta, who established a fund to provide portions for young women. Don Francisco Carballo, who founded the celebrated school of Belen (almost the only educational institution in Havana until the end of last century); and Father Espit (known as *Padre Valencia*), missionary of Puerto Principe.

STATISTICS OF CUBA, 1853.

POPULATION OF THE ISLAND.

JURISDICTIONS.	Area sq. m.	Whites.	Free Col.	Slaves.	Total Pop.	Chief Towns.	Popula.
WESTERN DEPARTMENT.							
Pinar del Rio..	3,713	21,843	3,824	9,998	35,665	Pinar del Rio...	1,500
San Cristóbal...	905	11,578	1,923	6,548	20,049	San Cristóbal...	270
Bahia-Honda ..	762	4,124	621	5,494	10,239	Bahia-Honda...	570
Mariel	572	15,921	2,849	19,422	38,192	Guanajay	3,000
San Antonio ...	154	12,284	1,721	10,188	24,193	S. Antonio Abad	2,890
Habana	893	87,916	32,594	26,850	147,360	HABANA	125,905
Santiago	214	7,194	1,597	4,964	13,755	Santiago	2,274
Bejucál	191	10,817	1,746	7,938	20,501	Bejucál	2,264
Guanabacoa ...	166	10,721	3,273	4,322	18,316	Guanabacoa....	8,100
Rosario	309	11,764	2,841	5,428	20,033	Rosario	450
Güines	1,131	18,214	2,442	16,918	37,574	Güines.........	3,542
Jaruco	512	10,218	1,875	8,136	20,229	Jaruco	611
Matanzas	856	34,721	5,948	40,728	81,397	Matanzas.......	26,000
Cárdenas	1,262	27,521	3,824	55,016	86,361	Cárdenas.......	6,173
Sagua	1,464	14,534	1,173	10,001	25,708	Sagua la Grande	2,510
Cienfuegos	2,558	17,811	4,124	11,318	33,253	Cienfuegos	4,708
Santa Clara	1,345	25,592	8,528	5,301	39,421	Villa Clara	6,604
Trinidad	869	15,208	7,324	9,318	31,850	Trinidad	14,119
Remedios	2,439	15,149	3,821	4,012	22,982	Remedios	5,270
Santo Espíritu ..	3,819	24,321	6,394	6,816	37,532	Santo Espíritu ..	9,982
Total	24,133	397,451	98,442	268,717	764,610		
EASTERN DEPARTMENT.							
Puerto Príncipe	6,009	26,893	10,318	9,321	46,532	Puerto Principe.	26,648
Nuevitas	2,261	2,721	397	1,742	4,860	Nuevitas	820
Tunas	2,725	3,818	1,821	722	6,361	Tunas	2,004
Manzanillo	1,880	7,321	11,143	917	19,381	Manzanillo	3,050
Holguin	2,523	19,427	3,271	3,827	26,525	Holguin........	3,754
Bayamo	1,309	10,721	11,217	2,724	24,662	Bayamo........	5,875
Jiguaní	702	6,721	4,318	684	11,723	Jiguaní	950
Cuba	3,177	21,524	29,718	34,000	85,242	Cuba	24,253
Guantánamo ...	1,595	1,574	2,281	5,928	9,783	Guaso..........	863
Baracoa	1,464	3,817	3,721	1,842	9,381	Baracoa	2,400
Total	23,145	104,537	78,205	61,708	244,450		
Western Depart.	24,133	397,451	98,442	268,717	764,610	Habana.	
Eastern Depart.	23,145	104,537	78,205	61,708	244,450	Cuba.	
Grand Total .	47,278	501,988	176,647	330,425	1,009,060		

STATISTICS OF CUBA.   119

POPULATION—1775-1851.

Census.	White Persons.	Free Col. and Black.	Slaves.	Total.
1775	96,440	30,847	44,333	171,620
1791	—	......	—	272,140
1811 (estimate)	274,000	140,000	212,000	626,000
1817	290,021	115,691	225,268	630,980
1825 (estimate)	325,000	130,000	260,000	715,000
1827	311,051	106,494	286,942	704,487
1841	418,291	152,838	436,495	1,007,624
1846	425,767	149,226	323,759	898,752
1849	457,183	164,410	323,897	945,440
1853	501,988	136,647	330,425	1,009,060

Absolute and Relative Movement.

Years.							
1775-1791	Absolute incr.	100,520	Incr. per cent.	58.5	Annual incr. per cent.		8.7
1791-1811	"	" 358,860	"	" 130.0	"	" "	6.5
1811-1817	"	" 4,980	"	" 0.8	"	" "	0.1
1817-1825	"	" 54,020	"	" 13.8	"	" "	1.7
1825-1827	"	decr. 10,513	Decr.	" 1.5	" decr.	"	0.7
1827-1841	"	incr. 303,137	Incr.	" 43.1	" incr.	"	3.1
1841-1846	"	decr. 108,872	Decr.	" 10.2	" decr.	"	2.0
1846-1849	"	incr. 46,688	Incr.	" 5.2	" incr.	"	1.7
1849-1853	"	" 63,620	"	" 6.7	"	" "	1.7

TOWNS OF 1,500 INHABITANTS AND UPWARD.

Cities, etc.	Pop. 1841.	Pop. 1846.	Pop. 1853.
Habana	137,498	106,968	125,905
Puerto Principe	24,084	19,168	26,648
Matanzas	18,991	16,956	26.000
Cuba	24,753	26,738	24,253
Trinidad	12,718	13,222	14,119
Santo Espiritu	9,484	7,424	9,982
Guanabacoa	—	6,519	8.100
Villa Clara	6,132	5,887	6,604
Cárdenas	1,828	3,103	6,173
Bayamo	7,480	4,778	5,873
Remedios	4,313	4,106	5.270
Cienfuegos	2,487	4,324	4,708
Holguin	4,199	3,065	3,754
Güines	2,515	2,612	3.542
Manzanillo	3,299	3,780	3,050
Guanajay	—	—	3,000
San Antonio	—	—	2 890
Sagua	—	—	2.510
Baracoa	2,605	1,853	2,400
Santiago	—	—	2,274
Bejucál	—	—	2,264
Tunas	—	—	2.004
Pinar del Rio	—	—	1,500

RURAL ESTABLISHMENTS.*

JURISDICTIONS.	Haciendas.	Ingenios.	Cafetales.	Potreros.	Cacaguales.	Algodonales.	Sitios de Labor.	Estancias.	Vegas.	Colmenares.
WESTERN DEPARTMENT.										
Pinar del Rio	92	4	—	180	—	—	4	—	2,096	85
San Cristóbal	29	11	19	177	—	—	502	—	879	17
Bahia-Honda	20	28	7	87	—	—	130	19	89	64
Mariel	—	64	87	84	—	—	1,302	9	—	22
San Antonio	2	11	139	107	—	—	1,050	—	14	140
Habana	44	—	—	23	—	—	59	501	—	12
Santiago	—	21	28	111	—	—	402	79	—	10
Bejucál	2	23	88	68	—	—	200	721	—	33
Guanabacoa	—	7	—	29	—	—	402	—	4	—
Rosario	—	9	21	96	—	—	1,365	196	21	16
Güines	5	47	49	247	—	—	1,901	79	—	31
Jaruco	—	29	27	260	—	—	930	1	—	60
Matanzas	3	204	67	271	—	—	1,785	10	5	37
Cárdenas	15	229	38	190	—	—	1,758	5	—	7
Sagua	9	79	1	375	—	—	1,277	—	—	121
Cienfuegos	42	97	—	702	—	—	1,126	2	98	127
Santa Clara	12	79	—	203	—	—	1,524	300	65	132
Trinidad	33	40	24	338	—	—	460	164	193	42
Remedios	150	44	23	684	2	—	682	279	83	272
Santo Espíritu	597	41	2	—	—	—	310	379	172	170
Total	1,055	1,067	620	4,488	2	—	17,169	2,744	3,714	1,398
EASTERN DEPARTMENT.										
Puerto Principe	1,124	91	2	602	—	—	42	701	129	39
Nuevitas	97	16	—	29	—	—	—	102	14	13
Tunas	8	3	—	14	—	—	32	100	31	178
Manzanillo	307	29	—	18	—	2	898	624	8	—
Holguin	487	173	2	60	—	—	4,102	3,915	1,160	116
Bayamo	252	26	3	78	—	—	90	1,265	210	430
Jiguani	110	27	—	65	—	—	1	1,124	69	78
Cuba	133	112	510	111	2	—	739	403	2,418	21
Guantánamo	48	14	60	18	—	4	40	78	215	18
Baracoa	40	2	21	—	9	218	260	10	11	—
Total	2,606	493	598	695	11	224	6,204	8,322	4,265	886
Western Depart.	1,055	1,067	620	4,488	2	—	17,169	2,744	3,714	1,398
Eastern Depart.	2,606	493	598	695	11	224	6,204	8,322	4,265	886
Grand Total	3,661	1,560	1,218	5,128	13	224	23,373	11,066	7,979	2,284

* For explanation of the provincial terms under this head refer to page 57.

reason this mediterranean city is named Santa Maria del Puerto del Principe, and its inhabitants are termed *Camagüeyanos.*.

San Juan de los Remedios was founded in 1545, at a town called Sabána, situated on a key, for which reason the term *cayo* is applied to the present town.

Guanabacoa was an Indian town where, in 1554, the Indians wandering about the country were ordered to reside, and which in 1743 obtained the title of villa. The other remarkable event during the administration of Velasquez was the erection of Baracoa into a city and bishopric in 1518, as the first town of the island, these distinctions being transferred to Santiago de Cuba in 1522. Velasquez died in 1524, in which year negroes were introduced to aid the Indians in their labors. The Spaniards then employed themselves chiefly in working the Cobre, Escambray, Jobabo and other mines, which, up to 1534, had yielded $260,000 of gold; in cultivating the soil and raising cattle.

The first government concession for an *ingenio*, or sugar estate, was made in 1535, and in the same year another was authorized near the Cerro (Havana); but the first known to have been established were—one at Guaicanamá (now Regla) in 1598, and others at Cidra and Canímar in 1669.

The sugar-cane was first introduced by Columbus from the Canaries into St. Domingo, on his second voyage, of the kind called *caña criolla*, or *de la tierra*. That of Otaheite was introduced in 1795, by Don Francisco Arango. In 1826 the striped and crystalline were brought from New Orleans; the purple, native of Java, having been introduced previously.

The territory of the island was at first distributed by the governors in assignments to the colonists, such as Cortés, las Casas, Vasco Porcayo, etc.; but the greater part in grants, under the denomination of *mercedes*, by the corporations of the towns. These *mercedes* were obtained on solicitation, the use of the land only being granted, and their extent was two leagues radius for *hatos* and *haciendas* for cattle breeding, and one league radius for *sitios* or *corrales*, or estates for raising swine, whence arose the circular form of such *hatos* and *corrales*. The first *merced* was granted for the *hacienda* Manicarágua in 1536, and farther grants were prohibited in 1729.

The first invasion of pirates, called buccaneers or fillibusters,* took place in 1538, when they reduced Havana to ashes. Governor Hernando de Soto went to assist the besieged on this occasion, leaving, as his lieu-

---

* From *fly-boat:* and buccaneer, from *boucan*, to make jerked beef, which they did, of the cattle obtained in their excursions.

tenant in Cuba, his wife, Doña Inés de Bobadilla, in conjunction with Juan de Rojas. He immediately after commenced to build the castle De la Fuerza, which he finished in 1544, thereby conferring more importance on the port of Havana, and inducing vessels bound for Mexico to touch there. The island was constituted a captain-generalship in 1589, when the authority was vested in Field-marshal Juan de Tejeda.

The first sugar-cane plantations of any note were established in the vicinity of Havana in 1580. Of the cultivation of tobacco in the Vuelta-Abajo, the earliest record is in 1719, a great deal being raised at Santiago de las Vegas about the middle of the last century.

The pirates successively invaded Puerto Principe, Trinidad, San Juan de los Remedios, Manzanillo, and Cuba. In the attack on Manzanillo in 1604, the pirate chief, Giron, passed to the town of Yara, and took prisoner Bishop Fray Juan de las Cabezas Altamirano, who was afterward ransomed with 200 ducats, hides, and other goods, and his detention revenged by the Bayamese, who captured the pirate in an ambush, and executed him.

Third Epoch.—ORGANIZATION : 1607-1762. This period was commenced by the division of the island into two governments. Piratical invasions continued, the most remarkable being that of Olonois, who murdered 90 men sent out in a vessel against him; Morgan, who sacked Puerto Principe; and the invasion by Lord Windsor, who, in 1662 (a century before the capture of Havana by the British), attacked Santiago de Cuba, destroying the sumptuous edifice called Alto de Osuna, and blowing up the Morro Castle; and finally, that of Vernon, who landed in the harbor of Guantánamo (which he named Cumberland), in 1741, and attempting to attack Cuba, was repulsed, and forced to re-embark with great loss. In 1693 Matanzas was founded on the site of the Indian town of Yucayo, and for the purpose 30 families were brought from the Canary Islands, during the governorship of Manzaneda. In 1722 shipbuilding for war purposes was commenced at Havana, upward of 125 ships having been built at the end of that century, viz., 6 three-deckers (2 of 120 guns each); 21 ships of 70 to 80 guns; 26 of 50 to 60; 14 frigates of 30 to 40; and 58 smaller vessels. In 1728 the first coffee estate was established in the district of Ubajay, with the seed brought from St. Domingo by Don José Gelabert, for the purpose of making rum. This plant was not, however, extensively cultivated till the end of the last century, when the French emigrants from St. Domingo settled in the island.

Printing was introduced into Cuba in 1695, and perhaps earlier into Havana. The Royal University was also founded during this epoch.

PHYSICAL, POLITICAL, AND INDUSTRIAL. 115

Fourth Epoch.—CIVILIZATION : 1762-1801. The social progress of the island dates chiefly from the capture of Havana by the British, when the supreme government recognized the importance of the territory. The said siege and capture of Havana occurred in 1762, in the reign of Charles III., and during the captain-generalship of Don Juan del Prado y Portocarrero. The 6th of June of that year a British squadron composed of some 200 vessels (including 24 ships of the line and 24 frigates) and 18,000 men, under Admiral Sir George Pocoeke, and conveying 14,000 troops under the Earl of Albemarle, laid siege to the city. Notwithstanding the unprepared state of the place, and the small force defending it (about 4,000 troops), the invaders met with a heroic resistance, especially from the Morro Castle, which was finally taken by storm, through a breach made by the enemy, the 30th of July. The British took possession of the place the 14th of August, under capitulation, and on the following day the nine Spanish ships in port were delivered to them, three others (Asia, Neptuno, and Europa) having been sunk at the mouth of the port to close it. The possession of the invaders, however, did not extend farther than Matanzas and Mariel. Among the Spaniards who distinguished themselves on this occasion, history makes especial mention of Don Luis Vicente Velasco, colonel in the navy and governor of the Morro, who valiantly defended his post until struck down by a bullet in the chest, and expired 24 hours after with the fortitude of a hero ; his lieutenant, Marquez Gonzales, who lost his life in the action ; Don Luis Aguilar and Don Rafael de Cárdenas, who defended the fort of Chorrera until commanded to abandon it, and then captured the heights of Taganana, which were fortified by the enemy ; Don Alejandro Arroyo, Don Francisco del Corral and Don Manuel Frias, who boldly assaulted the trenches of La Cabaña ; Chacon, Lujan, Zaldivar, Ruiz (who perished in an assault), and the countryman from Guanabacoa, Don José Antonio Gomez (known as Pepe Antonio), who, after performing prodigies of valor, perished miserably. The British continued in possession only a year, as, in consequence of the treaty of peace concluded at Paris between England, France, and Spain, the 10th of February, 1763, it was restored to Spain in exchange for the Floridas ; Count de Ricla, commissioned from Spain to take possion, arriving the 30th of July following, bringing 2,000 troops under General the Count O'Reilly.

During this period there was some immigration from Florida, and (in 1795) from St. Domingo, and mostly French ; the former introducing the Castilian bee, producing white wax, and the latter extending the cultivation of coffee. The Intendancy and the Commandancy of Marine were instituted ; the island was divided into two bishoprics, and in 1800 the

Royal Court of Judicature (*Audiencia*) was transferred from St. Domingo to Puerto Principe, where it continued until 1853. Improvements were made in the ecclesiastical department and the police regulations; the streets were named and lighted, and houses numbered; theatres and public walks were established; newspapers* and books were printed; economical societies, public libraries, almshouses, and asylums, and the Junta de Fomento (formerly Consulado) were instituted; scientific exploring expeditions through the island were undertaken, steam-engines introduced, etc.

Fifth Epoch.—Prosperity: since 1801.—During this period the island has increased in wealth and importance to such a degree that it takes a very prominent position among the countries of the world. Its progress is chiefly due to free trade; initiated in 1778, and extended from the commencement of the present century. The reverberatory apparatus for making sugar was introduced in 1801. The archbishopric and a great number of curacies were established. Vaccination introduced by Doña Maria Bustamente, who brought an inoculated infant from Porto Rico in 1804. The arrival of a multitude of emigrants from the dissenting Spanish-American countries. The large donations made by the inhabitants to Spain during the French invasion. The declaration of freedom of forests and plantations in 1815. The monopoly of tobacco abolished, and its cultivation, sale, and trade declared free. Slave trade abolished in 1817. Freedom to demolish *hatos* and *corrales*. Confirmation of grants made under the name of *mercedes*, 1819. The first steamboat established in the same year. Philharmonic societies instituted. Arrival of emigrants from Florida, in consequence of its final surrender by Spain. Several conspiracies and invasions in 1823–24 were smothered and defeated, the same as more recent ones. The publication of statistical returns, and a large topographical chart of the island. Copper mining extended. First appearance of cholera in 1833 (and subsequently in 1850). Excision in Cuba, 1836. The first line of railway (from Havana to Bejucál), in 1837. The establishment of a junta to propose especial laws for the island. The installation of the Real Audiencia Pretorial in 1839. The destructive hurricanes of October, 1844 and 1846. Gas light introduced in 1846. Electric telegraph, 1852.

Previous to free trade being declared, the expenses of the island were chiefly defrayed by the *situados* received from Mexico, while at present, notwithstanding the vast increase of the former, the revenue of the island affords a surplus of about $4,000,000.

---

* The first periodical was published in 1782, under the name of *Gaceta de la Habana*, and in 1793 the *Papel Periodico*, afterward called *Aviso*, and ultimately *Diario*.

STATISTICS OF CUBA. 121

DISTRIBUTION OF LAND—IN CABALLERIAS.*

JURISDICTIONS.	Under Cultivation.	Artificial Pasturage.	Natural Pasturage.	Mountains, Forests, etc.	Barren Land.	Grand Total.
WESTERN DEPARTMENT.						
Pinar del Rio..........	1,083	2,272	17,317	24,770	26,536	71,978
San Cristóbal	968	190	5,256	5,845	5,274	17,533
Bahia-Honda	170	260	219	8,391	5,724	14,764
Mariel	1,938	231	1,932	2,608	4,364	11.073
San Antonio	1,514	122	652	295	416	2,999
Habana, incl. I. de Pinos	5,355	150	7,842	967	2,988	17,302
Santiago	214	203	346	2,833	556	4,152
Bejucál................	1,608	67	854	290	852	3,691
Guanabacoa	308	94	674	656	1,497	3,229
Rosario	481	85	1,411	1,401	2.620	5,998
Güines	3,215	309	3,273	9,665	5,454	21,916
Jaruco	127	88	161	3,992	5,552	9,920
Matanzas..............	4,450	950	4,050	2,425	4,735	16,610
Cárdenas..............	7,049	1,325	7,469	1,082	7,529	24,454
Sagua	1,703	197	3,266	16,888	6,322	28,376
Cienfuegos	1,484	2,163	25,967	14,959	5.027	49,600
Villa Clara	767	514	14,733	6,150	3,855	26,069
Trinidad	782	1,529	1,543	5,325	7,662	16,841
Remedios	412	1,674	1,748	22,340	21,119	47,293
Santo Espiritu	470	2,740	3,259	43,529	24,056	74,054
Total................	34,098	15,183	102,022	174,418	142,138	467,859
EASTERN DEPARTMENT.						
Puerto Principe........	763	658	3,970	45,399	65,713	116,503
Nuevitas	172	67	78	40,502	3,014	43,833
Tunas.:...............	188	50	10,356	25,636	16,600	52,830
Manzanillo	260	1,248	13,401	3,232	8,620	26.761
Holguin...............	989	94	2,574	27,600	17,651	48,908
Bayamo...............	744	824	4,493	13,857	5,459	25,377
Jiguaní	394	50	1,194	5.897	6,076	13,611
Cuba..................	8,399	928	7,780	15,891	28,598	61,596
Guantánamo	602	1,118	2,004	17,765	9,424	30,913
Baracoa	1,963	121	1,376	6,802	18,114	28,376
Total................	14,474	5,158	47,226	202,584	179,269	448,711
Western Department...	34,098	15,183	102,022	174,418	142,138	467,859
Eastern Department ...	14,474	5.158	47,226	202.584	179,269	448,711
Grand Total	48,572	20,341	149,248	377,002	321,407	916,570

* The caballeria is equal to about 33 acres.

STATISTICS OF CUBA.

CHIEF AGRICULTURAL PRODUCTS IN 1852.

JURISDICTIONS.	Sugar, Arrobas.	Molasses, Puncheons.	Rum. Pipes.	Coffee, Arrobas.	Wax, Arrobas.	Honey, Barrels.	Tobacco, Cargas.
WESTERN DEPARTMENT.							
Pinar del Rio	41,001	200	260	2,907	1,427	497	49,702
San Cristóbal	186,900	14,821	960	29,508	1,321	1,601	10,324
Babia-Honda	460,428	4,881	1,500	2,801	326	370	1,120
Mariel	1,198,902	48,904	3,721	41,804	800	793	10,801
San Antonio	207,428	2,200	1,060	161,724	480	1,980	1,200
Habana	—	—	—	80	24,128	14	12
Santiago	160,876	4,100	260	113,524	290	381	70
Bejucál	130,996	1,900	892	70,965	290	899	500
Guanabacoa	77.853	973	—	—	80	15	—
Rosario	77,548	1,500	120	27,974	700	131	2.700
Güines	975,876	7,224	1,600	27,524	900	824	971
Jaruco	540,724	11,500	450	50,201	399	1,880	600
Matanzas	5,300,081	33,818	2,164	40,829	700	1,500	270
Cárdenas	8,871,302	60,800	11,001	16,124	2,400	480	1,100
Sagua	2,987,524	21,600	1,784	467	1,077	970	3,001
Cienfuegos	1,800,024	21,310	890	—	1,312	1,090	742
Santa Clara	506,821	5,825	524	870	1,519	5,090	16,351
Trinidad	880,476	9,724	570	42,924	810	1,400	8,500
Remedios	520,481	4,074	875	4,784	3,288	5,347	5,994
Santo Espiritu	472,528	4,348	1,180	4,309	7,505	16,432	4,449
Total	25,397,167	258,204	29,901	639,268	49,602	42,794	113,407
EASTERN DEPARTMENT.							
Puerto Principe	180,427	1,600	1,924	1,012	8,987	22,976	4,789
Nuevitas	313,521	970	40	—	374	1,073	290
Tunas	4,329	195	92	—	900	1,894	90
Manzanillo	5,700	1,349	308	684	2,998	1,724	4,191
Holguin	304,728	1,897	1,819	480	4,485	33,794	14,788
Bayamo	82,824	1,100	290	22,530	3,428	1,228	3,428
Jiguani	2,520	6	20	—	1,500	370	2,800
Cuba	2,785,426	1,784	4,727	396,180	629	♦100	78,597
Guantánamo	137,924	—	780	96,878	1,600	62	800
Baracoa	70	80	10	9,821	400	160	2,345
Total	3,767,469	8,981	9,510	527,635	25,301	63,381	108,618
Western Department	25,397,167	258,204	29.901	639,268	49,602	42,794	113,407
Eastern Department	3,767,469	8,981	9,510	527,635	25,301	63,381	108,618
Grand Total	29,165,236	267,185	39,411	1,166,903	74,903	106,175	222,020

COPPER.—In 1849 the four principal copper mines of the Del Cobre district produced 50,592 tons of ore, and in 1852 they produced only 17,117 tons. Nuevitas in 1852 exported 51 tons of that ore; and in the present year, 1853, the mines of Vuelta-Abajo are producing considerable quantities.

STATISTICS OF CUBA.

EXPORTATION BY THE AUTHORIZED PORTS OF THE ISLAND IN 1851.

AUTHORIZED PORTS.	Rum, Pipes.	Cotton, Bales.	Sugar, Boxes.	Coffee, Arrobas.	Wax, Arrobas.	Timber, Value.	Honey, Value.	Molasses, Puncheons.	Copper Ore, Quintals.	Tobacco, Pounds.	Cigars, Thousands.	Cocoa, Arrobas.	Ox-Horns.
Habana	5,801	80	849,918	150,253	49,666	$69,596	$23,832	44,439	3,360	4,193,569	261,989	1,862	145,482
Matanzas	1,293	—	337,862	14,505	—	1,491	4,085	86,525	—	288,826	1,495	—	—
Cardenas	—	—	40,707	—	134	—	792	97,743	—	—	57	—	—
Mariel	—	—	—	—	—	—	—	9,801	—	—	—	—	—
Trinidad	—	—	8,882	700	—	5,507	6,697	25,650	—	18,350	126	—	—
Cienfuegos	224	—	77,500	—	—	34,685	9,863	21,750	—	—	23	—	—
Nuevitas	80	—	4,969	5	2,806	43,556	7,350	7,776	641	—	1,352	18	11,200
Sagua	—	—	81,250	—	—	—	322	12,593	—	700	49	—	—
Remedios	—	—	13,003	—	—	—	3,018	27,727	—	8,523	60	—	—
Santa Cruz	—	—	588	—	—	20,428	2,043	945	—	22,525	—	—	—
Santo Espiritu	—	—	2,430	608	48	7,299	12	—	—	—	2	—	—
Cuba	1,842	441	58,190	455,222	4,145	44,654	1,086	1,777	428,880	1,488,923	3,115	5,159	2,400
Jibara	2	—	556	130	—	50	492	1,568	—	2,240,181	190	—	—
Manzanillo	13	—	8	2	598	163,870	5,400	3,363	—	179,781	463	—	—
Baracoa	14	—	83	3,657	56	4,070	178	12	—	1,055,265	1,856	—	—
Guantánamo	—	—	—	—	—	—	—	—	—	—	—	—	—
Total	9,221	521	1,549,898	625,118	57,453	$395,010	$62,604	341,594	432,882	9,316,593	270,313	7,039	159,082

STATEMENT OF NAVIGATION, COMMERCIAL MOVEMENT, AND CUSTOMS REVENUE IN 1851.

AUTHORIZED PORTS.	NAVIGATION.			COMMERCIAL MOVEMENT.			CUSTOMS DUTIES.		
	Vessels Entered. Number.	Tonnage.	Vessels Cleared.	Value of Imports.	Value of Exports.	Total.	Imports.	Exports.	Total.
Habana	1,749	591,572	1,622	$25,519,146	$16,577,001	$42,096,147	$4,776,571	$1,020,905	$5,797,476
Matanzas	499	100,076	578	1,889,478	5,373,370	7,262,848	568,136	305,088	873,274
Cárdenas	418	81,454	414	638,582	1,299,755	1,938,337	187,638	39,277	225,915
Mariel	33	5,576	—	3,527	7,350	10,876	1,000	—	1,000
Trinidad	197	38,392	188	706,987	1,608,017	2,814,004	181,197	74,415	255,612
Cienfuegos	266	51,102	230	571,403	1,273,368	1,844,771	179,754	73,900	253,654
Nuevitas	52	10,132	52	162,115	206,512	368,627	39,760	10,886	50,646
Sagua	129	23,779	129	128,221	1,217,108	1,345,329	64,976	72,874	137,850
Remedios	46	6,648	47	53,129	284,192	337,321	24,848	23,974	48,822
Santa Cruz	19	4,007	20	9,569	54,220	63,789	7,847	2,359	10,136
Santo Espiritu	11	1,358	11	29,834	42,206	71,590	8,129	2,972	11,101
Cuba	814	60,146	811	2,186,988	2,631,411	4,818,399	530,658	108,024	638,652
Jibara	37	4,306	34	233,734	300,171	533,905	36,463	32,931	70,394
Manzanillo	65	15,301	65	162,974	254,266	417,245	55,548	16,388	72,436
Baracoa	34	4,039	31	68,188	170,410	238,598	16,450	9,280	25,780
Guantánamo	1	207	1	2,320	—	2,320	310	181	491
Total	8,865	998,090	3,735	$32,315,145	$31,349,357	$63,665,102	$6,678,535	$1,793,984	$8,472,819

STATISTICS OF CUBA.

QUANTITY OF SUGAR EXPORTED, 1791-1850.

Years.	Arrobas.	Years.	Arrobas.	Years.	Arrobas.	Years.	Arrobas.
1791	1.360.224	1806	2,618.296	1821	4.348,840	1836	8.395.966
1792	1,165.664	1807	3,014,488	1822	4.910,856	1837	9.060,053
1793	1,347.520	1808	2,120,136	1823	5.781,682	1838	10.417,683
1794	2.458.064	1809	4,091,112	1824	4.986,264	1839	9.505.214
1795	1,241,128	1810	3.267.168	1825	4.498,939	1840	12.863.856
1796	2,040,120	1811	2,689.776	1826	6.287,390	1841	13.272.912
1797	2,003,192	1812	2.144,240	1827	5 878.924	1842	13.082.288
1798	2,272.008	1813	3,018.704	1828	5.967.066	1843	14,225.660
1799	2.768,768	1814	3.060.532	1829	6,588.428	1844	16,153.052
1800	2,387.688	1815	3.530.584	1830	7,868.881	1845	7,604,580
1801	2,671,592	1816	3.385.928	1831	7,133,381	1846	15.803.884
1802	3,384.600	1817	3.569 280	1832	7.588 413	1847	20.896 976
1803	2,642,824	1818	3.592.184	1833	7,624,553	1848	19.659.488
1804	3,217,416	1819	3.494,190	1834	8.408,281	1849	17,798,144
1805	2,906,838	1820	3,947,624	1835	8,718,300	1850	19,993.808

Quinquennial Average.

Quinquennial Periods.	Arrobas.	Quinquennial Periods.	Arrobas.	Quinquennial Periods.	Arrobas.
1791-1795	1,514.520	1811-1815	2,898.751	1831-1835	7.893.575
1796-1800	2,293.855	1816-1820	3,611,641	1836-1840	10,148.555
1801-1805	2.964,654	1821-1825	4.905,316	1841-1845	12,567.698
1806-1810	3,020,240	1826-1830	6,508,187	1846-1850	18,690,460

RUM, COFFEE, TOBACCO, ETC., EXPORTED 1826-1850.

Years.	Rum, Pipas.	Molasses, Bocoyes.	Coffee, Arrobas.	Wax, Arrobas.	Tobacco, Arrobas.	Cigars, Libras.
1826	2.597	68,880	1.773,798	22,918	79,591	197,194
1827	2,457	74.083	2.001.584	22,403	79,106	167.362
1828	2.864	86 891	1.284,088	21,404	70,031	210,335
1829	4.518	63,537	1.736.258	23,482	125.502	243.443
1830	5.594	66,218	1.798.598	38.740	160,858	407,153
1831	3,838	83.001	2.130.582	29.850	117.454	331.483
1832	3,423	100.178	2.048,890	30.203	76,430	448.128
1833	3.227	95,768	2.566,859	41.536	92,476	617.713
1834	3.648	104.218	1,817.315	35.258	87,154	616.020
1835	5,815	109.233	1,416.015	31,064	125,303	346,675
1836	3,888	109,549	1.610,441	28.259	228,519	518.443
1837	8,450	114.975	2.133.568	39.264	179,508	792.438
1838	5,408	134.802	1.550.341	28,296	194.799	916 466
1839	8,219	136.447	1.950 309	39.315	204,947	874,258
1840	10.209	146.464	2,143.574	26.132	169.671	849.824
1841	11,302	181.890	1,285,006	32,624	230,808	850.856
1842	10.227	119.188	1.998.816	33,884	287.713	751 445
1843	18,810	191.093	1.631.782	48.101	230,308	1,289.985
1844	6,326	172,431	1,240,032	34,276	287,713	792.525
1845	4.120	121.322	559.322	39.251	288,329	1,022.525
1846	9,082	203.597	817.662	41.716	353.041	766.782
1847	19,432	252.840	932,154	54,995	372,780	1,224,060
1848	16.339	228.726	694.137	50,110	251,025	807.400
1849	11.640	246.570	877,137	35,091	160,765	618.600
1850	11,825	269,044	520,134	58,194	319,125	1,063,200

Quinquennial Average.

Quinquennial Periods.	Rum, Pipas.	Molasses, Bocoyes.	Coffee, Arrobas.	Wax, Arrobas.	Tobacco, Arrobas.	Cigars, Libras.
1826-1830	3.606	71.921	1.718.865	25 789	102.915	245.097
1831-1835	3.991	98,478	1.995.832	33 582	99,768	471.993
1836-1840	6.285	128,447	1.877.444	32,253	195.487	790.285
1841-1845	9.157	147.074	1.392,997	37,407	244.872	941.467
1846-1850	13,653	240,155	768.244	48,141	291,347	896,008

COPPER EXPORTED—1841-1850.

Years.	Quintals.	Years.	Quintals.
1841	693,060	1846	635,654
1842	784,971	1847	565,495
1843	768,650	1848	656,491
1844	2,003,587	1849	583,310
1845	869,922	1850	552,283
Quinquennial average	624,038	Quinquennial average	598,647

VALUE OF COMMERCE WITH FOREIGN NATIONS—1850-1853.

IMPORTATION ON SPANISH VESSELS.

Countries.	1850.	1851.	1852.	1853.
United States	$40,971	$43,353	$295,935	$15,686
England	4,073,892	5,105,634	4,272,813	4,993,511
France	1,196,526	1,161,604	1,716,301	1,730,350
Germany	1,790,066	1,584,043	1,010,631	934,984
Spanish America	1,638,746	2,339,860	1,750,103	1,564,029

IMPORTATION ON FOREIGN VESSELS.

Countries.	1850.	1851.	1852.	1853.
United States	$6,612,289	$8,104,423	$6,255,350	$6,784,045
England	2,043,776	2,269,323	1,365,910	1,202,409
France	551,053	576,764	487.053	446,862
Germany	317,227	269,582	188,371	180,955
Spanish America	302,918	420,437	894,515	116,457

EXPORTATION ON SPANISH VESSELS.

Countries.	1850.	1851.	1852.	1853.
United States	$84,631	$32,774	$42,785	$60,805
England	722,145	1,048,067	1,044,927	1,713,505
France	450,139	624,126	528,856	436,140
Germany	674,045	804,512	610.886	655,786
Spanish America	516,683	915,940	580,074	454,129

EXPORTATION ON FOREIGN VESSELS.

Countries.	1850.	1851.	1852.	1853.
United States	$8,274,621	$13,190,080	$12,033,623	$12,074.290
England	6.338,921	11,829	4,441,749	6,709,330
France	1,412,402	889,042	984.512	2,857,248
Germany	1,197,474	1,487.708	1,079.279	818.232
Spanish America	60 554	131,128	221,085	60,702

STATISTICS OF CUBA. 127

COMMERCIAL MOVEMENT—1826-1850.

Quinquennial Periods.	Average Annual Value of Imports.	Average Annual Value of Exports.	Aver. Annual Value of Total Commerce.
1826-1830	$15.412,689	$12,717,929	$28,130,618
1831-1835	16,756,448	12,887,339	29,643,787
1836-1840	21,662,766	18,503,648	40,166,414
1841-1845	22,472,855	24.099,646	46,572,001
1846-1850	27,150,754	24,828,988	51,979,742
1851	32,315,145	31,349,357	63,665,102

REVENUE OF THE ISLAND—1826-1850.

	MARITIME REVENUE.			INTERNAL REVENUE.
Year.	Imports.	Exports.	Total.	Total.
1826	$3,782,409	$901,343	$4,683,753	$2,414,182
1827	4,412.963	1,246.916	5,659,879	2,810,094
1828	4,194,495	1,114,641	5,309.136	3,777,270
1829	3,938,596	1.255.371	5,193.967	3,948.642
1830	3,636,716	1,390,379	5,027,095	3.945,452
1831	3,932,505	862,959	4,795,465	3,501,739
1832	3,880,103	912.074	4,792,179	3,645.228
1833	4.208,706	1,026,664	5,235.371	3,660.185
1834	4,405,314	692,974	5,098,288	3,847.446
1835	4,791,777	634.256	5,426,033	3,371,140
1836	5,017,217	726,576	5,743,793	3,523,472
1837	4,997,780	811.995	5,809.775	3,027.390
1838	5,246,008	852.246	6,098.254	3,574.459
1839	6,113,508	1,249,570	7,363,078	3.841,355
1840	5,951,801	1,435,696	7,387,499	4,118.804
1841	5,943,819	1.322.644	7,266,464	3,848,881
1842	6.005,683	1,377,714	7,383 346	4,288.626
1843	5,396,339	1,590,677	6,987,017	3.407,040
1844	6,020,403	1,140,228	7.160 631	3,329.621
1845	5.396,416	574,831	5,970,748	3,221,329
1846	5,413,422	739.379	6.152.802	4,987.976
1847	6,601,233	893,094	7.494,331	5,314 891
1848	6,174,533	709,325	6,883,858	6,038,715
1849	5,844,788	584.477	6,429,260	6,235,068
1850	5,964,147	757,103	6,721,260	5,527,462

Quinquennial Average.

Quinquennial Periods.	Imports.	Exports.	Total.	Internal.
1826-1830	$3,938,086	$1,181,730	$5,174,766	$3,379,128
1831-1835	4,243,681	825,786	5,069,467	3,605.149
1836-1840	5,465,263	1,015,216	6,480,480	3,617,096
1841-1845	5,752,522	1,201,119	6,953,641	3,619,099
1846-1850	5,999,624	736,675	6 736,300	5,620.720

APPENDIX.

1st. According to the general trade returns of Spain for 1849 and 1850, the mercantile movement of the entire peninsula in 1850 amounted to $59,295,478, exclusive of bonded goods amounting to $2,189,723, but including the Balearic and Canary Islands. Of that sum, $34,606,544 was in imports and $24,688,934 in exports; and $47,949,643 in foreign trade, and $11,345,835 in trade with its ultramarine possessions. The foreign importation amounted to $29,033,807, and the exportation to $18,915,836. Of the trade with the distant possessions, the importation was $5,572,737, and the exportation $5,773,098, being a total of $11,345,834, of which $9,658,464 corresponds to Cuba, $909,923 to Porto Rico, and $777,448 to the Philippine Islands; consequently Cuba alone supports nearly the whole of this trade, which may be divided thus:

	Imports.	Exports.	Total.
Cuba	$4,587,897	$5,120,567	$9,658.464
Porto Rico	504,618	405,305	909.923
Philippines	530,222	247,226	777,448
Total	$5,572,737	$5,773,098	$11,395,835

The comparison of the returns of 1850 with those of 1849 show a decrease in the imports from Cuba and Porto Rico, and an increase in the exports.

The total amount of trade of the Peninsula of Spain and adjacent islands is as follows:

	Imports.	Exports.	Total.
Under Spanish flag	$29,193,220	$10,818,211	$40,011,431
Under foreign flag	3,700,969	11,520,780	15.221.749
By land	1,712,355	2,349,943	4,062,298
Total	$34,606,544	$24,688,934	$59,295,478

The total estimated expenditure of the nation for 1853 amounted to $61,414,826, and the revenue to $61,629,876, of which $2,222,150 was to be contributed by Cuba, $300,000 by Porto Rico, and $400,000 by the Philippine Islands.

APPENDIX.

2d. Statement of production and consumption of cane-sugar, coffee, and tobacco on the globe.(a)

Producers.	Sugar.	Coffee.	Tobacco.
Cuba (1852)	6,340,554	184,800	269,000
Porto Rico (1852)	1,000,000	124,600	88,500
St. Domingo	—	375,000	40,000
British West Indies (1851)(b)	3,859,214	—	—
British East Indies (1851)	1,763,867	—	—
Mauritius (1851)	1,108,388	—	—
Martinique (1851)	127,828	—	—
Guadaloupe (1851)	52,100	—	—
Dutch Guiana (1846)	300,000	—	—
St. Eustatia	500	—	—
Curacoa	375,000 ?	—	—
French and Dutch possessions in America(c)	—	100,000	—
Danish W. I. (St. Thomas, St. Croix, and St. John)	24,000 ?	—	—
Brazil(d)	2,000,000	3,139,240	—
Venezuela	—	400,000	—
United States (1850)*(e)	2,441,093	—	(f)1,997,000
Mexican States (1844)	450,000	—	—
Spanish Peninsula (1849)	10,000	—	—
Philippine Islands	125,000	81,250	150,000
Bourbon Island	425,512	—	—
Java	100,000	1,250,000	—
Sumatra	—	50,000	—
Sandwich Islands (1852)	52,000	—	—
China, Siam, etc., in Asia	500,000	—	—
Ceylon	—	375,000	—
Celebes	—	22,500	—
Malabar	—	47,500	—
Arabia	—	45,000	—
Hindostan	—	40,000	—
France(g)	—	—	262,500
Switzerland	—	—	2,750
Pontifical States	—	—	17,500
Sardinia	—	—	3,000
Naples	—	—	15,000
Austria and her possessions	—	—	375,000
Germany	—	—	500,000
Holland	—	—	50,000
Belgium	—	—	10,000
Denmark	—	—	2.250
Russia† (Poland 30,000)	—	—	250,000
Wallachia	—	—	18,850
Total quintals	20,549,556	6,184,890	4,051,850

* United States crop of maple sugar in 1850, 340,000 quintals (one-third in New York State and one-fifth in Vermont).
† Russia produces 522,000 quintals of cane and beet-root sugar.

Consumers.	Sugar.*	Coffee.	Tobacco.
England (1852)	(h)7,552,362	375,000	275,000
France	2,000,000	—	350,000
France and southern Europe (except Spain)	—	1,250,000	—
Holland, Belgium, Germany, Prussia, and Austria (including Lombardo-Venetian territory, and deducting re-exportation to Russia, etc.), of which 625,000 to Bremen, Hamburg, and Lubec	2,125,000	—	—
Germany without Austria	—	—	500,000
Austrian dominions	—	—	4,250
Germany and Northern Europe	—	1,750,000	—
Holland (31,250) and Belgium (45,000)	—	1,250,000	76,250
Trieste, Venice, etc.	625,000	—	—
Spain(i)	1,000,000	(j)1,500,000	(k)152,846
Portugal	200,000	—	2,000
Russia	810,000	—	5,000
Denmark	—	—	12,500
Denmark and Sweden	225,000	—	—
Sweden and Norway	—	—	22,500
Italy (exclusive of Lombardo-Venetian territory), Sicily, Malta, Turkey, Greece, and Levant in general	112,500	—	—
Italy	—	—	20,000
United States	4,250,000	750,000	—
Canada, Australia, Cape of Good Hope, etc.	600,000	—	—
Canada	—	160,000	—
Total quintals	19,499,862	7,035,000	1,420,346

NOTES TO APPENDIX.

(a) The want of uniformity in statistical arrangement among the few nations that publish such records, is a great obstacle to their usefulness. It often happens that in statements of exports no mention is made whether the place has produced or merely exported, and we have consequently been obliged to make use of data referring to exportation, and not to production, the latter having scarcely any existence. Cuba in 1852 appears to have produced 29,165,238 *arrobas*, and exported 25,362,216 *arrobas*. In 1851 the exportation attained the enormous amount of 1,549,893 boxes, or about 23,000,000 *arrobas*.

(b) The reduction to Spanish weight has been calculated at 110.434 lbs. Spanish to the British cwt., and 2.173 lbs. Spanish to the French kilogramme. The production of Jamaica included in the above was 627,769 cwt. Said island in the four years ending 1803 produced 135,331 hogsheads; in 1844–48, 41,872 hhds., and in the three years ending 1851, 38,937. Its largest crop was 150,000 hhds., in 1805. (*Henderson's Jamaica Almanac*, 1853.) British Guiana in 1852 exported 739,120 cwt.; this colony and Barbadoes being the only ones of the British possessions that do not evince decay. According to official data there were in Jamaica, in 1852, 128 estates entirely abandoned

---

* Tropical and colonial.

and 71 where the cultivation of the cane had been partially relinquished. Consequently the situation of that island is the most wretched among all the British possessions, but it is yet to be seen to what point her more fortunate sisters will be able to withstand the equalization of duties in 1854.

(c) Martinique produced in 1851, 110,938 kilog. of coffee, and 149,033 of cocoa.

(d) Rio Janeiro exported during the year ending May, 1853, the amount of 1,968,625 bags of coffee, of which 1,066,311 to the United States. In 1838 Cuba sent 33.051,061 lbs. of coffee to the United States, while Brazil sent only 27,411,986 lbs. In 1851 Cuba sent to the same markets 3,099,084 lbs., and Brazil 107,578,257 lbs. (See De Bow's Industrial Resources, etc.)

(e) The crop of Louisiana for 1851-52 was 236,547 hhds.; that of 1852-53 was 321,934 hhds.; and that of 1853-4 was 449,324 bhds. The quantity of molasses was 27,500,000 gallons. This result was produced by 1,481 establishments, of which 943 were worked by steam, and 538 by horse-power. The crop of Texas in the year 1852-3 was 11,023 hhds., averaging 1,000 lbs. In 1850 there was produced by Louisiana 226,001 hhds., South Carolina 77, Georgia 846, Florida 2,750, Tennesse 3, Alabama 87, Mississippi 8, and Kentucky 10 hhds.—total of United States, including crop of Texas, 237,133 hhds., which, at the rate of 1,000 lbs. per hogshead, gives a total of 237,133,000 lbs., or in round numbers 2,370,000 quintals. The crop ending January, 1855, has exceeded all previous ones.

(f) According to the census of 1840 the yield of tobacco in the United States was 2.191,633 quintals, showing a falling off of 224,177 quintals in 1850.

(g) France—crop of beet-root sugar in 1852-53, 1,635,731 quintals. According to the monthly official statements published by the French government, the production of beet-root sugar in France from 1st September, 1852, to 31st August of the present year, was 75,275,235 kilog., equal to about 400,000 boxes, and being an excess of 6,692,120 kilog. over the crop of 1851-52; but as the latter showed a decrease of 7½ millions kilog. on that of 1850-51, it may be considered nearly an average yield. This result has not corresponded with the expectations entertained during the first months of the crop. However, the number of establishments seems to indicate progress as it increases. There were 304 at work the 31st August, 1851, 329 at the same date in 1852, and the number at present is 337.* In Russia there are 880 manufactories of cane and beet-root sugar (77 of which are worked by steam), producing annually 522,000 quintals. We have no late statements of the production of beet-root sugar in Belgium, Prussia, Austria, etc., and in Great Britain it is insignificant as yet.

(h) 6,519,267 quintals British colonial sugar, and 1.033,095 foreign.

(i) In 1852 were shipped from this island to the Peninsula 190,848 boxes of sugar.

(j) Coffee from Cuba to Spain in 1852, 106,666 *arrobas*.

(k) As follows: 8,200,000 lbs. Kentucky and Virginia, 145,814 lbs. also of Virginia, 1,115,962 Marron-Kentucky, 14,379 Holland, 4,967,821 Philippine Islands, and 851,458 lbs. Cuba tobacco. (See Sr. Rodriguez-Ferrer's work, El Tabaco Habano.) In 1852 there was exported from Cuba to Spain 2,104,312 lbs. leaf tobacco, 11,247 thousand cigars, and 467,041 packets of cigarettes.

---

* According to the official returns last published, the number of beet-root sugar manufactories in France at the end of April last was 208, being 95 less than at the corresponding period of last year. The quantity of sugar made was 43,955,970 kilogrammes, being a decrease of 31,551,945 kilogrammes as compared with the same period of 1854. The amount given above for the sugar crop of Curaçoa is much too large, in my opinion, while that of the Danish West India Islands is underrated.—*Translator.*

A MEMOIR

OF

THE ISLAND OF PORTO RICO.

BY J. T. O'NEIL, OF ST. JOHN'S.

PHYSICAL GEOGRAPHY.

The Spanish Island of Puerto Rico (San Juan Bautista de), the smallest and most easterly of the Great Antilles, and meriting, by its beauty and fertility, the appellation of "The Cup of Gold," bestowed upon it by the figurative Spaniards, is situated in the Atlantic Ocean, between latitudes 17° 54' and 18° 30' 40" north, and longitudes 65° 37' 40" and 67° 16' 6" west of Greenwich.

Relative Position.—Lying immediately west of the Virgin Islands, east of Cuba and Hayti (which lies between), north of the continent of South America, and open to the north: added to its compact form and comparatively clear coasts, the island is eminently qualified for a centre of trade.*

Extremities.—The most prominent are, Punta de San Francisco on the west, Cabeza de San Juan on the north-east, Cabo de Mala-pascua on the south-east, and Los Morrillos de Cabo Rojo on the south-west.

Form.—Parallelogramic, and greatly resembling the trunk of an ox; the headland of Cabeza de San Juan at the upper end of the neck; Cabras islets and Punta Corcho, the lower; Cabo Mala-pascua at the curve of the chest; Punta Aguila and Los Morrillos de Cabo Rojo at the lower part of the buttock; Punta San Francisco projecting like the

---

* From the Island of Porto Rico you may escape from the region of the general or trade winds into that of the variables merely by steering to the north; and as this island is so far to windward, it is easy to gain all the easting that is necessary for going to the Lesser Antilles or Caribbee Islands. You may gain thus to windward, and beating with the breeze, without being under the necessity of running into high latitudes to catch the variables. From this island you may on one stretch catch any point of the Columbian main, from La Guayra to leeward.—*Blunt's Coast Pilot.*

stump of a tail; Puntas Peña-agujereada and Bruguen, or Peñas-blancas, at the rump; and Fronton de Vacia-talega and Punta Miquillo at the curve of the shoulder.

Boundaries.—On the north the Atlantic Ocean; on the north-east the reefy space that connects it with Culebras island (separated from the island of St. Thomas by a narrow passage); on the south-east the passage between it and the island of Vieques; on the south the Caribbean Sea; and on the west Mona Passage.

Neighboring Land.—The island of Hayti or St. Domingo on the west; that of St. Thomas on the north-east, and that of St. Croix on the southeast, each of the three being distant about sixty miles. On the north the nearest land is the island of Bermuda, and on the south the island of Curaçoa and the South American continent.

Extent.—Length from Cabeza de San Juan on the east to Punta de San Francisco on the west, 96 miles. Breadth from the city of St. John's on the north to the port of Jobos on the south, 35 miles. Mean length about 86, and mean breadth 34 geographical miles.

Area.—2,706 geographical, or 3,695 statute miles; and adding 257 estimated for the islands of Vieques, Culebras, Mona, etc., the total area is 3,865 square statute miles.

Circumference.—About 270 miles, of which about 195 are nearly equally divided between the north and south coasts, and 75 between the east and west coasts.

Coasts.—The coasts of the island are, in general, well defined and of easy access, although in some places (especially on the south-west and north-east) obstructed by reefs and banks of mud and sand. They do not contain more than seven harbors meriting the name, but there are many commodious bays, roadsteads, and anchorages. Vessels may run along either the north or south coast without risk, at a distance of three miles from the former, and five from the latter, taking care to avoid the islet of Caja de Muertos, which lies about four miles from the centre of the south coast. Nearer the island the north coast is rugged and uneven, having many rocks and keys on which the sea breaks heavily, and the whole south coast, from the Morrillos de Cabo Rojo to Cabo Malapascua, is of double land, and very foul, with reefs, islets, and shoals stretching out from it. On the east coast also are numerous islets and rocks, which can not be approached by large vessels, and lie between the island and the islets of Culebras and Vieques. Though the passages among these islets and rocks are generally deep, they should only be attempted by practiced pilots. Vessels coming from the north may sail round the north-west point of the island within a mile of the shore, and in 20 to 25 fathoms. The northernmost half of the west coast is pretty clear, but the southernmost is beset by many shoals and reefs, which imperatively demand the erection of a light-house.

Capes and Points.—The north-western extremity of the island is formed by Punta Bruguen or Borinquen (a high and steep cliff), and Punta de Peña-agujereada, whence, eastward, the principal ones are— Punta de la Isabela; Punta del Manglillo and the Morrillo de Arecibo, with the roadstead of Arecibo between; Punta de Caracoles; Puntas Marunguey and Lavadero, with the anchorage of Palmas Altas between; Puntas Boquilla, Puerto-nuevo, Cerro-gordo, Frailes, and Salinas, which last is the northern extremity of the Cabras islets, which, with the Morro (on which is a light), form the mouth of the harbor of St. John's; Fronton de Vacia-talega, Punta Miquillo, Punta San Diego, and Cabeza de San Juan, the north-eastern extremity of the island. On the east are Puntas Marunguey and Corcho, between which are the islets of Palomino, Piñero, and Cabras, and the port of Fajardo; Punta de la Lima (northernmost point of the bay of Fajardo), and Punta de Candeleros (southernmost point of the bay of Humacao), with Cayo Santiago between; Punta de Baracoa, Fronton de Guayanés, Puntas Quebrada-honda, Yeguas and Naranjo, and Cabo de Mala-pascua, which is the south-eastern extremity of the island. On the south are Puntas Viento and Guilarte, with the roadstead of Patillas between; Punta Colorados or Figuras, and Punta Barrancas, with the roadstead of Guayama between; Puntas Pozuelos and Colchones, with the port of Jobos between; Puntas Arenas and Fama, with the port of Salinas de Coamo between; Puntas Coamo and Boca-chica; Puntas Caballon and Cucharas, with the bay of Ponce between; Peñon de Tallaboa; Peñon de Guayanilla and Punta Vaquero, with the bay of Guayanilla between; Punta Picua and Fronton de Brea, with the harbor of Guanica between; Puntas de Guanica, Salinas, isla de Cabras, and de la Parguera; Los Morrillos de Cabo Rojo* and Punta del Aguila at the south-western extremity of the island. On the west are Punta de Palo-Seco; Puntas de Melones and Guaniquilla, with the bay of Boqueron between; Puntas de Pedernal and Ostiones, with the port of Cabo Rojo between; Punta Arenas; Puntas de Guanajibo and Algarrobo, with the bay of Mayagues between; Puntas Cadena and Rincon, with the small bay of Rincon between, and the cape called Punta de San Francisco projecting a little below the north-western extremity of the island, and between which and Punta de Peñas-blancas, a little above, is the bay of Aguadilla.

---

[1] * These rest on a coral bank, close to the outer edge of which no bottom has been found. Two or three leagues to the eastward and westward there are 10, 12, and 15 fathoms water.

Adjacent Islets* **and Keys.**—On the north, the islet of Cabrita without, and Cabras within, the entrance of the harbor of St. John's, and forming the west side of it. On the east, the islet of Hicacos, east of Cabeza de San Juan; islet of Palominos, east of Fajardo; islet of Piñero, east of Ceiba; islets of Cabras, Cayo Algodones and Cayo Santiago; islets of Culebra, Culebrilla, Culebrita, and Peluda, which are also known as Little Passage Islands, and extend nearly up to St. Thomas; and Vicques or Crab Island, south-south-west of the former; it is large, and contains a town. On the south are Cayo Berberia, islet Frio, islet of Caja de Muertos or Dead Man's Chest, the two islets of Cañagorda, near the port of Guanica, and Cayo Ratones. On the west, Cayo Fonduco, the islets of Mona, Monito, and Desecheo or Zacheo.

Reefs and Shoals.—On the north coast they are not well determined, but do not extend far from the shore. On the east are many reefs and shoals stretching out between the main island and the numerous islets in its close proximity; but the passages between them are deep, and readily made by good pilots. Those on the west coast comprise—Bajo Gallardo, which is about three cables length in extent, six and one-half miles due west (nearly) from Punta de Melones: least depth of water on it three fathoms, with rocky bottom: its bearings are, Zacheo, north by west (three-fourths west), Atalaya, south by west (three-fourths west), and the southern extremity of the Morrillos, east-south-east; Las Coronas and Coronitas, which are shoals of sand, on which the sea breaks at times, and extending scarcely a mile in any direction: distance from the coast about three and one-half miles, and bearing nearly south-west by south from Punta de Guanajibo, and south one-half east from Punta Giguera; Bajo Media Luna, a reef about five miles from the coast, two-thirds of a mile in length, north and south, and about two and one-half cables in breadth: the sea always breaks on it, the same as on three rocks distant from it half a mile east-north-east, and showing above water: the northern extremity of the reef is nearly south-west by west from Punta de Guanajibo, and south from Punta Giguera; a shoal westward two miles from Punta de Guaniquilla, about two cables in extent, with three fathoms water on it, and a rocky bottom: it bears south by west (three-fourths west) from Punta de Guanajibo, and south three-fourths east from Punta de Giguera; the rocky shoal Las Manchas, extending about three miles west-north-westerly from Punta de Algarrobo: there are two and one-half to four fathoms water on it, but vessels may pass very well between it and the shore, there being a good channel inside from the bay of Añasco; Bajo Rodriguez, a

---

* The largest islets will be especially mentioned in the sequel.

little without the line of Puntas Algarrobo and Guanajibo, and about half way between them: it is a rocky shoal, dry in several spots, and always showing itself, stretching nearly north and south, about half a mile long, and not much less at its broadest part: there is a passage through the midst of it, about north-east by east, with least depth of 12 feet; a great reef stretches out from the northernmost point of the port of Cabo Rojo, and, doubling Cayo Fonduco, ends at Punta de Veras; Bajo del Negro, a very small reef, with the sea constantly breaking on it, about three and one-half miles from the nearest coast, and lying west-south-west (one-half west) from Punta de Guanajibo, and south three-fourths east from Punta Giguera; Bajo del Negrillo, near the former, and smaller; Bajo Figueroa; and Bajo del Algarrobo, which is nearly bare and bold to the south-west, and on which it has been intended to erect a light. Among those on the south coast are—a shoal two or three miles in length, and three or four miles from the coast, and containing the roadstead of Guayama; a reef near the entrance of the bay of Ponce; there are also several reefs and shoals about the mouth of the port of Guanica, and in other parts of this coast. The number of shoals immediately bordering the coasts of the island is a natural consequence of the many rivers that empty into the sea in all directions.

Channels.—These, with the exception of the passages between the immediate islets, keys, etc., are few in number, the principal one being Virgin's passage, between Vieques and the islets of Culebras and St. Thomas, in which are soundings with 20 fathoms on the west side, but on approaching any one of the islets it is shoaler. The currents set through this channel strong to the westward.

Mountains, Valleys, and Savannas.—A range called the Sierra de Luquillo, rising in some places 8,700 feet above the sea, commences at Cabeza de San Juan, and with frequent and extensive gaps ends at the Silla de Caballo, south of Arecibo. Its highest point, called El Yunque (anvil), near the eastern coast, is visible at a distance of 70 miles. Another range, called the Sierra de Cayey in its eastern part, distinct from the former, and almost continuous, traverses the island from east to west southward of the centre: it commences near Yabucoa on the east, and after various convolutions forks out near St. German into various branches extending to the coast on the west and south-west. The highest points of this ridge are—La Atalaya (watch-tower)* in Añasco, Cerro Montuoso in Mayagües, Tetas de Cerro Gordo in San German, and El Torito in Cayey: it appears as a regular vertebra, and,

---

* This is an important guiding point to navigators, being seen along the whole of the west coast. It is the highest of the two peaks on the highest part of the range near that coast, and stands south-east by east from Point San Francisco.

like the Sierra de Luquillo, throws out numerous lateral branches which extend to the north and south coasts, and inclose many fertile valleys and savannas, some of which, when viewed from the heights, afford a most charming prospect. The mountains are thickly wooded, and the source of a multitude of streams.

Rivers.—The number of streams watering the island is exceedingly great, rendering irrigation unnecessary except on the south side, where drought is most prevalent. Besides upward of 1,200 brooks—the majority permanent and suitable to the purposes of life—and numerous smaller streams, there are 51 rivers emptying into the sea. Several of them are navigable by small craft for some six miles from their mouths, such as the Loiza, Toa, Bayamon, Manati, Arecibo, and Añasco. The greatest are—the Rio Grande de Loiza, which rises in Cerro Gordo, south of the town of Hato-Grande: flows northward, winding to the east and west, traverses the districts of Caguas, Gurabo, Trujillo-Alto, and Trujillo-Bajo, and, after receiving various rivers and a great number of brooks in its course, empties into the sea near Loiza; the Rio de Añasco, which rises on the north of Sierra de Cain, in San German, runs north-west and west, and, enlarged by many tributaries, empties into the sea at Añasco·; and the Rio de la Plata, which rises in Cerro Pelado in Cayey, runs north, with many convolutions, to the east, south, and west, takes the names of Caribe, Grande, Vegas, Cayey, and La Plata near Aibonito, traverses the districts of Cayey, Aibonito, Cidra, Sabana del Palmar, Naranjito, Toa-Alta, Toa-Baja, and Dorado, and, after having received, like the others, a large number of rivers and brooks in its course, disembogues in the sea with the name of Toa, at Boca-Habana, on the north of Toa-Baja.

Water-Falls.—There are few in the island, and none deserving of especial notice.

Lagoons.—There are several lagoons bordering the coasts, the principal ones being—Laguna de Peñones, east of St. John's, and formed by the sea; Laguna de Tortuguero, north-north-east of the town of Manati; Lago Joyuda, south-south-west of Mayagües; Laguna de Guánica, north-north-west of the port of Guánica: it is extensive, and abounds in ducks and fish.

Swamps.—Cienaga Salitrales, in the south-western extremity; Cienaga del Flamenco, east of Guanica; and Cienaga de Augustin, east of Humacao, are the most extensive.

Salt Ponds.—The principal ones are—Salinas de Palo-Seco, also called de la Sierra de Peñones, near the Morrillos de Cabo Rojo, on the south-west coast; and Salinas de Coamo, toward the centre of the south coast. There is besides a bed of fossil-salt at Isabela, on the north coast.

PHYSICAL, POLITICAL, AND INDUSTRIAL.   139

Harbors, Bays, Roadsteads, etc.—The chief ones on the north coast, which is not much indented, are—the spacious and well-sheltered harbor of St. John's, the roadstead of Arecibo, the anchorage of Palmas-Altas, and the small bays of Toa, Cangrejos, and Boca-Vieja. On the east—Ensenada-Honda (a fine harbor), the port of Fajardo, and the bays of Naguabo, Humacao, and Ensenada de Majagua. On the south—the first-rate harbor of Guánica, the good ones of Salinas de Coamo and Jobos, the bays of Guayanilla, Ponce, and Puerto Aguirre, and the roadsteads of Guayama and Patillas. On the west—the bays of Aguadilla, Rincon, Añasco, Mayagües, and Boqueron; and Puerto Real de Cabo Rojo, an excellent harbor. Those of Guánica and Ensenada-Honda are the finest harbors in the island. There are, besides, numerous creeks, coves, and small estuaries.

Currents.—The currents set from east to west, as usual in the tropics, although under certain positions of the moon they are reversed; but, this point has not been well determined. Their mean velocity is about half a mile an hour.

Climate.—The climate is warm and moist, but salubrious, except in low and marshy places. The extremes of temperature on the plains are about 62° and 95° Fahrenheit, but it must be several degrees cooler on the highlands, especially the mountainous regions north and east. The atmosphere is very humid, but least so on the south side. No hygrometric nor rain-gauge observations are recorded. The wind generally blows from the east and north-north-east, except from November to March, when northers prevail, though seldom with great violence; and during the wet season it often blows from the south-east. The land breeze is light and fitful. Whirlwinds sometimes occur during the dry season, but seldom strong enough to occasion much damage.

The period wherein a hurricane may be looked for extends from July to October (the great one of Santa Ana occurred the 26th of July, 1826, and the almanac, though usually fallacious in this respect, predicts one the 10th of October of the present year, 1855). These fearful visitations appear to be much less frequent than in former times, when a violent gale was almost of annual occurrence; the losses (and there was little to lose in those days) sometimes exceeding $500,000, besides 7,000 houses demolished or seriously damaged, numberless cattle and poultry destroyed, cultivated fields entirely denuded, large portions of forest uprooted, and upward of 1,500 persons killed or wounded. Since 1837 (August 2d), when upward of thirty large vessels were wrecked in the close harbor of St. John's, and proportionate damage done throughout the north coast, both on sea and land, hurricanes have been unfrequent and light. They are especially afflictive to the peasantry, whose "staff of life" is the plantain tree, so readily prostrated by the gale. The wind on such occasions seems to blow from nearly every quarter at the same time, and comes in gusts or waves, but its maximum intensity fortunately lasts little more than an hour. Hurricanes are often immediately succeeded by slight shocks of earthquake. Dew falls very copiously throughout the year, especially on clear nights, which are the most numerous. Fogs are rare. The year may be divided into two seasons—the wet and the dry, or summer and winter—the first never so oppressive as in more northerly countries, and the last somewhat similar to the autumn of the south of Europe. The rainy season usually lasts from July to January, with occasional dry spells of several weeks. Some years the rain pours down in torrents for several hours on many successive days, and streams that were insignificant before become raging torrents, overflowing the land, and carrying every thing before them. A flood in 1851 was preceded by three days of continuous rain. Almost every part of the island suffered from it; a number of lives were lost, thousands of cattle destroyed, bridges and houses swept away, and entire cane-fields swept bare. The south side is subject to drought, and is the only part of the island where irrigation is used. The loftiest mountain peaks are said to be sometimes capped with snow. Hail-storms are unfrequent. About the breaking up of the dry season violent thunder-storms occur, and silent lightning is frequent during the evenings of June, July, and August. Meteors are often seen, and the aurora borealis is sometimes visible. The sea about the coasts, as usual in the tropics, is highly phosphorescent, especially in summer, and long luminous belts (cestus veneris) are occasionally observed in the harbors and bays. Slight shocks of earthquake, or rather earth-tremor, being entirely superficial, and apparently caused by a sudden electric discharge from the earth, often accompany the first rain after long drought.

Diseases.—The most prevalent during the dry season are—common catarrhal affections, epidemic influenza, under a new form every season, whooping-cough, attacking even adults, light and intermittent fevers, and rheumatism. Consumption also has its victims. During the months of hot and rainy weather—hepatic affections, intermittent, bilious, typhus, and brain fevers, derangement of the digestive organs, smallpox, and erysipelas. Yellow fever visits the island only at intervals of several years, and soon subsides, rarely attacking any but the unacclimated. Although Asiatic cholera has raged so fiercely in nearly all the West India islands, including St. Thomas, which is so near to Porto Rico, the latter is yet a stranger to the disease. Among chronic diseases are—dropsy, hydrocele (very common), and gravel, and the great and permanent swelling of one or both legs, known to the faculty as elephantiasis, or Barbadoes-leg, is frequently encountered, especially among colored people. A few cases of goitre exist, but no scrofula, although leprous affections are sometimes met with. There are several complaints peculiar to the negroes—one proceeds from eating earth, and another is called yaws. It is somewhat remarkable that ophthalmia does not prevail at St. John's, where all the buildings are whitewashed outside, and reflect the sunlight most dazzlingly. Instances of great longevity are numerous in the island, especially in the interior, and several might be enumerated where the "span of life" has extended over one and a quarter centuries. Generally speaking, the women seem to live longer than the men.

Animals.—QUADRUPEDS.—The variety is small, and the only indigenous one is the jutía, seldom met with. Horned cattle, horses, and swine are extensively raised. Oxen are generally lean, but the beef of those exported is excellent, although that consumed in the island, being badly slaughtered, and usually of old and hard-worked subjects, is tough and dry. They are still much used in the sugar-cane mills, and almost exclusively for drawing carts. Their price ranges from $20 to $40, those trained to draught commanding the highest rate. They are invariably yoked by the forehead. Cows afford very good milk, yet the butter and cheese is poor (doubtless from improper manipulation), and far from sufficient to the consumption. Veal is rarely eaten. The horses are of the Andalusian breed (originally Arabian). They are generally small, but finely formed, mettlesome, and swift, and remarkable for the ambling gait called *paso*, so agreeable to the rider, while rapid. Those used by the peasantry in their journeys are undersized, lean, and rough, but exceedingly endurant of fatigue, and independent of grooming: $1,000 is sometimes paid for a racer, but very good traveling horses may be had for $150 to $300, and baggage carriers at from $30 to $60. Private carriages are usually drawn by American horses, imported expressly at a cost of $200 to $400 (duty paid), or purchased of an occasional circus company. Asses and mules are not much used, and consequently scarce. Hogs in the rural districts feed chiefly on the berry of the royal palm. The pork is lean but well flavored, and generally consumed in the fresh state, no hams nor bacon being prepared from it. Wild hogs are met with in the district of Naguabo. Sheep and goats are few, the flesh of neither being much used. As happens throughout the tropics, the wool of the first is substituted by short coarse hair, like that of the second. Camels and deer have been introduced, but have not multiplied. There are rabbits and guinea pigs, or cavies. Hydrophobia being almost unknown, dogs are allowed to multiply greatly, and there are numerous varieties, among which the *chino*, small, short-legged, and generally black, is remarkable for being entirely devoid of hair. Cats, rats, and mice are, almost of course, very abundant. Some of the first have run wild in the woods. Bats also are common.

BIRDS.—Besides those usually classed as poultry, there are tame and wild pigeons, parrots of various size and color, turtle doves, a species of partridge, canaries, linnets, nightingales, cardinals, robins, woodpeckers, humming-birds, *tomeguines*, scarce three inches long, swallows, owls, widgeons, wild ducks, pelicans, sea-gulls, flamingoes, king-fishers, *cocos*, snipe, and many other.

REPTILES.—These are few. There are no alligators, and the largest lizard is only about a foot and a half in length. The snakes are not venomous, and rarely exceed five feet in length. Small frogs and toads are common.

FISH—Abound in many of the rivers, and about the coasts and harbors. Among the best are the *liza*, or mullet, *pargo, carite, viajaca, dajao, mojarra*, king-fish, calamary, red-mullet, etc. Sharks are common about the coasts, and the *manatí* or sea-cow is frequently met with. Whales, porpoises, dolphins, etc., are often seen, and even seals sometimes visit the north coast. There are several kinds of shell-fish, including lobsters, shrimps, crabs, clams, and oysters (small, but savory, and usually growing on the submerged stems of the mangrove bushes). Land-crabs (*cangrejos*) are numerous, and, together with the rats, do great damage to the sugar-cane. There are also sea-urchins, starfish, polypi, beautiful anemones, conches and shells in great variety, sponges, corals, etc.

INSECTS—As in all warm and humid climates—are abundant. Those best known are—two kinds of fire-flies, bees, yielding excellent honey, wasps, butterflies of many kinds, cockroaches, grasshoppers, a species of locust, mosquitoes, sand-flies, and many other kinds of flies; weevils, moths, and several species of worms destructive to grain, vegetable leaves, and paper; scorpions, centipedes (both causing inflammation and fever by their sting); *gongolis* or millepedes, spiders, among which the large and hairy *guabá*, also called tarantula, is often fatal to cattle. Ants are very numerous, and the *comejen* will destroy the timbers of a house, leaving nothing but a thin outer shell. They are destroyed with difficulty, and only by repeatedly putting arsenic in their nests. Chigoes (a species of flea) are a great torment to the unshod, penetrating under the skin of the feet, and often rendering the negroes (especially children) quite lame. Fleas, lice, and bugs are plenty. There is also in the fields a diminutive, bright red insect called *abúse*, which attaches itself to the skin.

Vegetables.—The island is singularly rich in vegetable productions, and affords an exceedingly extensive and interesting (the more because little explored) field for the botanist. The variety of hard wood most suitable for building and for cabinet work is very great. For the latter purpose there are none more beautiful in any part of the world. Dyes and medicinal plants of most valuable properties abound, and the number of distinct fruits, growing spontaneously, is truly surprising. We do not attempt to enumerate any more than those most generally known in the island, and of the majority of these only the native nomenclature can be given. Among precious woods are the aceitillo or satin-wood, mahogany, ebony of several kinds, collor, walnut, palo-vacas, algarrobo or locust, veined, common, and red; odorous cedar, box, laurel de llamas, guásima (very medicinal), sabina or savin, moca, and many others. Besides these, the best for building—some for solidity, others for flexibility, and others again for both qualities—are the guayacan or lignumvitæ, which also affords the valuable gum-guaiac; white and black capá, cojoba, roble or oak, maricao, ortegon, úcar; yellow, black, and red maga; tortugo, ausubo, higuerillo, guaraguao, espejuelo, zapote, jagua, granadillo, pendola, quiebra-hacha (axe-breaker), the lofty sciba, etc. There is also the fountain-tree, with a stream of pure water running through its tubes. The chief dyes are Brazil-wood, tumeric, indigo, annatto, guatapaná, granadillo, mora, fustic, aroma, maricao, and dividiví, all of which grow wild. For tanning, the bark of the mangrove is excellent. Among resinous plants are that which produces the copaiba balsam, two kinds of tabanuco, which is very aromatic and medicinal, and its fruit affording good food for hogs; the male maméy, used in cutaneous diseases; copéy, guaiac, copal, algarrobo, and the pajuil or cashew.* Other medicinal plants comprise liquorice, tea, sage, stinkingweed, balsamillo, cojitre, tibéy, guaco (so famous in South America as an antidote to the poison of serpents), vervain, cepí, higuillo, sacabuche, corazon, cow-itch, parietaria, senna, nigua, zarzabacoa, chicory (very abundant), curía or garden balsam, violeta, caña-fístola or cassia-lignea, llantén (plantago), tamarind, mallows, malagueta or pimento, panic or couch-grass, green-pepper, mint, purslain, chamomile, mastich, rosemary, sanguinaria or knot-grass, etc. Besides these there are numerous poisonous plants, such as the seed of the poma-rosa and of the sand-box tree, the manzanilla or manchineel-apple, the yuca when not cooked, and many others. The cinnamon tree and a species of nutmeg also grow in the island. There are several kinds of palms, including the collor, ex-

---

* The nut of which (very palatable when roasted), growing attached to the pear-shaped, juicy and astringent, but refreshing fruit, contains a resinous oil which, on application for the removal of ringworm in a certain instance, is said to have produced an extraordinary growth of hair on the place rubbed with it.

otic date, cocoa-nut, and royal palm,* which last is doubtless the most valuable tree in the island, from the variety of its uses; also the beautiful and most useful bamboo, the wild cane, various kinds of calabash, medicinal, and affording gourds of all shapes and sizes, from a capacity of seven or eight gallons to a quarter of a pint, serving the country people for barrels, tubs, cups and saucers, spoons, etc.; and the guano, which affords a most excellent substitute for feathers in stuffing pillows and beds. Among fruit trees are the almond, aguacate or alligator-pear, also called vegetable marrow, bread-fruit, a species of chestnut, excellent pine-apples of two kinds, and oranges of three kinds, nispero or mess-apple, papaw and mango; five kinds of plantain and banana, constituting the chief food of the country people; guava of several kinds, cocoa-nuts, anón, corazon, two kinds of caimito, citron, shaddock, ausubo, several kinds of plums, two of gooseberries, dates (rare), algarrobo, cunde-amor, guanábana or sour-sop, guamá, granadilla, pomegranate, hicaco, fig, cashew, jobo, jácana, jagua, jobo de la India; five kinds of limes and lemons, maméy, zapote, several kinds of melons, múltas or guava-berries, pita-haya (a cactus), pepino-angolo (medicinal), parcha or bell-apple, poma-rosa, tamarind, two kinds of grape, peanuts, etc. Strawberries have been raised in some of the mountainous districts; and on the *estancia* of Vives, near Ponce, are several apple trees producing good fruit. Many other exotic fruits might be raised, but this branch of cultivation is not attended to. Among esculent roots and other alimenticious plants are the yuca, which affords the excellent manioc bread or *casabe* (though the fresh juice is a deadly poison), and fine starch; arrow-root, several kinds of yams, potatoes, sweet potatoes, yautías, ápio or celery, ginger, radishes, beets, turnips, carrots, lerén, gunda, egg-plant, tayon, tayote, gumbo or ocra, cabbage, lettuce, asparagus, beans and peas of various kinds (some peculiar to the island), green-peas, tomatoes, sweet and pungent pepper, pumpkin, squash, etc. Rice and maize are produced abundantly, and cocoa is also raised in small quantities. Sugar, coffee, and tobacco are the chief productions of the island. Cotton grows finely, but of late years is little cultivated. There is a great variety of fibrous plants suitable for making paper, and the plantain-stalk affords a material equal to flax.

Minerals.—This branch has been very little investigated, but the

---

* The palm-tree is said by Ray to "supply the Indians with whatever they stand in need of—bread, water, wine, vinegar, brandy, milk, oil, honey, sugar, needles, clothes, thread, cups, spoons, basins, baskets, paper, masts for ships, sails, cordage, nails, all the material for their houses, etc." This variety of uses, however, is much reduced, and in part almost forgotten in civilized countries. The price of a standing palm-tree in Porto Rico is $4.

island certainly contains its full share of metallic and combustible substances, and other valuable minerals. Gold has been found in the Luquillo Mountain, although a mining company, formed within the last two or three years, has failed of encouragement and relinquished the undertaking. The sands of the Luquillo River, and at the head of the Mayagües River, are auriferous. Particles of iron and steel are found in the vicinity of the rivers in Loiza; pyrites and marquesites in the mountains of Añasco; traces of iron, bismuth, etc., in the hills near the town of Mayagües; a bed of coal in Manatí, on the lands of Mr. Kortright, not worked. There are quarries of white stone in the districts of Ponce and Juana Diaz; of grindstone, in La Moca; of schistose and other good building stone in Cabo Rojo and Mayagües; of marble in Caguas, and masses of rock-crystal in the mountain of Mala-pascua. The principal salt-pits are—that of the Sierra de Peñones, in Cabo Rojo, very productive; the lagoon of Salinas de Coamo; and one in Isabela, containing fossil salt. There are thermal and sulphurous springs in the district of Coamo, resorted to by invalids; at Ponce, where the waters have lately begun to be used with benefit; at Hato-Grande; and the Guatemala River, in Pepino, is of thermal temperature.

POLITICAL GEOGRAPHY.*

Population.—According to the last census (in 1846) the number of inhabitants in the island was 447,914, of which 220,045 were whites (112,840 males and 107,205 females), and not more than ten per cent. of the whole were slaves. The following statement shows the steady increase during the last ninety years.

1765..44,883	1787..93,877	1794..127,183	1801..158,051	1824..261,268
1778..66,000	1788..101.398	1795..129,758	1802..162,192	1827..287,678
1782..81,120	1789..103,051	1796..132,982	1808..174.902	1829..321,661
1783..87,904	1790..106,679	1797..138,753	1812..183,014	1830..330,051
1784..91,845	1791..112,712	1798..144,525	1815..220,892	1834..358,836
1785..93,800	1792..115,557	1799..153,230	1817..221,772	1846..447,914
1786..96,238	1793..120,022	1800..155,426	1820..230,622	

At the same rate (nearly 2½ per cent. per annum), the present population should be about 550,000, with a proportion of slaves of probably not more than 9 per cent., as a considerable number become free every

---

* "Previous to 1776 the revenue of the island was chiefly derived from the customs dues on its small trade with Spain (not being allowed to trade with foreign countries), and nearly all the expenses of government were defrayed by the *situado*, or aid annually afforded by Mexico, and amounting to $4,324,498. Great, therefore, was the embarrassment when that supply was cut off by the insurrection, obliging the government to resort to extraordinary expedients, and even to make use of the most sacred deposits, without, however, filling the void. The penury of the situation becoming daily more aggravated, recourse was had to the issue of paper-money, which, although it temporarily relieved the necessities, soon banished both confidence and coin to such a degree that it fell to 10 per cent. of its original value, compelling the prohibition of its circulation, and the institution of measures to withdraw it. It was then considered advisable to separate the treasury department from the general government: to establish custom-houses at St. John's, Aguadilla, Mayagües, Cabo Rojo, Ponce, and Fajardo; and to organize a Tribunal of Commerce and an Economical Society, all in virtue of a Royal order of 28th November, 1811, from which period dates the existence of the Superintendency of the island, although all its attributions were only completed by Royal order of 28th July, 1846. These measures might not have failed of early and materially favorable results if the pecuniary embarrassment had merely arisen from want of protection to commerce and agriculture; but the evil had other roots. The enormous deficiency of the *situado* could not be covered in a short time, especially in the chaotic state of the administration, and with the smuggling that prevailed with the connivance of those whose duty it was to prevent it. Although many of the abuses were soon suppressed, such was the magnitude of the rest that no considerable improvement could be experienced for some time. In 1825 greater vigor was infused into the measures of the administration, who appointed officers termed *celadores*, men of known probity, whose duty it was to supervise the management of the respective custom-houses, subjecting them to certain regulations, and requiring greater method and perspicuity in their accounts. The greatest vigilance was also

year, either by paying for themselves with money accumulated from the produce of the patches of ground they are allowed to cultivate on holidays for their own benefit, or by being paid for (as many are) by their free relatives, who retain no legal claim on them. In neither case can the owner refuse manumission, or demand more than cost price, or such as may be adjudged by the *Sindico*, and usually ranging from $25 for an infant just born, to $300 and $500 for adults. Premising that the population at present is 550,000, the proportion per geographical square league is nearly 1,827 (152 per square statute mile), while in Cuba it is but 254; in Jamaica less than 1,000, and in Hayti about 382, supposing a population of 936,000. Were the Island of Cuba as densely peopled, it would contain 6½ millions of inhabitants. The proportion between slaves and freemen is no less satisfactory. According to the census of 1834, of the 358,836 inhabitants of Porto Rico, 54 per cent. were whites, 35 per cent. free colored, and 11 per cent. slaves. At the same period, according to Humboldt, the proportion per cent. in the other slave-holding countries was as follows:

	Cuba.	Jamaica.	Brit. W. I.	United States.	Brazil.
White	46	6	9	81	23
Free colored	18	9	10	3	26
Slaves	36	85	81	16	51

---

exercised against smuggling, and ere long the revenue was doubled. In the statistical returns of 1816 the production of the island was set down as $2,057,932, on a capital of $14.546,911. In 1820 the production had increased to $3,060,040; in 1827 to $3,529,668; in 1833 to $6,702,012; and in 1844 to $8,935,794, although in 1824 it was only $2,582,337. Previous to the Royal decree of 10th August, 1815 (exempting the inhabitants of the island from assessments and tithes for 15 years), the exportation (in 1813) amounted to $339.940, while in 1818 and 1819 it rose to $980,692 and $1.098,033 respectively. The prosperity of the island is almost entirely due to the Royal decree above mentioned. Thereby were permitted—the importation of slaves from the neighboring colonies; and the immigration of foreigners with capital and slaves, such colonists being accorded all the privileges of Spaniards after a residence of five years ; the exemption, as before stated, from assessments and tithes for 15 years, although an inland tax was imposed to defray the expenses of government; direct trade with the Peninsula free of duty, three per cent. being levied on the entry and clearance of shipments, by Spaniards, in Spanish bottoms, to foreign countries in Europe, the goods being transferable from one vessel to another free of further duty; the importation of slaves by Spaniards free of duty, and by foreigners under a duty of three per cent. *ad valorem ;* and of agricultural implements, gold, silver, and ships on the same terms, whence-ever proceeding; the direct trade by foreigners with the United States and Europe for one year, and with the neighboring colonies for six months, under a duty of 15 per cent. on manufactured goods, 10 per cent. on provisions generally, $1 per ton as tonnage duty on United States vessels, and 4 rials on those of other nations, and 5 per cent. on the value of domestic produce exported. These were the chief bases of the progress of the island, although they suffered many restrictions, and some of the measures were not properly carried out."—(*Coello's Descriptive Map, Madrid*, 1851.)

These statements prove how unjustly some writers have exclaimed against the numerous slavery of the Spanish Antilles, and that this fertile and well-situated island not only ranks among the most populous countries, but that slavery therein is gradually becoming extinct. The number of foreign settlers (except those from Spain and South America, who are proportionately few) in the island is very small. French emigrants, chiefly from Hayti, and holding several of the coffee plantations, are probably the most numerous; next, Italians and Corsicans, several of whom are sugar planters, a few Germans employed in commerce, and Danes (from the neighboring islands), the majority of whom are managers of sugar estates. There are also a few Dutch and English, but of Americans there are probably not twenty in the whole island. A large number of the so-called white population are, in reality, colored—probably one half. The *Jibaro*, or native of the rural districts, is supposed to be, generally speaking, of Indian descent; but of the pure aboriginal breed, said to have numbered 600,000 at the discovery, we do not believe that one remains.

Religion.—As in all Spanish countries, the Roman Catholic and Apostolic is the only form of worship tolerated, and it must be professed by all foreigners previous to domiciliation or marriage, or proofs given of such profession, in order to obtain burial in consecrated ground.

Administrative Division.—The island is governed by a captain-general appointed by the Crown, and who presides over the Real Audiencia or court of judicature, and all the tribunals except those of Commerce and Exchequer. No important measures, however, are carried into effect without the approval of the Crown. The Real Audiencia is composed of a president (the Captain-General), a regent, four judges, an attorney-general, and a recorder, and tries all suits and administrative affairs under appeal, criminal causes in all cases, and exercises authority in various other matters, referred to it by the laws. The administrative division of the territory comprises eight districts, and sixty-seven townships, viz.: the district of *San Juan* (the capital), comprising the townships of Luquillo, Rio-grande, Loiza, Trujillo-alto, Trujillo-bajo, Cangrejos, Rio-piedras, Guainabo, Bayamon, Toa-alta, Toa-baja, Naranjito, Corozal, Vega-alta, Vega-baja, and Dorado; *Arecibo*—Hatillo, Camuy, Quebradillas, Utuado, Manatí, Ciales, and Morovis; *Aguadilla*— Aguada, Rincon, Moca, Pepino, Lares, and Isabela; *Mayagües* — Añasco; *San German*—Cabo Rojo and Sabana-grande; *Ponce*—Juana Diaz, Santa Isabel de Coamo, Villa de Coamo, Aibonito, Barranquitas, Barros, Peñuelas, Adjuntas, Guayanilla, and Yauco; *Caguas*—Gurabo, Juncos, Hato-Grande, Aguas-buenas, Sabana del Palmar, Cidra, Cayey, Guayama, and Salinas; and *Humacao*, with the townships of Fajardo, Ceiba,

Naguabo, Piedras, Yabucoa, Maunabo, and Patillas. A chief justice, residing in each of the eight districts, decides, without appeal (aided by two *hombres buenos*), in all suits not exceeding $100, and takes immediate cognizance of all other causes not subject to the special tribunals of the general government, church, war, navy, artillery, engineers, exchequer, commerce, and estate of deceased persons. An *alcalde* in each town, at the head of the ayuntamiento or corporation, acting as justice of the peace, deciding without appeal all lawsuits under $50, in which cases he consults the opinion of the *hombres buenos* (sponsors of the parties), issuing writs, apprehending delinquents, and exercising generally the authority delegated to him in judicial matters by the chief justice of the district. There are also sub-alcaldes for the different wards, and the sergeant-majors of the country militia exercise authority in certain petty matters.

Exchequer.—This branch is conducted by an intendant of the army, and general delegated superintendent, and four offices established at the capital, viz.: the chief accountant's office and tribunal of accounts, the liquidating office, the chief treasury of the army, and chief administration of internal revenue, for the accountantship of land-taxes. The revenue is collected by seven custom-houses of the first class, five of the second, and nine of the third, making monthly remittances to the chief treasury, and fifteen receptories, whose collections are likewise remitted every month to the treasury, through the administration of internal revenue, to which they are subject. The custom-houses of the first class are those of St. John's, Mayagües, Ponce, Guayama, Aguadilla, Naguabo, and Arecibo, and are authorized for all export and import trade, and to issue permits or dockets for all goods transmitted to the other authorized places in the island. Of the second class are those of Cabo Rojo, Fajardo, Humacao, Guayanilla, and Salinas de Coamo, authorized for the exportation of the produce of the island, the admission of goods from the first-class custom-houses in coasting vessels of the island, the issue of permits for such goods to the other authorized ports, and the importation of provisions and lumber from the United States. Of the third class are those of Manatí, Luquillo, Añasco, Peñuelas, Guanica, Santa Isabel de Coamo, Patillas, Jobos, and Isabela, authorized for the admission of goods docketed by the first and second-class custom-houses, and to clear domestic goods to all parts of the island. Each of the principal custom-houses is administered by a collector, an accountant, a treasurer, a chief of the tide-waiters, an inspector, and a weigher. There are two receptories at St. John's, and one in each of the following towns: Mayagües, Ponce, Guayama, Aguadilla, San German, Arecibo, Manatí, Añasco, Cabo Rojo, Caguas, Humacao, Guayanilla, and Juana Diaz.

One of those at St. John's is for the collection of the estate of regulars, rent of crown lands, fines, and for the indemnification of stamp-paper. The rest are for the sale of stamp-paper, papal bulls, tickets in the government lottery, and for the collection of subsidies and land-taxes.

Church.—There is a bishop nominated by the Crown, confirmed by the Pope, and suffragan of the archbishop of Cuba; a chapter composed of a dean, an archdeacon, and a precentor, four canons, and two distributors of rations; six vicars corresponding to St. John's, San German, Arecibo, Coamo, Aguada, and Mayagües, and a curate for each town in the island.

Army.—The territory of the island is divided into eight commandancies or military departments, whose chiefs have charge of the armed forces. The latter consist of three Peninsular regiments of 900 men each, a brigade of artillery, six battalions of disciplined militia infantry, and a regiment of militia cavalry, composed of three squadrons. The superior officers are—the captain-general, director-general of militia (infantry and cavalry), sub-inspector of the royal corps of artillery and engineers, and the second general in command, sub-director of the Peninsular corps.

Navy.—The coast is divided into six districts or adjutancies—St. John's, Aguadilla, Mayagües, Ponce, Guayama, and Naguabo, under a commander-in-chief, who resides at St. John's, and is subject to the commandant-general of the station at Havana, in Cuba. The force consists of a coast-guard schooner, at the orders of the captain-general and the superintendent, and the arsenal contains 18 gun-boats and 4 auxiliary boats, to be manned when necessary by the artillerymen and marines of the establishment. The district of St. John's extends 61 miles on the north from the mouth of the Camuy River, exclusive, which lies west of the port, to the Mameyes River on the east, and comprises the sub-delegations of Manatí and Arecibo on the west, and Loiza on the east. That of Aguadilla extends 36 miles from the mouth of the Camuy River on the north coast, to the Caño de Barrero on the west coast, and comprises the sub-delegation of Isabela on the north. That of Mayagües extends 44 miles from the Caño de Barrero to Punta Jaboncillos, windward* of the port of Guanica on the south coast, and comprises the sub-delegations of Cabo Rojo and San German de Lajas on the west. That of Ponce extends 38 miles on the south coast from Punta Jaboncillos to Punta Salitral de Aguirre, and comprises the sub-delegations of Gua-

---

* Windward means eastward, whence the wind usually blows, and leeward means westward.

yanilla and Salinas de Coamo. That of Guayama extends 25½ miles on the south coast from Punta Salitral de Aguirre to Cabo de Mala-pascua, and comprises the sub-delegation of Patillas.· That of Naguabo extends 42½ miles along the east coast, from Cabo de Mala-pascua to the mouth of the Mameyes River on the north, and comprises the sub-delegations of Yabucoa, Humacao, and Fajardo, and Cayo Santiago, Vieques, Culebras, and other islets and keys windward of Fajardo.

Laws.—The island, like that of Cuba, is subject to special laws, pending the formation of which are in force the laws, royal decrees, regulations, and orders dictated by the Supreme Government, and communicated to the island. Next in order are the local regulations instituted by the Governor, the Audiencia, and the respective corporations of the towns. Then follow the Ordenanzas de Intendentes de Nueva Espana, which especially regard the exchequer. Next the Recopilacion de leyes de Indias; and finally, the following codes: Novisima Recopilacion, consisting of the occasional Royal edicts; Nueva Recopilacion; Leyes de Toro; Ordenamiento de Alcalá; Fuero Juzgo, which is chiefly an abridgment of the Theodosian Code originally promulgated by Alacic, who succeeded Euric, one of the Gothic conquerors of Spain; with the addition, from time to time, of numerous other laws; and the Leyes de las Siete Partidas, mostly formed of Roman, Gothic, and Canon laws. The military, naval, and commercial branches are especially legislated by the Ordenanzas del ejercito, Ordenanzas generales de Marina y Matriculas, and the Código de Comercio.

Education.—This branch was greatly neglected until 1837, many of the towns being without even a primary school; but since the institution of the Provincial Committee on primary instruction in that year (incorporated in 1851 in the Royal Academy of Belles-lettres) much progress has been made. There is at present a public school in every town, besides private ones in those of the first and second class. The city of St. John's contains six public and four private schools—four of the first for girls and two for boys, and of the last, two for each sex—besides a seminary, founded in 1831, with three professorships proper to the institution, and those of the French and English languages, mathematics, and design, which are supported by the *Sociedad Económica de Amigos del Pais*. According to the statement published by the Academy in 1852, the schools of the island were attended by 2,981 scholars. A large number of the boys are sent to Europe or the United States for education. The young creoles are exceedingly apt scholars, and very few attain manhood without a knowledge of reading, writing, and arithmetic, as, unfortunately, despising mechanical pursuits, their great aim is to qualify themselves for clerkship. The education of the females has, until recently, been much less attended to, and many can not write (very few can do so correctly), although their musical abilities, which are very good, may be cultivated; at present, however, a knowledge of letters is becoming gradually diffused among them, and, like their brothers, they learn readily. They are in general excellent and industrious needlewomen. At St. John's there is a circulating library (the only one in the island) and two semi-weekly papers are published—the "Gaceta de Gobierno" and the "Boletin." The "Semanario" is issued at Mayagües, and the "Ponceño" at Ponce—both semi-weeklies.

Character and Customs.—The Porto Riqueneans, like the inhabitants of all warm countries, are generally indolent, owing both to the enervating character of the climate, and the bountiful provisions of nature against their necessary wants; but they are temperate, honest at heart though thriftless, courteous, hospitable, and devout, especially in the rural districts. The poor (?) tenant of a hut built entirely of the palm-tree, and bound together with the strong and pliable *bejuco*, whose only habiliments are a check shirt, osnaburgs pantaloons, straw hat, and an innocent *machete* strapped to his waist; who spends most of the time in his hammock smoking and playing on the *tiple* (a small guitar), doing nothing, or sleeping; divested of care for the future by the present possession of a few coffee and plaintain trees, a cow, and the indispensable horse, and anticipating the pleasures of the next holiday's cock-fight or dance, will extend the most cordial and polite welcome to the benighted traveler, set before him the best of his plantains, milk, and cheese; relinquish to him his rustic bed; unsaddle and feed his horse, which at break of day he will have in readiness, and dismiss his guest with a "vaya usted con Dios," refusing with a gesture of pride or offended delicacy all proffer of payment. Such is the *Jibaro* of the interior. Proximity to the coast, and therefore to *civilization*, renders him interested, salutationless because not answered on first occasions, and deceitful in ratio of the increase of his wants. Dancing, cock-fighting, and the card game of *monte* are the favorite amusements of the men. The women are passionately fond of dancing, which they learn almost instinctively, and are great church-goers. They are small, graceful, and pretty, and their natural graces are enhanced (in the towns) by the draping *mantilla*, which used to be worn on all out-of-door occasions, but is at present unfortunately giving way to the bolder and far less becoming European hat, except at church, although there too the innovation has recently been permitted at the instance of some foreign ladies. It is also common to see them at the *paseos* with none but nature's covering on their heads. The nature of the climate and the want of systematic exercise soon mar the beauty of the women, and, marriageable at the early age of twelve to fourteen, at thirty-five they rank as old.

The *Jibaros* are sallow, lean, and not very well formed, but wiry and active, and endurant of great fatigue, though consuming very little animal food. St. John's day (June 24) used to be celebrated much more gayly than at present, at the capital, by horse-racing through the streets during that and the preceding day, and the greater part of both nights, at which time especially the unaccustomed beholder would be struck with astonishment. Hundreds, perhaps thousands, of horses brought in from the country around, coursing through the streets at full speed; some with single riders, but the majority bearing a couple— the lady being seated behind and firmly grasping the handle-shaped rims of the *banastas;* the shouted jests of both spectators and performers; the clattering of the thousand hoofs; the detonation of fire-arms; the crackle and blaze of the bonfires, over which the most venturesome leap their horses, and clouds of smoke and dust, render it altogether a most singular, wild, and exciting spectacle. The amusement is partaken by all classes, and although complete license prevails and merry jests are rife, the bounds of decency are very rarely trespassed. Accidents occur, of course, but are soon forgotten, and few ladies would be deterred by having nearly broken their necks the year before. This custom is gradually yielding to the increasing opposition of the government, the same as the lively masquerades, egg-shell pelting in carnival, and the musical gift-begging parties at new year's, which last is now confined to the lower classes, though formerly participated in by the gentry, who in large bands of both sexes would play and sing at the doors of their acquaintance until invited in to refreshment and dancing. The horses are not shod, and instead of the European saddle, which only lately has been adopted among the higher classes, the harness consists of a *rodilla* or double pad of plantain-stalk, over that an *aparejo*—a thick, wide, and broad cushion of straw, surmounted by the *banastas*— a pair of strong wicker baskets, held together by bands of ox-hide, and strapped tightly around the horse, fitting on each side of the cushion, over which the rider throws his great-coat or blanket, and uses the *banastas* as saddle-bags. The women ride on them sideways, as on a saddle, to which they are preferred by many travelers as being less fatiguing. The baskets or panniers are sometimes quite large, serving to carry plantains, etc., and the writer has seen a whole family borne by one horse—a man with a child on his lap, one in each basket, and his wife *en croupe*. The doors of the houses are always open, except at night, and there being no porters, knockers, or bells, the visitor has to announce himself *viva voce* with an "a Dios gracias" (thanks be to

God), or "Ave Maria" (Hail Mary), which is answered from within—
"a Dios sean dadas" (to God be they given), or "sin pecado concebida"
(conceived without sin), with the addition of "adelante" (come forward).
Of late years, however, the knuckles begin to be found sufficient. The
houses are never more than two stories high, and are usually provided
with spacious balconies and jalousies, but have no glass window-shutters.
Twenty or thirty years ago the furniture of the majority of them was
limited to a few hammocks, benches, and ordinary deal tables, but at
present many are furnished in the best European style. Matting and
oil-cloth begin to be introduced for the houses of the better class, though
bare floors are still the rule. The churches being unprovided with
pews, the women alternately sit and kneel on the floor, or carpets
brought for the occasion by their servants, while the men stand and
kneel. Rich and poor, white and black, free and bond, adore God together, the coarse garment of the field-negro in contact with the silk
and broadcloth of his master. The slaves in general are well treated,
and allowed many privileges, but none are taught to read or write.

Ox-carts are generally used for drayage, except at St. John's, where
carts are not allowed in the streets, and heavy burdens are slung on
poles which are borne either by mules or on the shoulders of men.

PHYSICAL, POLITICAL, AND INDUSTRIAL. 155

INDUSTRIAL GEOGRAPHY.

Manufactures and Arts.—The chief manufacture is that of muscovado-sugar, the quality of which is not excelled in any part of the world. It is generally of a fine yellow color and strong grain, and is much esteemed in foreign markets for immediate use, as it does not require to be refined. Cattle-mills, and a few wind-mills, were, until within a few years, the only ones used, but at present steam-power is employed on many of the estates. A steam sugar-refinery and iron-foundry combined was estab'ished at Mayagües about three years ago by a Liverpool firm, but in consequence of the failure of the owner, was not sustained long enough to test success. Rum is made, but in small quantity. There is a steam-mill for sawing lumber and grinding maize near Cabo Rojo, and another in the district of Ponce. In the interior they make excellent sweetmeats of guava, orange, etc., *casabe* or yuca-bread, starch from the same root, arrow-root flour, coarse cotton cloth for hammocks, tiles, bricks, and coarse pottery, shingles, tubs hollowed out of the trunk of the cedar tree, mats, baskets, straw hats, tallow candles, soft soap, and cocoa-nut oil. In several of the towns there are, besides shoemakers and other trades, manufactories of chocolate, friction-matches, cigars, tortoise-shell combs, carts, cart-wheel tires, and other petty iron work, and several tanneries. Ship-building is limited to small schooners and lighters, whose chief merit is great strength derived from the excellence of the timber.

Agriculture.—Agricultural science in the island is still in a very primitive condition. The antediluvian wooden plough continues in use in the interior, although European implements are being generally adopted on the sugar plantations. Manuring is not practiced, owing to the great native fertility of the soil, and where a constant and numerous succession of crops has impoverished the land, it is abandoned. The latest official statement of the number of acres under cultivation is of too old a date for present reference. The staple productions, constituting the wealth of the island, are sugar, coffee, and tobacco, as, although cotton of excellent quality was extensively cultivated eight or ten years ago, the quantity produced at present is small. Besides the above are raised plantains, maize, rice, sweet potatoes, pulse, *yuca*, and other vegetables. The fruit of the island is independent of cultivation. The average yield of sugar per *cuerda* (nearly an English acre) is about 3,500 pounds, though 5,000 to 6,000 pounds is often produced by the best lands, and even 8,000 and 9,000 pounds in some instances, and this without the modern improvements in manufacture which so much increase the production. The annual crops of the estates average about 300 to 400 hogsheads (of 11 to 12 quintals each), while the largest make from 600 to 1,500 hogsheads. The proportion of molasses is about 4 gallons per 100 pounds of sugar. On plantations that are short of slaves, the *Jibaros* or country people are employed during the season of cane-cutting at the rate of two *reales* (twenty-five cents, per diem and fed, and they would be far more advantageous to the planter than slaves if their attendance could be relied on, but being indolent, impatient of control, and having few wants to supply, they will seldom be induced to work more than three or four days out of the week, and not very hard then. The cane planted from cuttings matures in 9 to 12 months. The crop usually extends from the beginning of January to May or June. Sugar is very profitable to the Porto Rico planter, paying full interest on the outlay at the rate of $2½ the quintal, and it is rarely worth less than $3, and frequently a good deal more. Coffee and tobacco are almost exclusively raised by free labor. The former is superior to that of Brazil, than which it commands nearly one dollar per quintal more in the German markets. There are two distinct qualities—the *native* or double-shell, and the *plantation* or single-shell. The first is grown by the peasantry and brought to the shops in small parcels of 25 to 100 pounds in payment of advances in goods and provisions at usurious prices, and is produced at the rate of 15 to 35 pounds per tree, which grows very high, and even spontaneously in the forests. The grains are allowed to dry in the berry, and though comparatively small and dull-colored, are of excellent flavor. On the regular plantations, which are few in number, and whose annual crops vary from 200 to 800 quintals, the trees are pruned low, and do not average much over a pound each. The grain is usually large and of fine color, because it is divested of the pulp and outer skin constituting the berry very soon after being picked. The primitive mode of removing the inner shell, still generally practiced, consists in beating the grains in a large wooden mortar with a pestle, which is sometimes tipped with lead to improve the color of the grains. A coffee plant requires about four years from the time of planting to that of fruition. The coffee market opens in November. Three-fourths of the tobacco is produced on the north coast, and were it not exclusively in the hands of the non-progressive peasantry, might be grown of nearly as good quality as in Cuba. As it is, it commands a fair price for the German markets, and in Sabána del Palmar, near the centre of the island, it is of very fine and peculiar flavor, and known as *tabaco de Comerio*. Plantains and Indian corn or maize are indigenous to the soil. The root of the first is perennial, or rather annually renewed by three off-sets, each giving one stalk, which grows up in 8 or 9 months and produces a cluster of 100 and upward. Maize gives three crops a year. In many districts it is raised only for the leaves and stalks to feed horses. The reason why a great deal of rice is not produced is doubtless the want of proper mills to clean it, instead of the mortar and pestle, which, besides the attendant labor, breaks the grain and gives it a dirty appearance. Notwithstanding the suitableness of the soil for both maize and rice, the cultivation of them (especially of the second) is quite inadequate to the consumption, and it seems to be a rule that wherever sugar, tobacco, coffee, or cotton are the staple products, that country, though capable of producing the necessaries of life, will depend upon others for the most of them. Cocoa and indigo grow spontaneously in many parts of the island, but only the first has there been any attempt to cultivate, and but very recently, and it will no doubt prove eminently successful.

Porto Rico, although essentially agricultural, did not produce much in early times. In 1783 the production was only 273,675 pounds of sugar, 111,875 pounds of cotton, 701,775 pounds of tobacco, 1,126,225 pounds of coffee, 8,300 horse-loads of plantains, 1,550,000 pounds maize, and 2,009,000 pounds rice, while in 1834 it rose to 41,989,700 pounds sugar, 402,200 pounds cotton, 2,624,900 pounds tobacco, 11,596,500 pounds coffee, 823,530 loads plantains, 11,548,000 pounds maize, and 8,049,800 pounds rice, besides a million gallons of rum; and in 1851 the *exportation* amounted to 118,416.300 pounds sugar, 366,600 pounds cotton, 6,478,100 pounds tobacco, 12,111,900 pounds coffee, 4,827,400 gallons molasses, and 34,700 gallons rum, showing a remarkable degree of advancement, especially in the production of sugar, in spite of innumerable disadvantages which might readily be obviated. According to the official returns for 1846, the capital invested in agriculture amounted to $40,796,464, and the value of agricultural products for the same year amounted to $6,896,621, or very nearly 17 per cent. on the capital.

Navigation and Commerce.*—The number of vessels entered at the

---

* There is neither a bank nor insurance office of any kind in the island. In former years the trade of the island, both import and export, was done almost entirely through St. Thomas, which to this day continues to be the depôt for dry goods which are obtained by the shop-keepers on a credit of 9 to 12 months, but at prices sufficiently high to compensate both for the time and the great risk of insolvency (the security required being merely nominal), the amount of indebtedness arising from which is estimated at several millions of dollars. The shop-keepers in turn sell on long credits at broadly-margined rates, and the fact that but a minimum of the sales for immediate consumption is for cash, at the same time that there is no imprisonment for debt, is a great disadvantage to the community, the members of which are thus rendered improvident, tempted to extravagance, and constantly involved, besides suffering from the conse-

several custom-houses of the island in 1851 was 1,324, registering 160,586 tons, of which the proportion per cent. was, 42 American, 22⅜ Spanish, 21¼ British (chiefly Nova Scotian), 5 Bremen and Hamburg, 1⅝ Hanoverian, Oldenburgian, and Prussian, 1¼ Sardinian, 2⅝ Danish, 3⅛ French, and ½ Swedish, Dutch, South American, and Dominican. The proportion per cent. at the respective ports was: St. John's 27 (15½ Spanish); Mayagües 20⅞ (11½ American); Ponce and Guayanilla 16¼ (8⅜ American); Guayama 13½ (8 American); Aguadilla 5½ (1½ American, 1¼ German); Arecibo 7⅞ (3⅜ American); and Naguabo, Humacao, Fajardo, etc., 9 per cent. (3½ American). The number of vessels cleared in the same year was 1,209, registering 154,042 tons. The total value of the trade in 1851 was $11,835,844. Of the imports, which amounted to $6,073,870 (including $763,475 in coin), 19½ per cent. was from the United States, 32¾ from the foreign West India Islands (chiefly St. Thomas), 21¼ from Spain, 12¾ from South America (chiefly in cocoa); 4⅝ from Great Britain, 4⅜ from British North America, 4 from Cuba, and 1¼ from Germany, Sardinia, and France; the same being in ratio of 49⅞ per cent. to St. John's (8⅝ in bond), 16⅜ to Mayagües, 14¼ to Ponce and Guayanilla, 8¾ to Guayama, 3½ to Aguadilla, 3 to Arecibo, 3¼ to Naguabo, and ¾ per cent. to Humacao, Fajardo, etc. The exports amounted to $5,761,974, of which 14½ per cent. from St. John's (6¼ from bond), 23¼ from Mayagües, 22⅞ from Ponce and Guayanilla, 13¼ from Guayama, 6½ from Aguadilla, 8¾ from Arecibo, 5⅜ from Naguabo, and 5¼ from Humacao, Fajardo, etc., distributed in the proportion of 43¾ per cent. to the United States, 5¼ to the foreign West India islands, 9⅜ to Spain, 21¾ to Great Britain, 6⅛ to British North America, 7⅝ to Germany, 1¼ to Austria, 3 to Sardinia, 1½ to France; and ⅜ to Cuba and South America. Of the value of the imports about 62 per cent. was in Spanish bottoms, 22 per cent. in American, and 10½ per cent. in British, and of the exports—37½ per cent. in American, 23½ per cent. in British,

---

quent demoralization. In 1850–51 the colonial administration attempted to put an end to the intermediation of St. Thomas by imposing a differential duty of 15 per cent. *ad valorem* on imports from that island and other "non-producing" countries, and by establishing bonded warehouses at several ports besides the one already existing at St. John's, and also to encourage the direct importation and exportation of produce, by returning a portion of the inward dues provided the vessel loaded entirely with produce of the island. Except a differential duty of 2½ per cent., none of these measures, however were approved of at Madrid, in consequence, evidently, of good, though perhaps expensive management on the part of the emissaries of the merchants of St. Thomas and none were realized. St. Thomas also is the chief market for the bills of exchange on Europe and the United States drawn in Porto Rico during the shipping season, and likewise for chartering vessels which arrive there in search of freight after discharging their outward cargoes at the Windward Islands.

PHYSICAL, POLITICAL, AND INDUSTRIAL.   159

and 14¾ per cent. in Spanish, besides the smaller proportions in bottoms of other nations.

Of the imports entered for consumption, $1,099,443 was in breadstuffs, $1,016,522 in textile fabrics, $798,921 in metals, $381,208 in fish, $337,399 in liquids, $233,701 in candles, soap, and wax, $209,416 in tobacco, $200,659 in cooperage materials, $138,942 in lumber, $121,449 in skins and furs, $182,564 in hardware and cutlery, $120,568 in lard, butter, and cheese, $92,607 in provisions, $91,468 in fruit and vegetables, $90,739 in machinery and sugar-pans, $74,223 in agricultural implements, $45,756 in upholstery, $40,252 in earthen and glass ware, 27,741 in haberdashery, $25,249 in coal, $41,000 in clothing and hats, $21,794 in garlic, $17,355 in perfumery, $14,895 in spices, $20,374 in drugs, $23,429 in sugar, $3,882 in playing-cards, $10,479 in ice, and $180,305 in sundries. The imports comprise 44,333 barrels of flour (37,934 from Spain and 2,973 from the United States), 675 puncheons and 9,653 barrels corn meal (515 puncheons and 7,686 barrels from the United States), 200 bushels corn, 65 barrels rye flour, 10,402 quintals rice (9,400 from the United States), 290 quintals oats and barley, 3,881 quintals pilot-bread (3,605 from the United States), 2,709 quintals vermicelli (2,310 from Spain), 16,761 quintals potatoes (8,361 from Spain, 5,764 from the United States), 7,725 quintals onions (3,398 from Spain, 3,105 from the United States), 612 barrels apples (545 from the United States), 816 quintals figs (762 from Spain), 5,852 quintals peas and beans (5,793 from Spain), 23,123 quintals cocoa (from South America), 97,574 quintals dry fish (22,854 from the United States, 64,218 from British North America), 13,860 barrels mackerel (5,208 from the United States, 7,485 from British North America), 6,152 barrels herrings (4,630 from British North America, 714 from the United States), 2,033 quintals smoked herrings (1,388 from the United States), 15,542 gallons fish oil (8,286 from the United States, 4,988 British America), 2,939 barrels pork (2,700 from the United States), 848 barrels beef (650 from the United States), 2,155 quintals jerked-beef (244 from the United States, 1,911 South America), 2,180 quintals hams (1,647 from the United States), 5,030 quintals lard (4,868 from the United States), 1,519 quintals butter (1,275 from the United States), 3,697 quintals cheese (2,051 from the United States), 15,688 quintals soap (14,682 from Spain, 427 United States), 119 quintals sperm candles (97 from the United States), 4,211 quintals tallow candles (3,861 from the United States), 390 quintals stearine candles (163 from the United States), 10,663 quintals leaf tobacco (7,178 from Cuba, 1,213 St. Domingo, 2,272 United States), 1,580 quintals chewing tobacco (1,506 from the United States), 2,798 thousand cigars (1,478 Cuba, 995

Germany), 149 quintals refined sugar (49 from the United States), 2,603 quintals clayed sugar (from Cuba), 4,575 thousand feet of white-pine lumber (2,936 from the United States, 1,234 British North America), 2,267 thousand feet of pitch-pine lumber (1,904 from the United States), 4,727 thousand shingles (3,413 from the United States, 1,034 British North America), 112,628 hogsheads hoops (98,425 from the United States, 6,524 British North America), 2,081 thousand staves (1,822 from the United States, 696 British North America), 1,947 thousand wood hoops (1,491 from the United States), 3,410 empty hogsheads (2,255 from the United States), 15,400 dozen bottles malt liquor (8,791 England), 64 quintals cassia (47 from the United States), 717 quintals black pepper (705 from the United States), 1,041 pounds tea (504 from the United States), 1,002 barrels tar and pitch (862 from the United States), 3,000 tons coal (1,500 England), 28 horses (25 from the United States), 2 mules (from the United States), 8,545 quintals nails (1,023 from the United States, 3,072 England), 5,307 gallons brandy, 41,215 gallons gin, 86,248 gallons rum, 4,880 dozen liquors, and 580,739 gallons wine. The exports comprised 1,184,163 quintals sugar, 121,110 quintals coffee, 64,781 quintals tobacco, 4,827,400 gallons molasses, 6,827 quintals hides, 3,666 quintals cotton, 347 puncheons rum, 5,881 head of cattle 105 horses and 67 mules, 6,167 gallons bay-water, 1,429 thousand ears of Indian corn, 40,363 coco-nuts, 90 quintals cocoa, 6,925 ox-horns, 1,669 thousand oranges, 675 thousand plantains, 85 thousand cigars, 4 tons lignum-vitæ, 178 tons logwood, 68 quintals pimento, 8,017 logs cabinet wood, 128 quintals rice, 7,862 pounds annatto, 600 quarts castor oil, besides some cassia-lignea, ginger, tumeric, coco-nut oil, etc.

Revenue.—The revenues of the island are divided into maritime and inland. The first are derived from the customs and harbor dues, and amounted in 1851 to $1,069,448, which is a good deal less than the average of the previous decade, owing to the repeal of the export duties in 1850. The above amount includes $88,477 for tonnage dues, $3,108 for anchorage, and $2,543 for light-house dues. There are no official returns published of the inland revenue, nor of the expenses of government.

Communication.—The roads of the island have been until very recently so bad as to be almost impassable in the wet season. Within a few years, however, measures have been taken to improve them, and, if present projects are realized, there will soon be carriage roads communicating between the principal towns. At present, except for very short distances, the island can only be traversed on horseback. The project of a railroad between St. John's and Arecibo has been discussed, but is not likely to be realized for many years. There are several small coasting vessels running between the various ports, and to and from St Thomas, but affording very indifferent accommodation to passengers. A steamer (the Borinqueño), of 450 tons, built in New York in 1850, for a joint stock company in the island, communicated between the chief ports and St. Thomas for a short time, and promised to be a profitable investment, besides the facilities it afforded to trade and the traveling public, but her machinery soon proved defective, and notwithstanding expensive repairs in New York, in 1853, she now lies useless. There is a monthly steamer from Cadiz to Porto Rico, arriving from the 28th to the 30th, and proceeding to Havana. Twice a month a British Royal Mail Packet steamer from Southampton to St. Thomas, Porto Rico (arriving the 3d and 18th, at 3 P.M.), Jacmel in Hayti, and Jamaica, and thence back to Jacmel, Porto Rico (arriving the 15th and 30th, at 8 A.M.), and St. Thomas. Time from Southampton to Porto Rico, 15 days 21 hours. From St. Thomas the steamers of the above-mentioned company afford communication as follows: 1st. Leaving St. Thomas the 18th for Havana, Vera Cruz, and Tampico, retouching at Vera Cruz and Havana, and returning to St. Thomas the 15th. 2d. Leaving St. Thomas the 4th and 19th for Santa Marta, Carthagena, Chagres, and Greytown, and *vice versa* (excepting Santa Marta), arriving back at St. Thomas the 15th and 30th. 3d. Leaving St. Thomas the 3d and 18th for St. Kitts, Nevis, Monserrate, Antigua, Guadaloupe, Dominica, Martinique, St. Lucia, Barbadoes, and Demarara, and *vice versa*, arriving back at St. Thomas the 30th and 15th. Connecting with the above are the following: From Barbadoes the 6th and 21st for St. Vincent, Carriacon, Grenada, Trinidad, and Tobago, and *vice versa*, arriving back at Barbadoes the 12th and 27th. From Jamaica, the 7th, for Honduras, and arriving back at Jamaica the 25th. A British steamer between New York, Bermuda, and St. Thomas used to transport the Porto Rico mails and passengers, but the route was changed some time since to Halifax, Bermuda, and St. Thomas, and at present the only communication with the United States is by sailing vessels. The trade of both St. Thomas and Porto Rico greatly needs a regular and speedy means of intercourse with the United States, and it is to be hoped that steam communication will soon be reestablished. The mail betweeen the principal towns of the island is carried twice a week by mounted couriers, and the service is pretty well performed, the postage on a single letter ranging from 6 to 31 cents, according to the distance.

Weights.—These are the same as used in Spain, viz.:

The quintal=$4a$ or arrobas=100 libras=200 marcos=1,600 onzas= 25,600 adarmes=76,800 tomines=921,600 granos. The libra is equivalent to 460 French grammes, or, in English weight, 1.01423 pounds avoirdupois, or 1.23258 pound Troy. In apothecaries weight—the libra =12 onzas=96 dracmas=288 escrupulos=6,212 granos.

The arrelde used in weighing beef is equal to 4 libras.

Lineal Measure.—The Burgos or Castilian vara=8 pies=36 pulgadas of 12 lineas each, and is equivalent to 836 French millimetres or 32.91332 English imperial inches. The palmo=9 pulgadas or 12 dedos. The braza=2 varas. The paso=5 pies. The estadal=4 varas. The Castilian league=6,666⅔ varas, and the provincial league=5,000 varas.

Agrarian Measure.—The cuerda is a square of 75 varas or 5,625 square varas=4,701¾ square English yards, or nearly an English acre. The caballeria=200 cuerdas or nearly 6 Cuban caballerias, and is usually 10 cuerdas front by 20 deep. The vara de tarea used in clearings and cane-cutting=3 lineal varas. The solar or building lot varies in the different towns.

Dry Measure.—The fanega=12 almudes, contains 4,822¾ Spanish or 3,439 English cubic inches, equal to 1.550 English imperial or 1.600 Winchester bushels. The cahiz, used only to measure lime=12 fanegas. The hogshead of sugar ranges from 10 to 18 quintals (tare 10 per cent.), and the barrel 250 to 280 pounds (tare 20 pounds). The bag of coffee 110 to 120 pounds (tare 1 pound). The fanega of cocoa 110 pounds. The pack of cotton 120 pounds.

Liquid Measure.—The cuartillo (quart) is nearly one-fifth larger than the Castilian, and contains 725 French millitres or 44.225 English cubic inches. The Spanish arroba of wine or great arroba=1,237½ Spanish or 981 English cubic inches, equal to 3.538 imperial gallons. The arroba of oil or small arroba=2.780 imperial gallons. The pipa or pipe of wine=27 arrobas. In guaging molasses the standard used is the American gallon, equal to 4½ cuartillos or common bottles. The puncheon of molasses contains 110 to 140 gallons.

Currency.—The coin generally used in the island consists of unmilled and roughly-stamped bits of silver of exceedingly irregular shape, minted in Caracas, and denominated *macuquina*, of the respective values of 1-16, ⅛, ¼, and ½ of a *peso* or dollar. The whole dollar is very scarce, and the *macuquina* gold pieces have become cabinet curiosities. The original fullness of weight and purity of this silver coin, added to the facility of counterfeiting it, resulted, soon after the ports of the island were thrown open to foreign trade, in its exportation to a considerable extent, and the introduction of spurious pieces, so that the quantity in the island at present is estimated at less than a million of dollars, and characterized by the opposites of the above qualities. The vexed questions constantly arising from its depreciation have caused the government to deliberate on the expediency of withdrawing it, but no direct measures having yet been taken, it continues to be the general medium, done up in paper packages of $50, which, however, on passing from one hand to another are always opened, counted over, and in part rejected, for which purpose the larger commercial establishments sometimes require two clerks. The copper coin is chiefly thin discs weighing about the fourth of a cent, and current at 272 to the dollar. English pennies and American cents also pass, in parts of the island where the proper coin is scarce, at 4 to the *medio* or 1-16th of a dollar.

The gold and silver money of Spain, Mexico, and Spanish South America is current, the first usually at 12½ and the latter at 6¼ per cent. better than the *macuquina;* but this rate varies with the supply, which is rendered necessary by the exacted payment of one-fourth of all the customs-dues in Spanish or ex-Spanish gold. Very recently the circulation of other foreign coin has been authorized at the rates stated in the appendix to this work.

DEPENDENCIES.

Vieques (*Crab Island*).—This island, constituting the eighth and last of the departments into which Porto Rico is divided, lies 10⅜ miles east of the main island, in latitude 18° 10′ north and longitude 65° 23′ 14″ west of Greenwich. It is trapezoidal in shape, 24 miles long from east to west, 6 miles broad, 62 in circumference, and 167 square statute miles in area. The land is moderately high and well wooded: the south-west end hilly, and westward low and uneven. There are numerous shoals and reefs between it and the main island. The soundings 1½ miles from shore are 6 fathoms. Like Porto Rico it is beautified by a luxuriant perennial vegetation, and divided through its length by a mountain chain of little height, the chief eminences of which are Cerro Jaloba on the south-east, and Cerro Tinajas on the west. There are few rivers in the island, and none permanent nor of pure water, and among the numerous brooks only one (the Quebrada Mulas, near the town) is constant, but small and brackish. There are nine shipping places, viz.: Puerto Mulas on the north, Punta Arenas on the north-west, Puerto Ferrer or Ferro, and Ensenada Honda on the south, Puerto Mosquito and Puerto Real on the south-west, Puertos Diablo and Salinas on the east, and Playa-Grande on the west: none of these, however, merits the name of harbor. The climate is warm and damp, and unhealthy in the numerous swampy places. The soil, especially in the lowlands, is good, and the vegetable kingdom is rich, affording excellent timber for all purposes, such as úcar, tachuelo, capá, cojoba, tortugo, zapote, maria, canelo, etc. Pimento and yams abound in the woods. Sugar, coffee, and cotton are produced, besides plantains, rice, and other vegetables, grains and fruits. There is a copper mine in the south-western extremity of the mountain chain near Puerto Real, and three salt-ponds on the north coast, but none of them are worked. The animals are cattle, horses, mules, and sheep; ducks, flamingoes, doves, partridges, parrots, pigeons, etc.; abundance of shell-fish and crabs of great size, and on the south coast tortoise-shell and other turtle are numerous. History is silent in regard to the aboriginal inhabitants of this island, neither is there any record of the first settlement of Europeans. It is, however, upward of forty years ago that several persons from St. Thomas, St. Croix, and other vicine islands settled in it and established a few farms and sugar plantations. In 1846 the population numbered 1,275.

The island is immediately governed by a commandant of the army, under the orders of the governor of Porto Rico, and assisted by a *Junta de visita* or circuit court. He resides in the town of Isabel Segunda, which is the only one in the island, and was founded in 1843 on the north side in a spacious plain. In 1846 it contained 5 streets, 66 wooden houses and 32 huts, with a population of 354, a church, a temporary hospital, a fort, and a square.

Until 1846 the trade was limited to barter of timber and other productions of the soil, for merchandise from the neighboring islands, but in consequence of the privileges subsequently accorded by the government, warehouses and shops are being multiplied, and the affairs of the island in general are progressive. The productions in 1846 were valued at $83,494, on a capital of $1,091,901.

Culebras, also called Carlit and Serpent's Island on English maps, and sometimes Great Passage Island, lies north-east of Vieques and off the east end of Porto Rico, and is more than six miles in length and about three in breadth. There are many reefs and keys about it. Off its east side is Culebrita or Little Passage Island, from the south end of which a dangerous reef extends to the south-south-west and south-west, three miles. To the west of the south part of this reef is the harbor of Culebra, which is two miles in extent at the entrance. There are two channels into this harbor which are divided by a bed of rocks and bordered by reefs; but the interior is clear and secure, and there is a pilot in the port. Plenty of water, wood, and fish may be obtained here, and the neighboring keys are famous for a great number of tropical birds which breed there.

Caja de Muertos (*Dead Man's Chest*).—This small islet is situated in lat. 17 °50' north and long. 66° 33' west, about five miles from the centre of the south coast of Porto Rico. It is shaped like a wedge : the north end high, centre low, and the south end has a sugar-loaf mountain, which appears at a distance like a detached island. It is foul on both north-east and south-west sides. The anchorage is on the west side off the lowland, and half a mile off shore, in eight fathoms.

Desecheo (*Zacheo*), **Mona, and Monito.**—These islets, lying off the west end of Porto Rico, are only frequented by fishermen, and we have no special description of them. They are said to contain wild goats, and even cattle; and abound in fish, turtle, birds, and fine conches. Mona, the largest (probably 20 square miles in area), is high and well wooded. Its eastern extremity, which projects considerably, is in latitude 18° 07', longitude 67° 47'. Monito lies north-west of it in latitude 18° 11', longitude 67° 52'. Zacheo is about 18 miles almost due west of Point San Francisco and in latitude 18° 24', longitude 67° 27'.

EARLY HISTORY.

PORTO RICO was discovered by Columbus in 1493, on St. John's day (24th of June), which was being celebrated on board when land was descried, for which reason the admiral gave it the name of the saint, though the natives called it Borinquen. The beautiful aspect of the country, and the facilities afforded by a fine harbor,* decided Columbus to anchor and land, but at the sight of the Spaniards the natives fled to the woods, and Columbus, inferring that they would prove intractable, and not wishing to run the risk of a doubtful undertaking, weighed anchor and proceeded on his course toward St. Domingo. Among his companions was Don Juan Ponce de Leon, who in 1508 reconnoitered and took possession of the island. The friendly reception given him by the chief cacique, Agueinaba, added to the fertility of the soil and the gold which was found in abundance, determined Ponce de Leon to form a colony, and he returned to St. Domingo to seek the appointment of governor. But Don Miguel Serron had forestalled him, and at the head of 200 picked men, including the said Leon, Añasco, Sotomayor, Gil, Toro, and Diaz, overcame the resistance of the natives with little loss, and effected a settlement, founding the town of Caparra in 1510, at the place now called Pueblo-viejo, on the southern shore of the harbor of St. John's. In the same year were begun the settlements of San German and Aguada. In 1511, the Indians, displeased with the distribution made of them by Ponce de Leon among his companions, revolted,† and greatly annoyed the intruders; but after several fierce encounters they were completely subjected on the field of Yagüeca or Añasco. However, the incursions of the Caribs were so frequent, and the hurricanes so destructive, that the new settlers became discouraged, and the island was almost deserted in 1530-32.

According to history, the population of the island at the time of

---

* It is uncertain what part of the island Columbus first visited, but from the description of the Indian town and surrounding country, it was probably Aguadilla.

† Though the Spaniards had already occupied the territory for some time, the Indians still entertained doubts of their mortality, and the cacique Aguciuaba (successor to him who had so amicably received Ponce de Leon), and the other Indian chiefs, desiring to test the matter, resolved that one of them, the cacique Broyoan, should, if possible, put to death the first white man found in his dominions. Salcedo, a young Spaniard, traveling through the province of Yagüeca (now Añasco), was met by several Indians and accepted their offer to carry him across the Guaurabo River. Midway they let him fall and held his head under until life was extinct. This proof of mortality was immediately communicated to all the chiefs in the island, and the general revolt ensued.

its discovery was 600,000. They were peaceful, affable, generous, and hospitable, and punished theft with their severest penalty. They believed in a good spirit from whom they derived all their benefits, and an evil spirit to whom they attributed all their ills. Their chief amusements were dancing and the game of ball. Their weapons were bows and arrows, and a species of club formed like a hatchet, no doubt the same as the North American tomahawk. The men employed themselves in hunting and fishing, and the women in cultivating maize, sweet potatoes, yams, plantains, etc.

The island was invaded by the British as early as 1519. In 1595 the adventurer Drake besieged the capital with a numerous fleet and sacked it, after having burnt the vessels that were in the harbor. This hastened the conclusion of the fortifications of the Morro begun by Philip II. In 1598 the Earl of Cumberland landed with 1,000 men and took possession of the Morro, whose garrison of 400 men capitulated; but an epidemic which broke out among his troops soon obliged him to re-embark, after sacking and firing the town and leaving the fort in ruins. This invasion cost the colony, besides 80 brass-pieces, a large amount of provisions, and the release of many prisoners. In 1615 a powerful fleet, commanded by the Dutch general, Baldwin Henry, took possession of the capital and laid siege to the Morro castle, where the citizens and the small number of troops had taken refuge. The besieged, headed by Captain Juan de Amezquita y Quijano, sallied against the enemy and fought so valiantly that in a few hours the Dutch were defeated and Baldwin Henry slain by the intrepid Amezquita. In commemoration of the event there is a monument on the field of the Morro. In 1625 great ravages were committed by the buccaneers and fillibusters, who, however, were completely defeated in 1650. In 1678 the capital was again attacked by a British squadron commanded by Earl Strain, but a violent storm destroyed their vessels against the coast before the troops could be landed. In 1702 another British squadron landed troops on the shores of Arecibo, but so impetuous an onslaught was made on them by a small band of militia cavalry under Captain Correa, that they were forced to retreat to their ships, leaving many dead and wounded. In 1797 the capital was again besieged by the British under Abercrombie, with a large fleet and over 10,000 troops, but so heroic was the defense made by the inhabitants during thirteen successive days, that the besiegers were compelled to re-embark with great loss in dead, wounded, and prisoners, and in ammunition and stores. Aguadilla also was attacked at the same time and made a brave resistance, and in 1825 repelled some privateers who had taken possession of the fort. Fajardo, too, made a brave defense against the privateers.

THE CAPITAL AND THE DEPARTMENTS.

San Juan Bautista de Puerto Rico, called St. John's in English, is situated on the north coast, about 30 miles west of Cabeza de San Juan, on an islet about 2¾ miles in length and little over 500 yards in breadth. This islet is connected by the bridge of San Antonio with a larger one, which is united to the mainland by the Aurora bridge. The city, which with its suburbs occupies an area of 87 acres, was founded in 1511 by the Governor Juan Ponce de Leon, whose fortified residence, now known as the *Casa-blanca*, was the first edifice of any note therein. In 1846 the number of houses was 918, including the public and state buildings, with a population of 15,867. There are 13 streets—6 running east and west, and 7 north and south—straight and very well paved, with a concave centre instead of gutters at the sides, and, as few wheeled vehicles are used, and the land slopes, every shower washes them thoroughly. The city proper is encircled by a high and exceedingly thick wall,[*] plentifully surmounted by cannon, and embracing two strong fortresses (the Morro on the north-west, at the entrance of the harbor, and San Cristóbal, with its labyrinthine outworks on the east) and pierced by three guarded gates—San Justo, San Juan, and Santiago. There are, besides, many well-situated batteries, and the place is altogether so well fortified, and protected moreover by the high and rocky nature of the northern coast, as to be almost impregnable. The principal edifices are—the Casa de Beneficencia (alms-house), with accommodation for 300 persons; the military hospital, with ample room for 350 beds; the building containing the treasury offices; the palace of St. Catherine or Real Fortaleza, where the Captain-General resides and has his office: the arsenal; the cathedral (a great, gloomy structure commenced in 1513 and not finished until very recently); the convents of Santo Domingo, San Francisco, and Carmelite nuns, which also serve as churches; the town-house, seminary of San Ildefonso, the bishop's palace, park of artillery, a fine theatre, custom-house, bonded warehouse, market-house, jail, and house of correction. The intramural dwellings are two stories high, built of brick with very thick walls, balconies, and terrace-roofs, to which the tenants resort in the evening. They are all whitewashed inside and out, and relieved by the green balconies and jalousies, combining with the clean and well-paved streets to give the city a very neat appearance. Water is supplied

---

[*] This wall forms a parapet over 40 feet thick, and, together with the two main fortresses, cost so much money that the king of Spain declared that they must have been made of solid silver.

by a cistern in every house, and drought seldom lasts long enough to occasion any inconvenience in that respect.* There are several squares, the principal ones being the Plaza de Armas and the Plaza de Santiago, which fronts the theatre and is finely shaded by almond-trees. Two fine military bands† play in them several evenings in the week. There is also a fine shady *paseo* extending to the bridge of San Antonio. The climate of the city is hot but dry, and comparatively healthy. A steam ferry-boat plies across the harbor‡ to the village of Cataño on the mainland. There is a long stone pier at which brigs can discharge.

The First Department‖ is situated on the north-east of the island, and contains 15 towns with their corresponding districts, viz.: Bayamon, Toa-alta, Toa-baja, Dorado, Naranjito, Vega-alta or Espinosa, Vega-baja or Naranjal, Corozal, Guaynabo, Rio-piedras, Trujillo-alto, Trujillo-bajo, Rio-Grande, Loiza, and Cangrejos. St. John's is the port of entry.

Bayamon, the head of the department, and founded in 1772, is situated near the southern coast of the harbor of St. John's, north of Naranjito, east of Toa-alta, and west of Rio-piedras. Population of the district 8,125. *Productions.*—Sugar, a little coffee, etc., amounting to $101,913, on a capital of $828,223. *Rivers.*—The Bayamon, rising in the Cidra mountains and emptying into the harbor of St. John's at Palo-seco, and its tributaries the Rio Hondo and Minillas, besides 13 brooks.

Toa-alta, founded in 1751, on the north coast of the island, toward the

---

* An attempt was made some years ago to bore an Artesian well in the principal square, but, owing to want of implements or to ignorance, the contractor, a Swede, we believe, failed, and was condemned to labor in the chain-gang. At the place called Miraflores, near the city, are some excellent springs.

† Probably as good as any in Europe.

‡ The harbor of St. John's is very capacious, and ships may lie with the utmost safety in five, six, and seven fathoms. The entrance is along the islet on which the city is erected, and between the Morro point (on which is a revolving light, in lat. 18° 28′ 40″ north and long. 66° 7′ 2″ west of Greenwich, showing 8 seconds of light to 114 of darkness) and three islets called the Cabras. South of the latter is a small islet occupied by a little square fort called the Cañuelo, which defends the west side of the harbor. The channel is generally buoyed. The west and south sides of the harbor are flat and shoal. The west side of the entrance is rocky, but in the channel the ground is generally gravel and sand, with depth of five, six, seven, and eight fathoms. From the south side of the town a low point of land extends to the southward, and is surrounded by a shoal. Ships generally ride to the east of this flat, and out of the wash of the sea occasioned by the trade wind, which commonly sets directly into the harbor. It is high-water in the harbor at 8h. 21min. on the full and change, and the greatest rise is about 1¼ feet.—*Blunt's Coast Pil. t..*

‖ These items are chiefly taken from Pastrana's Catechism of Geography. The statistics of population, production, etc., of this and the succeeding departments are from the census of 1846. In the agricultural productions only sugar, coffee, tobacco, cotton, and cattle will be mentioned.

interior, north of Corozal, south of Toa-baja, east of Vega-alta, and west of Bayamon. Population of the district 4,321. *Productions.*—Sugar and coffee in small quantity, cattle, etc., amounting to $38,862, on a capital of $256,997. *Rivers.*—The Toa, rising in Cerro-pelado, in Cayey; the Lajas, rising west of the town; the Mucarabones and Guadiana, rising in the southern wards; the Cañas, flowing from the heights on the south, and the Cancél, rising on the east. These are all tributaries of the Toa, which empties into the sea at the place called Boca Habana. There are also 14 brooks.

Toa-baja, founded in 1745, on the north coast, north of Toa-alta, southeast of Dorado, and north-west of Bayamon. Population of the district 2,979. *Productions.*—Chiefly sugar, and valued at $102,839, on a capital of $981,357. *Rivers.*—The Toa, before-mentioned, besides several brooks and drains.

El Dorado, founded in 1842, on the north coast, east of Vega-baja and north-west of Toa-baja. Population of the district 2,786. *Productions.*—Chiefly sugar, and amounting to $78,034, on a capital of $535,829. *Rivers.*—The Toa, Dorado, Cocal, and Lajas, besides several drains.

Naranjito, founded in 1824, in the interior, north of Sabana del Palmar, south of Bayamon, south-east of Corozal, and west of Aguas-buenas. Population of the district 2,835. *Productions.*—Some coffee, etc., amounting to $12,243, on a capital of $106,234. *Rivers.*—The Rio-Grande or Toa, with its tributaries the Naranjito and Cañas, besides 19 brooks.

Vega-alta or Espinosa, founded in 1775, on the north coast, north of Corozal, south-west of Dorado, east of Vega-baja, and west of Toa-alta. Population of the district 3,807. *Productions.*—Sugar and coffee, etc., amounting to $64,922, on a capital of $227,928. *Rivers.*—The Sibuco, emptying into the sea north of Naranjal, besides several brooks.

Vega-baja or Naranjal, founded in 1776, on the north coast, north of Ciales, east of Manatí, and west of Vega-alta. Population of the district 4,173. *Productions.*—Sugar, coffee, etc., amounting to $81,865, on a capital of $648,998. The forests abound in timber of ortegon, úcar, ausubo, etc. *Rivers.*—The Sibuco and Morovis, besides several brooks and three large drains.

Corozal, founded in 1795, in the interior, northward, south of Toa-alta, north-west of Naranjito, and east of Morovis. Population of the district 5,009. *Productions.*—All kinds of lesser fruits, amounting to $38,038, on a capital of $244,727. *Rivers.*—Maravilla, Congo, Corozal, Padilla, Negro, Maria, and Sibuco, besides a number of brooks.

Guaynabo, founded in 1723, in the centre of the department, north of Aguas-buenas, south-east of Bayamon, and west of Trujillo-alto. Population of the district 4,287. *Productions.*—Chiefly the lesser fruits, and amounting to $42,386, on a capital of $351,708. *Rivers.*—The Guaynabo and the Bayamon, besides innumerable brooks.

Rio-piedras (also called Roble),* founded in 1774, at the place called El Roble, in the interior of the territory which partly surrounds the harbor of St. John's, north-west of Trujillo-alto, south of Cangrejos, and east of Bayamon. Population of the district 3,576. *Productions.*— Several of the lesser fruits, amounting to $50,830, on a capital of $437,203. *Rivers.*—The Piedras, rising in the heights of Morcelo and emptying into the harbor of St. John's, at the place called Puerto-nuevo, besides several brooks—the one called Quebrada de Juan Mendez being noted for its pure and wholesome waters.

Trujillo-alto, founded in 1801, near the centre of the department, north of Gurabo, south-west of Rio-piedras, and east of Guaynabo. Population of the district 2,749. *Productions.*—A small quantity of coffee and the lesser fruits, amounting to $11,082, on a capital of $126,065. *Rivers.* the Loiza, rising in Cerro-Gordo, in Hato-Grande, besides many smaller streams.

Trujillo-bajo, founded in 1817, near the centre of the department, north-east of Trujillo-alto, south-east of Rio-piedras, and west of Rio-Grande. Population of the district 4,435. *Productions.*—Chiefly sugar, and amounting to $83,112, on a capital of $646,682. *Rivers.*—The Loiza and the Canobanilla, besides several smaller streams.

Rio-Grande, founded in 1840, near the north coast, east of Trujillo-bajo, south-east of Loiza, and west of Luquillo. Population of the district 2,884. *Productions.*—Coffee, etc., amounting to $58,866, on a capital of $267,274. *Rivers.*—Espiritu-Santo, Rio-Grande, Mameyes, and Herrera, besides several brooks.

Loiza, founded in 1719, on the north coast, north-west of Rio-Grande and Luquillo and north-east of Trujillo-bajo. Population of the district 3,528. *Productions.*—Sugar, etc., amounting to $147,157, on a capital of $615,320. The forests abound in timber of úso, ortegon, tortugo, cedar, satin-wood, etc, *Rivers.*—Rio-Grande or Loiza, Espiritu-Santo, Canobana, Canobanilla, and Mameyes, besides 18 brooks. The sands of the Rio-Grande and its tributaries in this district contain particles of iron, steel, and gold.

Cangrejos, founded in 1760, on an islet connecting with the one on which stands the city of St. John's by the bridge of San Antonio, and with the mainland by the bridge of La Aurora, is situated north of Rio-piedras, east of St. John's, and west of Loiza. The population, produc-

---

* This town is a favorite resort of the people of St. John's (whence there is a line of stages), and is famous for its excellent bread. The population, prcduction, etc., of Cangrejos was included in the census of 1846 in the numbers given for Rio-piedras.

tion, etc., of this district in the census of 1846 were included in the numbers given for Rio-piedras. *Productions.*—Several of the lesser fruits. *Rivers.*—The Piedras, besides the rivulet of Juan Méndez, which empties into the sea through the Caño de la Aurora. The soil is very sandy, and produces an abundance of the fruit called hicacos or cocoa-plums, and pajuiles or cashews. It was on the beach of this islet that the British landed when they besieged St. John's in 1797.

The **Second Department** is on the north side of the island, and comprises a *villa* and seven towns with their corresponding districts, viz.: Arecibo, Hatillo, Camuy, Quebradillas, Utuado, Morovis, Ciales, and Manatí.

Villa of Arecibo, the head of the department and port of entry of the first class, founded in 1778, on the north coast, north of Utuado, east of Hatillo, and north-west of Manatí. The town lies about nine and a half leagues westward of St. John's, on a tongue of land between the river and the sea, and on the western side of the roadstead, which, being open to the north wind, affords little shelter to vessels. Population of the district 11,187. *Productions.*—Sugar, coffee, tobacco, cattle, etc., amounting to $356,138, on a capital of $1,650,456. The forests contain trees of ortegon, maga, tortugo, zapote, capá, roble (oak), laurel, cojoba, úcar, and other fine timber. *Rivers.*—The Rio-Grande de Arecibo, rising in Adjuntas and emptying into the roadstead of Arecibo, and its tributaries, the Tanamá, Don Alonzo, and Limon, besides several brooks and drains. On the road to Utuado, and about seven miles south-east of the town, at a place called Consejo, is a cave worthy of being visited by the traveler. Near the town is the Ojo de Agua, a spring bubbling up out of a cavity in the rock, and apparently boiling. The soil of the district is exceedingly fertile.

Hatillo, founded in 1823, on the north coast, north-east of Quebradillas, east of Camuy and west of Arecibo. Population of the district 5,373. *Productions.*—Coffee, tobacco, much cattle, etc., amounting to $60,334, on a capital of $367,664. *Rivers.*—The Hatillo, which rises in Lares and disembogues in the sea north-west of the town, and the Tanamá, besides two brooks.

Camuy, founded in 1807, on the north coast, north-east of Quebradillas, east of Isabela, and west of Hatillo. Population of the district 5,382. *Productions.*—Coffee, tobacco, etc., amounting to $52,565, on a capital of $298,966. *Rivers.*—The Camuy, which is the Hatillo before-mentioned, and the Cibao, which flows into the Guajataca, besides two brooks.

Quebradillas, founded in 1823, near the north coast, south-east of Isabela and south-west of Camuy. Population of the district 4,618. *Productions.*—Coffee, tobacco, a little sugar, etc., amounting to $40,516, on a capital of $286,528. *Rivers.*—The Guajataca or Tuna, rising in Lares and disemboguing in the sea north of Isabela, besides several brooks. The district is famous for the sweetness of its oranges.

Utuado, founded in 1739, near the centre of the island, north of Adjuntas, south of Arecibo, south-east of Lares, and south-west of Ciales. Population of the district 7,804. *Productions.*—Coffee, sugar, etc., amounting to $65,566, on a capital of $375,109. The forests, which are very thick, afford excellent timber of various kinds. *Rivers.*—The Rio-Grande or Utuado, which is the same that traverses Arecibo, the Jayuga, Tanamá, Caricaboa, Lesama, Montaña, Saliente, Mamey, Haragan, Jauca, Limon, Yuni, Pellejas, Guanico, Bibí, and Caguanita, all emptying into the first, besides numerous smaller streams. There is a cave at the place called Caguana, supposed to have been used as a cemetery by the aborigines from the human remains found in it.

Morovis, founded in 1818, near the centre of the island, north of Barros, south of Vega-alta, east of Ciales, and west of Corozal. Population of the district 4,808. *Productions.*—Chiefly coffee, and amounting to $32,650, on a capital of $203,855. The forests abound in the best timber of the country. *Rivers.*—The Rio-Grande or Manatí, Morovis, Unibon, and Carrera, besides several brooks.

Ciales, founded in 1820, in the interior of the island, northward, west of Morovis, south of Manatí, and north-east of Utuado. Population of the district 3,074. *Productions.*—Coffee and tobacco in small quantity, etc., amounting to $25,057, on a capital of $159,713. *Rivers.*—The Rio-Grande or Manatí, besides one brook.

Manati (a port of entry of the third class), founded in 1738, near the north coast, north of Ciales, south-east of Arecibo, and west of Vega-baja. Population of the district 11,598. *Productions.*—Sugar, coffee, tobacco, etc., amounting to $149,712, on a capital of $997,144. *Rivers.* -The Manatí, rising in Barranquitas and emptying into the sea on the north. There is a bed of coal in this district on the estate of Mr. Cornelius H. Kortright.

The **Third Department** is situated on the north-west side of the island, and comprises one *villa* and six towns with their corresponding districts, viz.: Aguadilla, Isabela, Moca, Villa de la Aguada, Rincon, Pepino, and Lares.

Aguadilla,* the head of the department and port of entry of the first

---

* The town is in lat. 18° 24′ 57″, and long. 67° 8′ 15″ (as observed by Capt. John McKellar, R. N., and 18° 25′ 58″ and 67° 0′ 20″ as given by Spanish officers), about seven and a half miles north-east by east from Punta San Francisco, and about two miles south-south-east of Punta de Peñas Blancas, which is the northernmost point of the bay which fronts the town, and affords anchorage for the largest ships with shelter

class, founded in 1775, on the north-west coast, south-west of Isabela and north-west of Moca. The town contains several fine dwellings and warehouses and a theatre. Population of the district 10,458. *Productions.*—Sugar, coffee, tobacco, cattle, etc., amounting to $158,041, on a capital of $1,080,601. *Rivers.*—The Chiquito, which rises in the district, and the Culebrinas, rising in Lares—both disemboguing in the sea between Aguadilla and Aguada. There are also seven brooks. As previously stated, it is supposed that this was the port made by Columbus on the discovery of the islands. The town was attacked in 1797 by several British vessels, and in 1822 and 1825 was partly destroyed by fire. In 1825 the battery was taken by pirates, who were, however, soon put to flight.

Isabela (a port of entry of the third class), founded in 1819, on the north-west coast, north-west of Quebradillas and north-east of Aguadilla. Population of the district 9,405. *Productions.*—Sugar, coffee, tobacco, cattle, etc., amounting to $160,581, on a capital of $725,101. Fossil salt is found on a hill near the Guajataca River. *Rivers.*—The Guajataca or Tuna, besides two brooks.

Moca, founded in 1774, near the coast, north-west of Pepino, south-east of Aguadilla, and north-east of Aguada. Population of the district 8,213. *Productions.*—Coffee, a little sugar, etc., amounting to $89,837, on a capital of $481,837. The forests abound in capá, cedar, ausubo, algarrobo or locust, tortugo, and other hard woods, and there is a quarry of grindstone in the vicinity. *Rivers.*—The Culebrinas, rising in Lares and emptying into the sea between Aguada and Aguadilla, besides 22 brooks and several drains.

Villa de la Aguada, founded in 1506, on the north-west coast, north-west of Añasco, north-east of Rincon, and south-west of Moca and Aguadilla. Population of the district 8,103. *Productions.*—Sugar, coffee, tobacco (in small quantity), etc., amounting to $84,116, on a capital of $546,884. *Rivers.*—The Culebrinas, Rio-Grande, and Guayabo, which

---

from the sea-breeze; there being ten fathoms at about three cables length from shore, and no less than seven to eight fathoms at a distance of one-fourth of a mile anywhere front shore. The whole bay is perfectly clear with exception of the white reef, Puñas Blancas, extending from Punta de Palmas, which is the northernmost point of the bay. It may be entered easily and safely at any hour of the day, but not at night, when the breeze dies away and calm ensues. The sea in general is smooth, with the usual trade-wind, but becomes very rough with a norther. There is excellent water to be obtained from the Ojo de Agua, which passes through the middle of the town. There is also a good river of fresh water. There is a small battery of three guns commanding the north side. The bay is much frequented by vessels bound from Europe to Cuba, both on account of facility in obtaining refreshments and to procure pilots for the Old Bahama channel.—*B'unt's Coast Pilot.* There are no wharves or piers, and boats are beached.

empty into the sea, and their tributaries the Culebras and Cañas, besides seven brooks and two drains. Here was the residence of the chief Indian cacique, Agueinaba, and it must therefore have been the principal place in the island before the Conquest.

Rincon,* founded in 1770, on the north-west coast, south-west of Aguada and north-west of Añasco. Population of the district 4,385. *Productions.*—Cattle (abundant), sugar, a little coffee, etc., amounting to $25,623, on a capital of $162,960. *Rivers.*—The Rio-Grande, which separates the town from that of Aguada, besides four brooks and nine drains.

Pepino, founded in 1752, in the interior toward the north-west coast, north-east of Añasco and north-west of Lares. Population of the district 10,723. *Productions.*—Coffee, sugar, cotton, etc., amounting to $99,546, on a capital of $499,473. *Rivers.*—The Culebrinas, Guatemala (a thermal stream), Guacio, Sonador, Guajataca, Cibao, Arenas, and Juncal, besides 36 brooks.

Lares, founded in 1829, in the interior toward the north-west coast, south of Quebradillas and south-east of Pepino. Population of the district 6,035. *Productions.*—Coffee, sugar, cotton, etc., amounting to $58,040, on a capital of $272,803. The district abounds in excellent timber. *Rivers.*—Guajataca, Camuy, Prieto, Guallo, Cedrito, and Culebrinas, all having their sources in the district, and the Guacio, which rises in Adjuntas, besides 13 brooks.

The Fourth Department is situated on the west coast of the island, and comprises two *villas* and three towns, with their corresponding districts, viz.: Villa de Mayagües, Añasco, Cabo Rojo, Villa de San German, and Sabana-Grande.

Mayagues,† the head of the department and port of entry of the first class, founded in 1760 on the west coast, north of Cabo Rojo, south of Añasco, and north-west of Sabana-Grande. The town proper is situated at the base of a range of hills and about one mile from the bay, on which is a large number of dwellings, fine fire-proof warehouses, etc. The road between is flanked by dwelling-houses and shady sand-box

---

* The bay is well sheltered but small, of unequal bottom, and full of rocks.

† The custom-house of Mayagües is in lat. 18° 13' north and long. 67° 12' 45" west by French survey, and 67° 8' 0" on English charts. The anchorage is well sheltered from the north and fit for ships, provided they are not very large, there being five fathoms water inside the bar. A good knowledge of the entrance is necessary to avoid a shoal stretching about half a mile out from Punta del Algarrobo and a reef extending two cable-lengths from the little point called Puntilla. The river runs into the northernmost part of the bay, and in this estuary schooners and sloops, for the most part, lie up during the hurricane season, being the best anchorage on the west coast. The tides rise and fall two to four feet—time irregular.—*Blunt's Coast Pilot.*

trees. The town, which was almost entirely destroyed by fire the 30th of January, 1841 (loss estimated at two or three millions of dollars), and again partly burnt down the 2d of January, 1852, contains a number of fine two-story brick houses, some of them very large, with iron doors and balconies, and furnished in the best style; a large church, town-house, barracks (a large stone edifice with a battery of several guns), and a neat square where a military band plays twice a week. Water is supplied by a few wells, but chiefly by the river which runs close by, and an excellent spring at the foot of the hills above-mentioned. The custom-house is fire-proof and a striking building. On the north side of the bay is a small battery, and near by is a large iron edifice built for the foundry and sugar-refinery mentioned in a previous chapter. There are several sugar estates in the immediate neighborhood. It was here that about four years ago Commander Randolph, of the American sloop-of-war Albany, aided by the consul, Mr. Turull, exacted the liberation of the captain and crew of the schooner North Carolina (wrecked on the coast), who were detained by the authorities for the investigation of the wreck. The population of the district in 1846 was 20,952. *Productions.*—Sugar, coffee, etc., amounting in that year to $603,730, on a capital of $3,192,274. *Rivers.*—The Añasco, also known as the Rio-Grande or Guaurabo, which rises in Cerro Cain, in San German, and disembogues in the sea south-west of that town; the Cañas, Arenas, Mayaguesillo, Guaba, and Mucarabona or Bucarabones, which empty into the Añasco; the Casey, tributary of the Cañas; the Mayagües, that empties into the port; the Guanajibo, rising in Cerro Cain and emptying into the sea south-west of Mayagües, and its tributary, the Rio-Hondo. There are, moreover, 71 brooks. There is a quarry of good building stone near the town, and metallic substances in the hills.

Anasco* (a port of entry of the third class), founded in 1703, on the west coast, north of Mayagües, south-east of Aguada, and south-west of Pepino. Population of the district 11,714. *Productions.*—Sugar, coffee, etc., amounting to $286,554, on a capital of $1,128,574. *Rivers.*—The Añasco or Guaurabo, which rises in Cerro Cain, in San German, and disembogues in the sea south-west of the town; its tributaries the Casey, Cañas, Humata, and Daguey, and the Rio-Hondo, which empties into the Guanajibo, besides 36 brooks. This is a flourishing and fertile district, and was also a place of note among the aborigines, who called it Yagüeca. Pyrites and marquesites are found in the mountains.

Cabo Rojo† (a port of entry of the second class), founded in 1771, on

---

* The bay is fit for vessels of any size, and is completely sheltered from the north winds.

† *Puerto Real de Cabo Rojo*, about five and a half miles south of Punta de Guana-

the west coast, south of Mayagües and west of San German. Population of the district 17,892. *Productions.*—Sugar, coffee, cotton, a little tobacco, etc., amounting to $288,093, on a capital of $1,100,558. *Rivers.*—The Viejo and the Estero, which rise in Cerro Cain, in San German, and empty into the Guanajibo, besides several brooks and a number of drains. This district contains a quarry of laminous stone, and the salt-pits of Sierra de Peñones, which produced 931 *fanegas* in 1851.

Villa de San German, founded in 1511, on the west coast, inland, west of Sabana-Grande and east of Cabo Rojo. Population of the district 44,402. *Productions.*—Sugar, coffee, a little cotton, and tobacco, etc., amounting to $359,817, on a capital of $2,871,181. *Rivers.*—Rio-Grande or Guanajibo, rising in Cerro Cain, in the district; its tributaries, the Cruavo, Miraflores, Maunabo, Cain, Oconuco, Duey, Rosario, Estero, and Viejo; the Prieto, Guallo, Toro, Guaba, Lajas, Zapo, and Bucarabones or Mucarabona, which empty into the Añasco River, besides many brooks and several drains and lagoons. There are good grounds for believing that there are two veins of gold in the district—one in the hills that rise from the banks of the Oconuco River, and the other in a rivulet at the place called San Pedro. This district is mostly lowland, and therefore generally known as La Bajura. It is famous for fine sweetmeats (generally made by the women) and for embroideries.*

Sabana-Grande, founded in 1814, on the west coast, inland, east of San German and south-east of Mayagües. Population of the district 4,935. *Productions.*—Sugar, coffee, a little cotton, and tobacco, etc., amounting to $31,715, on a capital of $224,875. *Rivers.*—The Rio-Grande, which empties into the sea under the name of Guanajibo; the Cañas, Cruavo, Miraflores, Coco, and Subsúa, besides many brooks.

The Fifth Department is situated on the south side of the island and comprises two *villas* and nine towns, with their corresponding districts, viz.: Villa de Ponce, Barros, Adjuntas, Yauco, Guayanilla, Peñuelas, Juana Diaz, Santa Isabel de Coamo, Villa de Coamo, Aybonito, and Barranquitas.

---

jibo, is a fine harbor, nearly circular in figure, and about three-fourths of a mile in extent from west to east. In the centre there is 16 feet of water and 3 fathoms at the entrance, which is by a very narrow channel near the south point of the harbor. From the north point a great reef stretches out, which, doubling Cayo Fonduco, ends at Punta de Veras. South-south-west, about two miles from the southernmost point, is Punta de Guaniquilla, the north point of the *Bay of Boqueron*, which is so full of reefs as not to allow anchorage. Punta de Melones, the south point, is distant from the first about two and a half miles.—*Blunt's Coast Pilot.*

* Especially towels, some of which are so elaborately worked as cost $20 to $30.

Ponce,* the head of the department and a port of entry of the first class, founded in 1752, on the south coast, east of Guayanilla, southeast of Peñuelas, and south-west of Juana Diaz. The town is about one and a half miles distant from the bay, with straggling houses between, and separated by an unbridged, shallow stream, which becomes a torrent after heavy rains. The church, which is one of the finest in the island, is surrounded by a large square and fragrant acacia trees. Around this square are fine brick houses two stories high, but the rest are poor-looking one-story wood houses. The barracks is a large stone edifice, and serves as a fortress. The buildings on the bay are chiefly fire-proof warehouses and the dwellings of the merchants, many well built and in the European style, though generally but one story high. Population of the district 21,466. *Productions.*—Sugar, coffee, tobacco, etc., amounting to $803,607, on a capital of $3,989,382. *Rivers.*—The Jacaguas and the Inabon, both rising in Utuado and emptying into the sea south of Juana Diaz; the Bucaná, also rising in Utuado, and the San Patricio in Adjuntas under the name of Corcho, both emptying into the eastern side of the bay of Ponce; the Portugués or Ponce, which rises in Adjuntas, and the Marueño and Cañas, the three emptying into the western side of the bay. There are also several brooks and drains. In this district there is a quarry of white stone and several hot mineral springs in the ward of Quebrada Domingo. The town was almost entirely destroyed by fire the 27th of February, 1820.

Barros, founded in 1825, on the north of the department and in the centre of the island, south of Morovis and north-west of Barranquitas. Population of the district 2,810 *Productions.*—Coffee, etc., amounting to $11,416, on a capital of $87,065. The forests contain many kinds of timber for building and cabinet-work. *Rivers.*—The Orocovis and Barros, which rise in the district; the Bauta, which originates in the hills between the town and Ciales, and the Lamas, rising in Barranquitas: all emptying into the Rio-Grande of Manatí, besides many smaller streams.

Adjuntas, founded in 1815, on the south coast, inland, north-east of Peñuelas, south of Utuado, east of Sabana-Grande, and north-west of Juana Diaz. Population of the district 3,070. *Productions.*—Coffee, etc., amounting to $20,164, on a capital of $128,270. The forests abound in cedar, capá, oak, ortegon, guaraguao, higuerillo, laurel, canelo (a species of cinnamon), and other trees. *Rivers.*—The Portugués or Ponce

---

* The town and harbor are about five leagues east of Guanica. Land low near the water's edge and covered with mangrove bushes and some cocoa-nut trees. There is a low, sandy island and a reef near the entrance of the port.

and the Corcho, under the name of San Patricio, both of which disembogue in the district of Ponce; the Saltillo, Ciénagas, Pellejas, and Tanamá, which empty into the Arecibo River; the Vacas, a tributary of the Jacaguas of Juana Diaz, and the Viejas, Guilarte, Limaní, Cidra, and Guallo, which, under other names, disembogue in the district of Añasco. All these have their sources in the district, which is also watered by 218 smaller streams, and in this respect is probably without a parallel.

Yauco,[*] founded in 1756, near the south coast, west of Guayanilla, south-east of San German, and south-west of Peñuelas. Population of the district 11,468. *Productions.*—Sugar, etc., amounting to $98,138, on a capital of $459,987. *Rivers.*—The Yauco, which rises in the district and disembogues in the sea south of Guayanilla; the Subsúa, which, confluent with the Cañas of Sabana-Grande, empties into the port of Guanica, and the Duey, tributary of the Yauco, besides several brooks.

Guayanilla (a port of entry of the second class), founded in 1833, on the south coast, east of Yauco, south-west of Peñuelas, and west of Ponce. Population of the district 5,722. *Productions.*—Sugar, coffee, tobacco, etc., amounting to $94,502, on a capital of $637,572. The forests abound in úcar, yaití, cojoba, cedar, ausubo, capá, and other trees. *Rivers.*—The Guayanilla, rising in the Guilarte Mountain, and the Yauco, both emptying into the sea south of the town. There are also a brook and several drains. The place was invaded in 1797 by the British, who were repulsed by the inhabitants, and in 1838 and 1839 the town was partly burnt down.

Peñuelas (a port of entry of the third class), founded in 1793, near the south coast, north-west of Ponce, south-west of Adjuntas, and north-east of Yauco. Population of the district 7,561. *Productions.*—Sugar, coffee, cotton, tobacco, etc., amounting to $67,663, on a capital of

---

[*] The harbor of Guanica, a port of entry of the third class, lies immediately west of Yauco, 16 miles west of Ponce and about 15 miles east of the Morrillos de Cabo Rojo. "It is the best anchorage on the south coast, and fit for vessels of all classes, with from six and a half to three fathoms water, which latter depth is found in its interior. The bottom is sand and gravel. The mouth of the harbor is in the centre of the bay, formed by the Fronton (cliff or bluff) de la Brea on the west, and Punta Picua on the east, near which last are the two islets of Caña-gorda, between which and Punta de la Meseta, which is the east point of the entrance of the harbor, there is a reef which reaches out from the coast about a mile and nearly forms a circle, uniting at one end with the islets and at the other with Punta de la Meseta; there is also a rocky shoal stretching out about half a mile from it. Between Fronton de la Brea and Punta de los Pescadores, which last is the west point of the mouth of the harbor, the coast forms another bay, the mouth of which is shut by a reef, that running out from Punta de los Pescadores, ends on the south side of the bay, about a mile within the Fronton de la Brea."—*Blunt's Coast Pilot.*

$259,644. *Rivers.*—The Barreal, Guayanés, Yaya, and Jobos, which empty together into the sea south of the town, taking in their course the names of the various districts they traverse. There are also several brooks.

Juana Diaz, founded in 1798, near the south coast, north-east of Ponce and west of the Villa de Coamo. Population of the district 7,616. *Productions.*—Sugar, coffee, tobacco, etc., amounting to $106,929, on a capital of $756,583. Cattle abound. *Rivers.*—The Jacaguas, Guallo, and Toabaca, which empty into the sea south of the town; the Escalabrado, emptying into the sea south-east of the town, and the Inabon, which separates the district from that of Ponce, besides several brooks. There is a quarry of white stone in the vicinity.

Santa Isabel de Coamo, also called Coamo-Abajo (a port of entry of the third class), founded in 1841, on the south coast, south of Villa de Coamo and south-east of Juana Diaz. Population of the district 991. *Productions.*—Sugar, etc., amounting to $25,284, on a capital of $202,116. *Rivers.*—The Piedras-blancas and the Coamo, which empties into the sea south-west of the town. There are some fine hot mineral springs two and one-third leagues north-east of the town, which are resorted to by invalids.

Villa de Coamo, also called Coamo-Arriba, founded in 1646, on the south coast, inland, north of Santa Isabel, east of Juana Diaz, and south-west of Aybonito. Population of the district 3,805. *Productions.*—Coffee, tobacco, etc., amounting to $36,122, on a capital of $212,025. *Rivers.* The Coamo, which rises in the district and empties into the sea southwest of Santa Isabel, its tributaries the Minas and the Cullon, the Escalabrado and the Toabaca, which disembogue near Juana Diaz, and the Jueyes, which empties into the sea south of the town of Salinas, besides 29 brooks.

Aybonito, founded in 1822, on the north of the department in the centre of the island, north-east of the Villa de Coamo and south-east of Barranquitas. Population of the district 3,059. *Productions.*—Coffee, etc., amounting to $29,763, on a capital of $216,477. *Rivers.*—The La Plata, rising in Cayey, in Cerro-pelado; its tributary the Honduras or Usabon, and the Cullon, besides several brooks.

Barranquitas, founded in 1803, on the north of the department in the centre of the island, north-west of Aybonito, south-east of Barros, and south-west of Sabana del Palmar. Population of the district 3,600 *Productions.*—Cattle, coffee, etc., amounting to $19,296, on a capital of $179,092. *Rivers.*—The Usabon, tributary of the La Plata; the Piñona, which rises in the district in the hill called La Torrecilla and flows into the Usabon; the Rio-Hondo, another tributary of the La Plata, and rising in the district; the Barrancas and the Cuñabon, which rise in the Torrecilla and empty into the Manatí, besides several brooks.

The Sixth Department is situated on the eastern extremity of the island, southward, and comprises nine towns with their corresponding districts, viz.: Humacao, Naguabo, Ceiba, Fajardo, Luquillo, Las Piedras, Patillas, Maunabo, and Yabucoa.

Humacao, the head of the department and port of entry of the second class, founded in 1793, on the east coast, north of Yabucoa, south-east of Las Piedras, and south-west of Naguabo. Population of the district 6,165. *Productions.*—Sugar, a little coffee, etc., amounting to $116,916, on a capital of $670,123. The district abounds in cattle. *Rivers.*—The Humacao, which rises south of the town of Las Piedras and empties into the sea south-west of Humacao; the Anton Ruiz, rising in the district, and the Candelero, which rises in the south in Cerro-pelado and empties into the sea by the Boca de Candelero, south-west of the town. There are also many brooks. From some meteorological cause or other, phenomena in animal life are frequently met with in this district and its neighborhood, such as dwarfed men, distorted animals, etc.

Naguabo (a port of entry of the first class), founded in 1794, on the east coast, north-east of Humacao and south-west of Ceiba. Population of the district 5,841. *Productions.*—Sugar, cattle, a little coffee, etc., amounting to $83,049, on a capital of $643,888. In 1851 nearly 6,000 beeves were shipped from this port for the consumption of the neighboring French and Danish islands. The forests abound in ausubo, yellow and black cojoba, algarrobo, tachuelo, capá, and other hard wood, and wild hogs are sometimes met with. *Rivers.*—The Naguabo, called Blanco at its rise; its tributaries the Cubuí and Prieto, and the Santiago and Daguao, all rising in the Luquillo mountains and emptying into the sea south-east of the town. There are also many smaller streams.

La Ceiba, founded in 1838, on the east coast, north-east of Naguabo and south of Fajardo. Population of the district 2,024. *Productions.* —Sugar, a little tobacco, cattle, etc., amounting to $37,608, on a capital of $230,216. *Rivers.*—The Daguao and the Fajardo, besides several brooks.

Fajardo (a port of entry of the second class), founded in 1774, on the east coast near the headland of San Juan, north of Ceiba and south-east of Luquillo. Population of the district 5,009. *Productions.*—Sugar, cattle, etc., amounting to $113,901, on a capital of $475,807. The forests afford ausubo, tabanuco, masa, granadillo, guaraguao, and other useful timber. *Rivers.*—The Fajardo, which rises in the Luquillo mountains and disembogues in the sea on the south of the port; there are also eight smaller streams. The sands of the river are auriferous. Nearly the whole town was burnt down on the 29th of April, 1832, and the 11th of April, 1833.

Luquillo (a port of entry of the third class), founded in 1797, on the north-east coast, north-west of Fajardo and east of Rio-Grande. Population of the district 2,918. *Productions.*—Sugar, etc., amounting to $46,123, on a capital of $254,429. The forests abound in tabanuco, ausubo, laurel, sabina, algarrobo, úcar, and other trees. *Rivers.*—The Mameyes, Sabána, Pita-jaya, and Juan Martin, which rise in the mountains on the south of the district. The first and last empty into the sea on the north of the town, and the others together on the east. There are also 22 brooks. The sands of the streams are auriferous, and small nuggets of gold have been found in the Luquillo mountains.

Las Piedras, founded in 1801, on the east coast, inland, north-east of Hato-Grande or San Lorenzo, north-west of Humacao, south-west of Naguabo, and south-east of Juncos. Population of the district 4,801. *Productions.*—Coffee, tobacco, etc., amounting to $24,025, on a capital of $173,569. *Rivers.*—The Gurabo, which rises in the Luquillo mountains and empties into the Rio-Grande of Loiza, and its tributaries the Humacao and the Valencia, besides a large number of smaller streams.

Patillas (a port of entry of the third class), founded in 1811, on the south-east coast, north-east of Guayama and south-west of Maunabo. Population of the district 5,734. *Productions.*—Sugar, tobacco, cattle, etc., amounting to $90,119, on a capital of $579,788. The forests are well stocked with cojoba, péndola, tortugo, tachuelo, maga, cedar, jácana, jaya, palo de vaca, yaití, carne de doncella, and many other trees affording excellent timber and cabinet-wood. Large masses of rock-crystal are found in the Mala-pascua mountain. The town was half burnt down in 1841.

Maunabo, founded in 1799, on the south-east coast, north-east of Patillas and south of Yabucoa. Population of the district 2,633. *Productions.*—Coffee, tobacco, a little sugar, etc., amounting to $25,618, on a capital of $209,688. The forests abound in various fine timber. *Rivers.* —The Maunabo, rising in the mountain ridge which separates the district from those of San Lorenzo and Yabucoa, and emptying into the sea on the south of the town. There are many brooks besides.

Yabucoa, founded in 1793, on the south-east coast, north of Maunabo and south of Humacao. Population of the district 6,468. *Productions.* —Sugar, a little coffee, cattle, etc., amounting to $96,818, on a capital of $768,601. *Rivers.*—The Guayanés, rising in the mountain that separates the district from that of San Lorenzo, receives the Ingenio and Limones, and empties into the sea on the east of the town, besides 89 smaller streams.

The Seventh Department is situated inland toward the east coast, and comprises ten towns with their corresponding districts, viz.: Guayama, Hato-Grande, Juncos, Gurabo, Caguas, Aguas-buenas, Sabana del Palmar, Cidra, Cayey, and Salinas.

Guayama,[*] the head of the department and a port of entry of the first class, founded in 1736, on the south coast, south-east of Cayey and southwest of Patillas. The part of the town situated on the bay is called Arroyo, the town proper being some distance inland. Arroyo contains some fine dwellings and warehouses, and it is contemplated to erect a church there. Population of the district 12,244. *Productions.*—Sugar, etc., amounting to $616,295, on a capital of $3,801,864. The forests abound in úcar, algarrobo, capá, cojoba, tachuelo, etc. *Rivers.*—The Aguamaní, which rises in the Carite mountain, north-east of the town, and empties into the sea on the south; the Rio-Seco, called Charcas at its source, north of the port of Jobos, and spreading its waters over the land near said port, and the Yaurél, which rises north of Arroyo and disembogues in the sea south-east of the town under the name of Nigua. There are also 41 brooks. The prosperity of this district, and of nearly the whole south coast, is greatly retarded by the drought that usually prevails there.

Hato-Grande or San Lorenzo, founded in 1811, inland toward the east coast, south-west of Las Piedras and east of Cidra. Population of the district 6,672. *Productions.*—Sugar, a little coffee, etc., amounting to $63,832, on a capital of $275,701. *Rivers.*—The Rio-Grande or Loiza, which rises in Cerro-Gordo, south of the district, and empties into the sea north of Loiza, and its tributaries the Majáguas, rising in the Culebras mountain which separates the district from that of Caguas, and the Cayaguas, which rises in Yabucoa, besides 75 smaller streams. The waters of some of the brooks are hot.

Juncos, founded in 1797, toward the east coast, inland, north-east of Hato-Grande, north-west of Las Piedras and south-east of Gurabo. Population of the district 3,584. *Productions.*—Sugar, coffee, cattle, etc., amounting to $30,906, on a capital of $309,142. *Rivers.*—The Valenciano, rising in the Guineo mountain, south-east of the town, and the

---

[*] The anchorage is formed by a shoal two or three miles in length and three or four miles from the coast, and has no other shelter from the sea-breeze than the shoal. Vessels usually anchor in four fathoms one mile from the shore. The soundings of the entrance vary from five to seven and eight fathoms, gradually shoaling toward the shore. The land by the water side is low, but up the country high and uneven.—*Blunt's Coast Pilot.*

The port of Jobos also serves for the export trade of the district. It is a port of entry of the third class, and one of the best in the island, being, in fact, a regular wet-dock, but the entrance affords only 14 to 15 feet draft. The bottom throughout is soft mud.

Gurabo, rising on the north-east, both emptying into the Rio-Grande of Loiza, and there are besides 49 brooks.

Gurabo, founded in 1815, inland, toward the east coast, north-west of Juncos, south of Trujillo-alto, and north-east of Caguas. Population of the district 3,876. *Productions.*—Little sugar and coffee, cattle, etc., amounting to $24,816, on a capital of $167,434. *Rivers.*—The Rio-Grande or Loiza, which rises in Cerro-Gordo, in Hato-Grande, and its tributary the Gurabo, which rises in Juncos, besides 29 smaller streams.

Caguas, a considerable town and seat of the judicature of the department, founded in 1775, inland, toward the east coast, north-east of Sabana del Palmar, south-west of Gurabo, and south-east of Aguas-buenas. Population of the district 7,808. *Productions.*—Sugar, coffee, cattle, etc., amounting to $91,684, on a capital of $722,347. The forests abound in moca, granadillo, laurel, guaraguao, oak, and many other trees. *Rivers.*—The Rio-Grande or Loiza and its tributaries; the Turabo, which rises in the same district, in Cerro-pelado; the Cagüitas, rising in Sierra de Caguas; the Bairoa, whose source is in the ward De las Mulas, in Aguas-buenas, and the Caña which rises in the Jagueyes ward, in Aguas-buenas; the Quebradillas, rising westward near the district of Cidra and emptying into the Turabo; and the Caibonito, rising in the Alto de los Naranjos, in the district, and emptying into the Cagüitas; besides 40 brooks. There is a quarry of marble in the vicinity.

Aguas-Buenas, founded in 1838, in the north of the department, north-west of Caguas and south of Guaynabo. Population of the district 3,912. *Productions.*—Coffee, etc., amounting to $16,718, on a capital of $110,111. *Rivers.*—The Bayamon, rising in Cidra and emptying into the sea near St. John's, and the Cagüitas, Bairoa, and Caña, which empty into the Loiza; besides 21 brooks. In the ward of Sumidero, on the south of the town, is a very large cave whose limits have not been ascertained, but it is supposed to extend as far as the town of Sabana del Palmar.

Sabana del Palmar, founded in 1826, in the east of the department, near the centre of the island, north-east of Barranquitas, south of Naranjito, north-west of Cidra, and south-west of Caguas. Population of the district 2,533. *Productions.*—Tobacco of excellent quality, known as " *Tabaco de Comerio,*" coffee, etc., amounting to $9,422, on a capital of $96,881. *Rivers.*—The La Plata, which rises in Cerro-pelado, in Cayey, and its tributaries the Arroyato and Rio-Hondo, besides six brooks.

Cidra, founded in 1809, in the east of the department near the centre of the island, north of Cayey, south-east of Sabana del Palmar, east of Barranquitas, and west of Hato-Grande. Population of the district

PHYSICAL, POLITICAL, AND INDUSTRIAL. 185

5,926. *Productions.*—Coffee, etc., amounting to $23,850, on a capital of $219,944. The forests abound in anón, capá, oak, péndolo, maria, and many other trees affording fine timber. *Rivers.*—The Rio-Grande or La Plata, which rises in Cerro-pelado, in Cayey; its tributary the Arroyato, and the Bayamon, both rising in the district, and the latter emptying into the harbor of St. John's. There are also 21 brooks.

Cayey, founded in 1774, in the south of the department, inland, northwest of Guayama, south of Cidra, and south-east of Aybonito. Population of the district 5,201. *Productions.*—Sugar, coffee, cattle, etc., amounting to $53,435, on a capital of $457,719. The forests abound in cedar, capá, guaraguao, ausubo, and other timber. *Rivers.*—The Rio-Grande or Cayey, which is the same with the La Plata, which rises in Cerro-pelado, in the district; the Guavate, with the same source; the Carite and Maton, which rise in other mountains in the district and empty into the Rio-Grande, and the Jájome and Lapa, which also originate in the district and empty into the Salinas. There are besides 84 smaller streams. The finest valley landscapes can be viewed from the Cayey mountain, which is traversed by the main road.

Salinas* (a port of entry of the second class), founded in 1851, near the south coast, south-west of Cayey, north-east of Santa Isabel de Coamo, and west of Guayama. The population, production, etc., were included by the census in the numbers given for Guayama, of which district it was a ward until 1852. *Productions.*—Sugar and coffee in small quantity, etc. *Rivers.*—The Lapas and Majadas, which rise in Cayey, and the Jueyes, both disemboguing in the sea south of the town; besides eight brooks and numerous drains. The town and district derive their name from the salt-ponds (salinas) south of the former.

The Eighth Department is the island of Vieques, already described.

---

* Salinas is a good place to lie in. There are four or five fathoms anchorage in good ground, and a good watering-place afforded by a kind of lagoon near the water-side. —*Blunt's Coast Pilot.*

STATISTICS OF PORTO RICO.

EXPORTATION FROM THE ISLAND OF PORTO RICO.

	Sugar, Quintals.	Molasses, Gallons.	Coffee, Quintals.	Tobacco, Quintals.	Cotton, Quintals.	Hides, Quintals.
1828	197,886..	374,174..	111,610..	23,965..	4,792..	5,178
1829	277,154..	377,443..	121,870..	23.771..	4,820..	4,191
1830	340,104..	465,889..	169,119..	34,902..	4,978..	4.487
1831	307.733..	823,420..	104.858..	49,417..	4,526..	4.768
1832	346,534..	1,187.244..	168,181..	36,024..	5,373..	3,887
1833	342.794..	1,216,770..	102,862..	49,526..	8,780..	4.452
1834	358.722..	1,171,796..	182,305..	40,568..	5,749..	5,627
1835	438.574..	1,391,593..	72,623..	57,151..	7,400..	6,006
1836	498,889..	1,724,661..	52.772..	49,542..19.522..		8,686
1837*	456,642..	1,815,062..	93,453..	21,043..50,037..		13.359
1838	691,385..	3,203,243..	95,546..	23,866..12.408..		5,376
1839	692,458..	3,811,719..	85,384..	43,203..11,840..		6,786
1840	817,937..	3,033,084..	124,501..	42,274..	6,212..	6,074
1841	845,571..	3,148,755..	89,218..	54,067..	8,180..	5.440
1842	919,069..	3,037,725..	128,789..	66,939..	8,821..	5,670
1843	710,399..	2,280,115..	77,568..	74,531..	3,505..	5,097
1844	811,606..	3,063,870..	125,017..	63.587..	5,289.	6.519
1845	929.044..	3,742,760..	67.958..	75,186..	4.682.	5,772
1846	877,400..	3,444.152..	104.739..	39,345..	2,949.	6,895
1847	1,041,782..	4,487,021..	134,664..	22.706..	3.623.	6,771
1848	1,012,987..	3.867.474..	96,181..	24.574..	1,824.	7,456
1849	1,007,425..	4,328,135..	86,153..	24,305..	3.040.	5,191
1850	1,121,294..	4.905,318..	117,837..	29,733..	2,415.	5,443
1851	1.184,163..	4.827,400..	121,119..	64.781..	3,660.	6.827
1852	937,326..	3,717,831..	124,598..	58,070..	2,604.	4.618
1853	1,156,662..	4,751,842..	137,815..	20,995..	1,513.	6,636

In 1852.					N	Hides.
To the United States	726,688..	3,066,564..	2.206..	— ..	— ..	15
" Great Britain, Cowes, etc.	53,218..	184,604..	30,534..	2.180..	— ..	—
" British North America	52,588..	514.847..	482..	— ..	— ..	45
" Germany	80.549..	— ..	31,139..	53,758..	754.	47
" France	56,829..	— ..	4,000..	— ..	— ..	—
" Genoa and Trieste	2,286..	— ..	27.123..	— ..	970..	402
" Spain and elsewhere	15,666..	1,816..	29,109..	2,132..	880.	4,110
	937,324..	3.717.831..	124,598..	53,070..	2,604..	4,619

* The returns of 1837 Include $643,000 worth of cotton, hides, and coffee re-exported from ▴ond, the quantities of which are not recorded.

EXPORTATION—*Continued.*

In 1852.	Sugar, *Quintals.*	Molasses, *Gallons.*	Coffee, *Quintals.*	Tobacco, *Quintals.*	Cotton, *Quintals.*	Hides, *No.*
From St. John's	73,162	106,233	15,153	2,062	—	2,820
" Arecibo	103,659	286,963	5,332	33,391	70	47
" Aguadilla	19,001	7,680	25,222	11,063	1,011	208
" Mayagües	195,201	727,020	58,988	—	1,523	1,544
" Ponce	241,519	1,071,489	17.264	6.832	—	—
" Guayama	203,382	1,192,921	2,639	4,122	—	—
" Humacao, etc	101,400	325,526	—	—	—	—
	937,324	3,717,831	124,598	58,070	2,604	4,619

COST OF SUGAR AND MOLASSES.

Market Price. Macuquina.		On Board. Round Money.			Sterling. s.	d.
$2 50	per 100 lbs. Spanish	$2 68	Per 112 lbs. Eng.	$2 95¾	or 11	7¼
2 75	" "	2 95¼	" "	3 24	" 12	8½
3 00	" "	3 21½	" "	3 53	" 13	10
3 25	" "	3 47¾	" "	3 81¼	" 14	11¾
3 50	" "	3 74	" "	4 10¾	" 16	1¼
3 75	" "	4 00¼	" "	4 39½	" 17	2¾
4 00	" "	4 26½	" "	4 68¼	" 18	4¼
4 25	" "	4 53¾	" "	4 97	" 19	6
4 50	" "	4 79	" "	5 26	" 20	7½
4 75	" "	5 04¼	" "	5 54¾	" 21	9
5 00	" "	5 31	" "	5 83½	" 22	10¾

	Cents.		Cents.	s.	d.
8 cents per gallon	14 12	10 gallons per cwt.	141 2	or 5	6½
9 " "	15 17	" "	151 7	" 5	11½
10 " "	16 22	" "	162 2	" 6	4½
11 " "	17 27	" "	172 7	" 6	9½
12 " "	18 32	" "	183 2	" 7	2½
13 " "	19 37	" "	193 7	" 7	7½
14 " "	20 42	" "	204 2	" 8	0½
15 " "	21 27	" "	212 7	" 8	5½
16 " "	22 45	" "	224 5	" 8	10½

The above calculations are based upon Sterling being at $4 80 Round money, and Patriot Doubloons at $17 Macuquina each.

NOTE.—The above table corresponds to St. John's, but, with a trifling difference in local charges, may be applied to the other markets in the island. The charges on coffee at Mayagües, which is the chief market for it, is, per 100 lbs. Spanish, about 37½ cents in bags, and 62½ cents in casks, exclusive of commission of 2½ per cent. on cost and charges.

EXTRACT OF THE TARIFF OF PORTO RICO, FROM NOV. 1ST., 1851.

ARTICLES AND VALUATION.—*Class* 1.—Flour, $12 50 per barrel.

Class 2.—Corn meal, $4 per bar., and 16 per pun.; rye flour, $4 per bar.

Class 3.—Beans, 3c. per lb.; beer and ale, $3 per doz.; bread, pilot and navy, 6c. per lb.; candles, tallow, 12c. per lb.; crackers, biscuit, 7½c. per lb.; dates, 12½c. per lb.; figs, 4c. per lb.; hams, American, 9c. per lb.—other, 15c. per lb.; herrings, smoked

87c. per 100; horses, geldings, $150 each; mules, $51 each; oats, 1¼c. per lb.; onions, 2c. per lb.; pepper, black Castile, 12c. per lb.; prunes, in boxes, 5c. per lb.; rice, 4½c. per lb.; raisins, 6c. per lb.; soap, 10c. per lb.; wine, common Bordeaux, $23 per cask and $3 50 per box—Marseilles, red, $20 per cask and $3 per box—Cape, Rhine, and Champagne, $8 per doz.—Madeira, $3 75 per *arroba* and $6 50 per doz.

Class 4.—Beef, pickled, $9 per bar.; fish, dry, 3c. per lb.; hoops, wood, $25 per M; hogsheads, $3 each—$9 per 4 nest—$3 per 3 nest; herrings, pickled, $8 per bar.; lumber, per M ft., pitch pine, $20—white pine, $15; mackerel, $4 per bar.; pork, pickled, $15 per bar.; shooks, with or without heads, $1 each; staves, rough, $12 per M; salmon, pickled, 9c. per lb.; shingles, $3 per M; truss hoops, $6 per doz.

Class 5.—Apples, $3 per bar.; empty bags, $2 25 per doz.—do. barrels, 50c. each; beets, 2c. per lb.; beef, jerked, United States, 7c. per lb—Buenos Ayres and Brazil, 6c. per lb.—other, 5c. per lb.; bricks, fire, $16 per M; butter, 16c. per lb.; cassia, 25c. per lb.; cloves, 37½c. per lb.; cheese, European, 16c. per lb.—other, 10c. per lb.; candles, sperm, 32c. per lb.—composition, 28c. per lb.; earthenware, common, in crates, 75c. per foot; lard, 10c. per lb.; nails, iron, 6c. per lb.; nuts, 6c. per lb.; oil, sperm and linseed, 75c. per gal.—fish, 50c. per gal.; pepper, Guinea, 25c. per lb.—Tobacco, 8c. per lb.; ploughs, large, $25 each—small, $6 each; pitch and tar, $3 per bar.; potatoes, 1½c. per lb.; paints in oil, 8c. per lb.; tallow, 7½c. per lb.; tongues, smoked, 7c. per lb.; grindstones, $1 50 each; turpentine, oil, 12½c. per gal.—spirits, $1 per gal.

Class 6.—Refined sugar, 18c. per lb.—white, unrefined, 9c. per lb.; cigars, foreign, $3 per M—Cuba, $10 per M; tobacco, Virginia leaf, 8c. per lb.—chewing, 10c. per lb. —St. Domingo leaf, 12c. per lb.—Cuba, 20c. per lb.

Class 7.—Mineral coal, Roville ploughs, bark for tanning, horses (stallions), mares, asses, ice, leeches, temper-lime, gold and silver in bars, ingots, and coin. The following for sugar manufactories: gudgeons—if Spanish, grate-bars, doors, and mouth-plates for furnaces; cogwheels and rollers, iron or copper pans, clarifiers and molasses tanks, iron skimmers and ladles, duplicate pieces for steam and cattle mills. The following if from Spain under Spanish flag: steam sugar-mills, machines for cleaning rice and cotton, winnowing coffee or shelling corn, stills, manure, seed, and plants.

N.B. Foreign steam sugar-mills, manure, plants and seed, stills, and agricultural machines pay 1 per cent. on valuation.

Foreign Goods.	1.	2.	CLASSES. 3.	4.	5.
Under foreign flag	43½ p. c.	29¼ p. c.	29 p. c.	28½ p. c.	23 p. c.
" Spanish "	35¼ "	21¼ "	20 "	17¼ "	16 "
" " " from Spain	23¼ "	17¼ "	20 "	14¼ "	16 "
Spanish Goods.					
Under foreign flag	33 "	19 "	15 "	15 "	12 "
" Spanish "	6¼ "	6¼ "	7 "	6¼ "	7 "

Foreign Goods.	Sugar. Unrefined white. Refined.		CLASSES. 6.	7.
Under foreign flag	4c. per lb.	8c. lb.	Cigars $2 per M ..Free Toba'o, Virginia leaf, 4c. lb.	
" Spanish "				
" " " from Spain	2c. "	..4c. " ..	" chewing 5c. " ..	"
Spanish Goods.				
Under foreign flag	4c. "	..8c. " ..	" St. Domin. lf. 5c. " ..	"
" Spanish "	2c. "	..4c. " ..	" Cuba leaf 3c. " ..	"

Additional 1 per cent. on the amount of duty, except when specific, for "Balanza." One-fourth of the whole is payable in Spanish gold, at 12½ per cent. premium. Im-

STATISTICS OF PORTO RICO. 189

ports from non-producing ports pay a differential duty of 2½ per cent. on valuation, and from the neighboring islands the same under Spanish flag as under foreign. Exports, except timber, are free of duty, and when molasses is an entire cargo, or when vessels clear as they entered, no tonnage dues are exacted; else the charge is one dollar per ton on foreign vessels, and three-eighths of a dollar per ton on Spanish vessels. Vessels laden with mineral coal to the extent of their tonnage are subject to tonnage dues of only half a dollar per ton for foreign, and Spanish vessels nothing. Light-house dues of three cents per ton to 150, and one cent for each in excess, continue to be levied. At Mayagües there is a local charge of one rial or 12½ cents for each 400 lbs. of weighable imports or exports.

EXPORTATION FROM MAYAGUES, PORTO RICO—TOTAL CROPS.

	Hogsheads of Sugar.				Puncheons Molasses.		
	1847.	1848.	1849.	1850.	1851.	1847.	1848.	1849.
New York	6,020..	11,039..	7,072..	8,241..	7,039..:.	2,497..	3,442..	3,118
New Haven	47..	381..	274..	813..	959....	1,184..	2,807..	1,819
Philadelphia	1,828..	2,127..	1,343..	3,024..	3,489....	670..	397..	639
Baltimore	4,453..	2,005..	2,325..	459..	2,029.. :	585..	203..	852
Other ports	2,354..	1,801..	1,638..	975..	2,455....	946..	967..	500
United States..	15,302..	17,353..	12,652..	13,512..	15,971....	5,882..	7,816..	6,228
British N. Amer.	1,119..	1,291..	557..	1,528..	3,450....	848..	311..	304
G. Britain, Cowes	4,359..	3,288..	3,934..	4,626..	5,721....	2,249..	1,859..	1,632
France	2,285..	1,386..	755..	3,158..	403....	— ..	— ..	—
Spain	— ..	— ..	40..	— ..	28....	— ..	— ..	—
Germany	— ..	381..	— ..	181..	411....	— ..	— ..	—
Denmark	— ..	— ..	— ..	741..	—	— ..	— ..	—
Genoa and Trieste	239..	385..	216..	383..	—	— ..	2..	—
Total	23,304..	24,029..	18,154..	24,129..	26,044....	8,474..	9,487..	8,164

Weight of sugar 30,929,751 pounds in 1851 against 29,114,623 pounds in 1850.

EXPORTATION FROM MAYAGUES—Continued.

	Pchs. Molasses.		Quintals of Coffee.				
	1850.	1851.	1847.	1848.	1849.	1850.	1851.
New York	4,324...	2,849......	767..	949..	980..	9,505..	2,573
New Haven	3,584...	4,401......	— ..	10..	7..	— ..	—
Philadelphia	659...	339......	3..	460..	— ..	896..	604
Baltimore	27...	339......	5..	114..	40..	4,669..	130
Other ports	565...	1,003......	1.192..	327..	778..	360..	65
United States	9,109...	8,981......	1,967..	1,860..	1,805..	15,430..	3,378
British N. America	322...	1,408......	— ..	99..	36..	36..	122
G. Britain, Cowes	768...	380......	5,560..	2,085..	1,408..	3,606..	4,455
France	— ...	—	2,828..	3,095..	2,099..	557..	1,707
Spain	— ...	—	6,252..	8,549..	1.841..	3.759..	2,064
Germany	— ...	—	39,223..	25,052..	24,647..	13.477..	16,238
Denmark	— ...	—	— ..	— ..	— ..	— ..	—
Genoa and Trieste	— ...	—	8,096..	5,275..	6,286..	18,314..	17,305
Total	10,699...	10,769......	63,926..	46,015..	38,181..	55,179..	45,878

CHIEF IMPORTS OF PROVISIONS, ETC., AT MAYAGUES.

		1852.	1851.	1850.	1849.	1848.	1847.	Duties.*
W. P. lumber ..	m. ft.	1,278..	1,087..	1,108..	592...	1,699...	1,078..	$3 68
P. P. " ..	"	440..	498..	463..	178...	381...	573...	4 89
Hhd. staves	m.	111..	621..	585..	473...	983...	540...	2 94
" shooks & h'ds		17,404..	26,537..	33,312..	19,191...	16,189...	9.257...	24½
Wood hoops ...	m.	527..	585..	726..	468...	598...	618...	6 12
Shingles	"	1,506..	609..	399..	288...	453...	544...	73½
Pork	bbls.	543..	436..	594..	649...	304...	646...	3 67
Beef...........	"	162..	393..	223..	148...	223...	104...	2 20
Dry fish	quin.	30,792..	29,663..	27,177..	20,401...	28,684...	26,544...	76½
Mackerel	bbls.	3,112..	4,125..	4,254..	6,103...	5,701...	4.458...	98
Herrings.......	"	1,469..	1,377..	2,098..	1,037...	1.178...	906...	76½
Butter	kegs.	877..	947..	1.232..	1,124...	1.098...	1,223...	3 86
Lard	"	4,325..	3,191..	3,391..	3,067...	4,097...	4,176...	2 43
Flour..........	bbls.	9,754..	7,243..	7,874..	7,338...	8,870...	11,892...	5 67
Corn meal†	pun.	873..	303..	222..	333...	381...	796...	4 92
"	bb's.	6,314..	1,276..	1,121..	1,537...	1,067...	2.796...	1 23
Rice†..........	quin.	8,168..	2.243..	1.039..	1,890...	1,099...	3,763...	1 39
Tallow candles .	box.	6,086..	5,276..	5,094..	3,695...	3,674...	3,898...	3 62
Bread	blls.	1,415..	1,128..	988..	624...	671...	558...	1 84
Potatoes	"	1.598..	1,377..	813..	1,110...	1,025...	1,144...	39
Onions.........	quin.	1,199..	1.980..	651..	895...	1,817...	1,581...	63
Cheese, Amer...	box.	5,348..	3,402..	2,208..	1,823...	2,079...	3,415...	2 43
Hams, " ..		4,446..	3,391..	3,708..	2,714...	3,299...	3.702...	2 75
Manuf. tobacco.	pkgs	130..	375..	175..	471...	460...	554...	5 19
Leaf tobac., Vir.	hhds.	40..	36..	26..	32...	33...	58...	4 14

NOTE.—Of late years flour has been chiefly supplied by Spain and fish by the British North American provinces, which also provide lumber to some extent.

LEGAL VALUE OF FOREIGN COINS, 1ST OCTOBER, 1853.

Gold.	Round Money.	Macuquina.
Spanish doubloon	$16 —	$17 56¼
Patriot "	15 50	17 —
United States double eagle	19 37½	21 25
French 40 franc piece	7 60	8 83½
British sovereign	4 61½	4 90
Silver.		
Spanish, South America, Mexican, and United States dollar	1 —	1 12½
Pesetas Sevillanas	— 20	— 22½
French 5 franc piece	— 95	1 6¾
" 1 " "	— 19	— 21½
British crown	1 10	1 23¾
" shilling	— 22	— 24¾

And the aliquot parts in proportion.

The above data have been chiefly obtained from the reliable trade-circulars of the highly respectable houses of Latimer & Co., of St. John's, and Latimer, Turull & Co., of Mayagües.

* These duties are on foreign imports under foreign flag, and, with little difference, are the same throughout the island.

† The increase of importation of rice and meal in 1852 was in consequence of damage to the native crops by a gale in August, 1851.

www.ingramcontent.com/pod-product-compliance
Lightning Source LLC
Chambersburg PA
CBHW032143160426
43197CB00008B/757